NEXT GENERATION LEADERSHIP

Sherry Penney Dec. 2010

NEXT GENERATION LEADERSHIP

INSIGHTS FROM EMERGING LEADERS

SHERRY H. PENNEY AND
PATRICIA AKEMI NEILSON

NEXT GENERATION LEADERSHIP

First published in 2010 by
PALGRAVE MACMILLAN®
in the United States—a division of St. Martin's Press LLC,
175 Fifth Avenue, New York, NY 10010.

Where this book is distributed in the UK, Europe and the rest of the
world, this is by Palgrave Macmillan, a division of Macmillan Publishers
Limited, registered in England, company number 785998, of Houndmills,
Basingstoke, Hampshire RG21 6XS.

Palgrave Macmillan is the global academic imprint of the above companies
and has companies and representatives throughout the world.

Palgrave® and Macmillan® are registered trademarks in the United States,
the United Kingdom, Europe and other countries.

ISBN: 978–0–230–62069–8

Library of Congress Cataloging-in-Publication Data

Penney, Sherry H.
    Next generation leadership : insights from emerging leaders / Sherry
    H. Penney and Patricia Akemi Neilson.
        p. cm.
    Includes bibliographical references and index.
    ISBN 978–0–230–62069–8
    1. Leadership. I. Neilson, Patricia Akemi. II. Title.

HD57.7.P447 2010
658.4′092—dc22   2009036638

A catalogue record of the book is available from the British Library.

Design by Newgen Imaging Systems (P) Ltd., Chennai, India.

First edition: June 2010

10 9 8 7 6 5 4 3 2 1

Printed in the United States of America.

To Emerging Leaders Everywhere

CONTENTS

FOREWORD

THE TIME FOR NEW LEADERSHIP IS NOW, AND WE ARE PLEASED TO SEE THE hopeful messages conveyed in the chapters that follow. This book looks at leadership from the viewpoint of emerging leaders themselves. How do those who will lead see the future challenges to leadership? What goals do they have, what skills will they need, and what kinds of organizations do they want to lead? In this book, we also hear about the leadership aspirations of women and people of color, and the need for cultural awareness in institutions.

We speak as individuals from the private and the nonprofit sectors who have been in leadership positions and observed leadership in many forms. We both have been privileged to have met and worked with many of the over three hundred emerging leaders discussed in this book. We find them to be talented and inspirational. Leaders everywhere will benefit from their insights.

We urge you to read this book and learn what young leaders have to say about leadership for the future. The next generation of leaders is already among us. Our future is in their hands, and we ignore them at our peril. We must heed their voices now because leadership for the future cannot be left to chance. It is time to pass the torch.

Marshall N. Carter
Chairman, New York Stock Exchange Group
Chairman and CEO (retired), State Street Corporation

Hubie Jones
Dean Emeritus, Boston University School of Social Work
Founder and President, Boston Children's Chorus
Charter Trustee, City Year, Inc.

Authors' Notes

SHERRY H. PENNEY

It is perhaps presumptuous to think that anyone can actually teach leadership. So when I thought about offering courses in leadership and also establishing a unique executive leadership program late in my career, I reviewed my own evolution as an academic, civic, and business leader. What in my own values and experiences informed me and propelled me on this journey? Why did I want to establish an Emerging Leader's Program?

My values like those of many others come from my parents, and for me, my Dad's influence, in particular, was the formative event for my journey in and of leadership. It is a journey that involves values, experiences, and seeing a strong need. My father, Terry Hood, was a school principal and superintendent in Michigan while I was growing up and was the ultimate collaborative leader although such a concept was not used in the 1950s. As a school administrator, his values were an essential part of all that he did. He was attuned to issues of diversity although we rarely discussed it. He invited a black choir to our small town in Michigan to sing at our all white church. Our community was predominately white and quite conservative, but he was totally committed to justice and equality, and to seeing the best in everyone and believed that others should try to be this way too. There were gay and lesbian teachers—individuals whom he hired because they were outstanding teachers. I never heard him use words such as diversity, but he lived in such a way that it was evident that he valued all individuals equally and tried to foster in others an attitude of openness and acceptance.

He never allowed me to believe that there were any limitations to what women could do, and when at age 11, I announced that I wanted to be a lawyer, he encouraged that goal. (My mother told me I should train to be a teacher.) Later in my teens, he arranged for me to meet the congress-woman from Michigan, Martha Griffiths. Again, he placed no limits on what I might want to do. He supported equal educational opportunity for all and that is how he lived his life. When he was felled by a heart attack at a young age, he gave up administration and became a high school counselor and continued his commitments to helping all without regard to race, gender, or difference.

I pursued a pre-law curriculum as an undergraduate but ended up enrolling in graduate school with a generous scholarship rather than law school and set out to become a history professor. (History was also the discipline that my father taught before he became a principal.) As a doctoral student I was told, as discussed in chapter 4, that my university would never hire a woman in its history department, although the department would help me find a job elsewhere. I did not protest but listened carefully and probably from that moment on, I knew that I would find a way to see that no other woman ever had to hear those words. That I would strive to become a university president might have been ordained that day!

After graduate school, I taught history briefly at Union College in Schenectady, New York, but moved into administration soon after. I was fortunate to serve as associate provost at Yale University and vice chancellor for Academic Programs at the SUNY system office and acting president of SUNY Plattsburgh before becoming chancellor of the University of Massachusetts Boston. As chancellor, I occupied a major leadership position and tried to be the collaborative leader that I hoped to be. I'm sure all did not see it that way!

I also made real my commitment to diversity, and my senior staff of vice chancellors and deans included more women and people of color than white males. Moreover, during my tenure we added the Asian American Institute and the Gaston Institute (for research on Latinos) to the Trotter Institute for African American Studies that existed on the campus prior to my arrival. We also made a home for the Institute for Women and Politics whose goal is that more women run for and be elected to public office.

The university faced 11 budget cuts and reversions in my first four years on the job and the reaction in the university community was one of anger and disbelief. My attempts at collaboration worked sometimes better than others. One of the best was the formation of an inclusive committee to assist in making recommendations for the many reductions that had to be made. Together we learned much about collaborating to make difficult decisions.

I did not want collaboration to be seen as useful only in a budget crisis so looked for other ways to foster a more collaborative climate. With the help of an American Council on Education (ACE) fellow, we developed a leadership program for faculty and staff. We created a series of seminars on issues in higher education and invited individuals to apply to participate. Six months of very productive discussions followed as well as an expanded concept by all of what choices leaders have to make. I also worried about how the students viewed leadership. Around the same time I read the Ron Heifetz book *Leadership Without Easy Answers,* and it helped me realize how difficult it was for them to understand that many times the leader has to make the least objectionable choice among all difficult choices and that there were serious limitations on what could be done in a crisis situation. It was not possible to take serious reductions in the state support, keep fees and tuition low, and also offer all the classes needed. Working with colleagues in student affairs, we also began a student leadership program. It included seminars as well as mentoring and was a way for students to learn more about what leaders face and how individuals can be better leaders. It also created a stronger cadre of student leaders for the university. The Beacon Leadership Program for undergraduates continues to this day.

Fortunately, after four years of cuts we entered a more stable phase and were able to move the campus from state college status to doctoral, to undertake a major fund raising campaign, and to celebrate having the first two Fulbright students in the history of the campus. We also began a series of capital improvements including plans for a new campus center. A variety of initiatives related to leadership development in all our constituencies had been put in place. It was during this period that I was asked to serve as President of the University of Massachusetts system on an interim basis. That was my role during 1995, and again I was able to work with the senior staff in the President's office and with the chancellors toward a spirit of collaboration.

When I retired as chancellor in 2000, leadership was again on my mind. Fortunately, a major donor created an endowed professorship in leadership and I was to be the first holder of the chair. A major financial institution also provided a grant to establish an executive leadership program for young professionals. As outlined in the introduction and chapter 1, our region was changing dramatically in terms of demography, business enterprises, and the role of nonprofits. Where would we find the leaders of the future who would guide us in this new and more diverse setting? I was convinced, along with several others, that they were among us and that what we needed to do was find them and bring them together for an intensive leadership development experience. The Emerging Leadership Program was born and my leadership journey continues.

I have learned much from them and their thoughts are featured throughout this book.

PATRICIA AKEMI NEILSON

Who would have guessed that I would be at an urban university working with young professionals chosen by their companies to be the leaders of tomorrow given my circuitous career path. I am a *Sansei* (third generation) Asian American. Both my maternal and paternal grandparents immigrated to Hawaii from Okinawa, a prefecture of Japan, in the early 1900s. I was born and raised in Hawaii and grew up being part of the majority culture. After high school I was fortunate to attend Seattle University. Going away for college was my first venture outside the state and my introduction to being a "minority." My four years of education at Seattle University went far beyond academics, and exposed me to a completely new lifestyle and provided me with opportunities to navigate my new bicultural existence. My parents were blue collar workers and sacrificed much to send me to college on the mainland, but to them the sacrifice was necessary because providing an education for me and my two sisters was of utmost importance. Upon receiving my degree, I returned to Hawaii to start my first professional position as an outreach drug abuse counselor for the YMCA of Honolulu. This was the beginning of my administrative roles in the nonprofit community, designing, implementing, and leading programs that addressed the needs of underserved communities.

In the mid-1980s, my husband was offered a position at the headquarters of a major computer company in Massachusetts so we decided to move our family to the Boston area. My experience with grant writing, transformational curriculum development, program design, and implementation secured me a position at North Shore Community College as the director of the displaced homemaker program, an academic skill training program for single parents, divorced, and widowed women.

During this period I pursued a doctorate degree in Leadership in Education. My research interest in the under representation of Asian Americans in senior administrative positions in higher education has led me to advocate for the development of pipelines for this talent. In higher education although 6.4 percent of the national student enrollments are Asian Americans, less than one percent (.09 percent) are chancellors or presidents. Proportionately, Asian Americans are the most underrepresented group in senior administrative positions. Only 2.4 percent of the 145,371 administrative positions in higher education are held by Asian Americans, compared to 9.4 percent of such positions held by African Americans and 3.6 percent by Latin Americans.

Upon completion of my degree, I was appointed to the position of academic dean. While serving as dean, I participated as a Fellow in the Emerging Leaders Program. I was impressed with the speakers in the program and the cross sector networking opportunities, but what struck me was the mission and vision of the program: to create leaders who are collaborative, civically engaged and who represent the demographics of the region.

Toward the end of the ten-month Emerging Leaders Program, a posting for the associate director of the Center for Collaborative Leadership was circulated and was brought to my attention. I had been taken by the challenge of the mission and I considered applying for the position. Although it was not the ideal trajectory for my career path, I applied and was offered the position.

I made a mission based decision because I was intrigued with the idea that I could be part of changing the complexion of the leadership in the region. It has been nearly five years and I am now the director of the program. With almost 400 alums of the program and an active alumni association, there are strong indications that the program is having an impact on the region. Graduates of the program have been promoted to significant leadership roles in private industry, government, education, and the nonprofit community and serve on many nonprofit boards. And the interest in running for and holding elected office is growing. The Emerging Leaders Program is at critical mass and is definitely making a difference!

ACKNOWLEDGMENTS

THIS BOOK PROJECT HAS TRULY BEEN A COLLABORATIVE EFFORT. WE ARE especially grateful to the 20 emerging leaders who contributed essays and helped to make this book a reality: Sandra Bailly, Ron Bell, David Dance, Lisa DeAngelis, Hugh Drummond, Paul Francisco, Armindo Gonçalves, David Halbert, Chi Huang, MD, Andrea Hurwitz, Anne Marie Boursiquet King, Georgianna Meléndez, Nate Pusey, Michael Rawan, Pauliina Swartz, Amanda Trojan, Mary Tolikas, Deanna Yameen, Christie Getto Young, and one who wishes to remain anonymous.

We acknowledge, in particular, Senior Scholar Sue Reamer who provided the initial encouragement for this book. She has been with us every step of the way giving wise advice and guidance as we developed the program and as we moved ahead with this book.

We gratefully acknowledge State Street's initial grant that made the program possible. State Street Corporation and Foundation also provided two additional grants that provided support for research for this book. Our thanks go, in particular, to Marshall N. Carter, George Russell, and Jennifer Waldner from State Street.

We thank Alan Macdonald and J. D. Chesloff of the Massachusetts Business Roundtable, Tom Chmura, vice president for economic development, University of Massachusetts system office, and Chris Martin and Steve Dodman of the Greater Boston Manufacturing Partnership for information about the changing business climate in Massachusetts. Insights from Chris Carmody and Penny Connor, vice presidents at NSTAR, for observations on generational workplace challenges and leadership skills are also appreciated.

We also thank Patricia Peterson for her careful reading and editing of the essays and suggestions for this manuscript and Emily Rubin who co-authored several of the essays. Marjorie Arons-Barron of Barron Associates Worldwide provided valuable advice throughout as did Christine Green of the Trefler Foundation.

Dean Philip L. Quaglieri of the College of Management at UMass Boston provided consistent encouragement and faculty members Peter Kiang of Asian America Studies and Maureen Scully of the Management and Marketing

Department have assisted in the program itself and have been especially helpful as we prepared the manuscript.

The authors are also grateful for research assistance from graduate students Jennifer Leigh, Vinai Norassakundt, Ben Donner, Meredith Evans, Katia Canenguez, and Tom Robinson and for additional assistance from John Lozada. We thank Karen Bowen and Deanne Dworski-Riggs in the Center for Survey Research at UMass Boston for conducting the survey of our alumni. Suzanne Buglione, Jennifer Safford-Farquharson, and Donna Charbonneau of CommunityBuild also assisted with surveys and focus groups. Additional focus group sessions were facilitated by Ian Cross, Gina LaRoche, and Eleanor Chin, and we thank them all.

We especially thank Andrea Wight, assistant director for the Center for Collaborative Leadership, who provided technical service and valuable editorial and other advice to us throughout the whole process. Marcela Massarutto and Glendalys Cabrera of the Center for Collaborative Leadership also were helpful and we thank them.

We also extend special thanks to Laurie Harting, executive editor at Palgrave Macmillan and to Laura Lancaster, editorial assistant, for their assistance throughout the process. We are indebted to them and others at Palgrave Macmillan.

Finally, we thank our husbands, Jim and Joey. Jim Livingston (Sherry's husband) read drafts, assisted with technology dilemmas, and provided encouragement and hugs. Joey (Pat's husband) provided much needed technical support, kind words and patience during stressful times when writer's block set in.

INTRODUCTION

EMERGING LEADERS HAVE MUCH TO SAY ABOUT LEADERSHIP. THIS BOOK IS informed by what we are learning from them about what leadership should look like in the future, how it may differ from past models, and how our society can benefit from their insights.

If we are to have effective leaders in the future, we must find those potential leaders now and provide them with leadership training and development. That is what we set out to do. As we looked at our region at the turn of the century, it became clear that the leadership profile is in flux. Many of the businesses that once were prominent in our area as well as companies that had traditionally provided the business and civic leadership no longer exist. Others have felt the impact of mergers and acquisitions. New organizations are emerging, and individuals from them will be called on to play prominent roles in the future. In addition, demographic data show that people of color are now a majority in our city, but most leadership positions throughout the region continue to be held by white males with few females or people of color in those roles. A more representative body of leaders is needed. We believe that the leaders for the future are out there—they need to be found and provided with focused leadership development opportunities.

So we met with several individuals in the business and nonprofit communities to express our concern. We found much support for developing a leadership pool for the future, and that is what we did. We created an Emerging Leaders Program and a Center for Collaborative Leadership in 2001, and in 2002 we began our work with young professionals. For the past eight years we have been privileged to work intensely with groups of talented young professionals— "emerging leaders." Including all eight groups, 342 individuals, with an average age of 37, have participated in the program and 46 new emerging leaders joined us in January 2010 as this book was going to print. They come from all areas of the business community as well as from the nonprofit and governmental sectors and are representative of the demographic and organizational profile in many urban areas in the United States.

We ask organizations to seek out and then nominate individuals for their leadership potential, thereby encouraging them in their roles as future leaders.

This process also strengthens the commitment of those organizations to find and support their own emerging leaders, which in turn enhances their efforts to retain talented young professionals.

We work with each cohort over a ten-month period beginning with a week-long seminar in January followed by monthly sessions through July and a final session in September or October. The learning model is hands-on and focuses on collaboration, inclusion, and civic responsibility. We address many of the issues that emerging leaders face in their organizations such as: ethics in the workplace, how to work in teams, how to lead from the middle of the organization, how to communicate effectively, how to resolve conflicts and practice effective negotiation, and how to face work/family challenges. The program has four main elements: evaluation sessions analyzing one's own leadership style, seminars focusing on specific skills, team projects, and meetings with current leaders to learn about their paths to leadership. Over the course of the ten months, participants have an opportunity to hone their leadership skills and also to create new and expanded professional and social networks. Throughout, we encourage individuals to cross boundaries and sectors in meaningful and long-lasting ways. Individuals from the business world work closely with those from the nonprofit and governmental sectors. Differences of race or gender are no longer a central focus when these young professionals work together in forum sessions and on teams. Inclusion and collaboration become the norm.

The Emerging Leaders Program won the "Excellence in Practice" award from the European Foundation of Management Development in 2007 at a ceremony in Brussels and was cited as a unique model of cooperation between business and the academic world.[1]

We asked these emerging leaders to assist us in learning more about their thoughts on leadership by writing essays outlining their views. Those essays were compiled and printed in 2009: *Voices of the Future: Emerging Leaders.* Copies of the essays are available on our Web site (leaders.umb.edu.) and a list of the authors is in the appendix. Excerpts from those essays appear in this book, and these personal insights shed new light on the topic of future leadership. One essay mentions Leadership (capital "L") and leadership (small "l") and points out that both are important. This concept is one that others of the writers support. These young professionals see leadership in a more inclusive way than did many from previous generations. They do not favor the old "top-down" capital "L" leadership model. They value honesty and integrity as the most important qualities of leaders and they believe that everyone can be a leader and that it is important to enhance leadership qualities in everyone. Their vision of a new leadership model is clearly one that will change organizations in the future.

In addition, we interviewed several alumni of the program as well as their sponsors. We also held eight focus groups with alumni and participants.

Individuals from interviews and focus groups are not identified by name to protect confidentiality, but we have included quotations from many of them throughout this book. We also enlisted the Center for Survey Research at the University of Massachusetts Boston to survey these emerging leaders to obtain quantitative information about their views on leadership challenges and related issues. All of these sources have been helpful as we developed this book.

Their thoughts also alert us to the need for change in many organizations. Emerging leaders prefer to work in organizations that demonstrate corporate social responsibility. They want organizations to provide opportunities for their own professional development and growth, and they like to be in places whose policies permit and encourage family friendly work environments.

The next generation of leaders is among us. They are the talented young professional individuals who have been identified by their organizations as the emerging leaders of the future, and they now have developed the skills and experience needed to take on major leadership roles. These talented young professionals are our future, and it is time to listen to them.

Chapter 1, Who and Where Are Emerging Leaders: What Do We Know About Them?, outlines the characteristics of emerging leaders and provides a summary of some of the recently published work on emerging leaders.

In Chapter 2, How Do Emerging Leaders See Themselves as Leaders?, the focus is on the importance of reflection in leadership development. We discuss how young professionals think about their own styles as a first step in becoming stronger leaders. We discuss goals they set for themselves and then examine whether the goals have been met.

In Chapter 3, What Qualities Make Effective Leaders?, the skills and behaviors that will benefit emerging leaders in the future, how they see their skills develop and their behavior change over time, are discussed.

Chapter 4, Women and Leadership: Progress and Roadblocks, addresses the issue of gender—how do young professional women develop their leadership styles, what barriers do they face and what roles will they play in the future? How are they dealing with work/family issues and how do these affect their paths to leadership?

Chapter 5, Inclusive Leadership, looks at issues of cultural differences, diversity, and inclusion. Over 40 percent of our participants have been individuals of color. What have they experienced in their organizations? How do they see themselves as future leaders? Are their challenges different from those of other young professionals?

Chapter 6, The View from Generation X: Organizations Need to Change, discusses what we have learned from emerging leaders about the challenges they see for leaders in the future. We also examine their views on how organizations must change and on the importance of corporate social responsibility.

In addition, we discuss what emerging leaders want to see in the organizations where they work and how organizations can make themselves attractive to young professionals.

In Chapter 7, Leadership for the Future: Passing the Torch, the views of Generation X and Generation Y about the future are discussed as well as the roles they hope to play.

CHAPTER 1

WHO AND WHERE ARE EMERGING LEADERS: WHAT DO WE KNOW ABOUT THEM?

WHY DO WE NEED ANOTHER BOOK ABOUT LEADERSHIP? IF YOU CHECK Amazon or other sources, you will find thousands of such books. But most of them focus on leadership from the point of view of established leaders and academic researchers. Studies from leaders who have been CEOs, political, or nonprofit leaders are helpful and have provided the basis for much current thinking about leadership. And much leadership development work focuses on executive training for senior managers. We know less about the views of the leaders of the future and how to prepare them, but that discussion is now more important than ever before.

The voices of young professionals often called Generation X (born between 1965 and 1980) and Generation Y (also sometimes called the Millennials and born between 1980 and 2000) need to be heard. How do they (X and Y) differ from Baby Boomers (born 1945–1964)? How do they relate to the Traditionalists or The Silent Generation (Tulgan calls them the Schwarzkopf generation—those born before 1946)?[1] How will Generation X lead and work with Generation Y? How do they view themselves as leaders? What qualities do they stress? How do they see leadership in the future? Their characteristics and thinking can tell us much about where we are going and what leadership styles will take us there. These voices need to be heard because leadership for the future cannot be left to chance. Their insights also are helpful to organizations where they work who must deal with recruiting and retaining talented people. And their voices are useful to other young professionals embarking on their own leadership journeys. In the pages that follow we will bring you the views and thoughts of emerging leaders, primarily those from Generations X and Y.

DEMOGRAPHICS

We begin by describing these young professionals. Who are these emerging leaders? This book focuses on the 342 individuals who participated in our program from 2002 to 2009 and includes 150 men and 192 women with people of color some 40 percent. These emerging leaders have diverse professional backgrounds with 210 (61 percent) from the corporate sector, 89 (26 percent) in the nonprofit sector, and 43 (13 percent) from the governmental sector. They are primarily Generation X with a few Boomers and a few from Generation Y.

They represent the major businesses and nonprofit organizations in our region. Although our study focuses on a region in the Northeast, these young professionals are representative of what one would find in other large urban areas in the United States. They come from organizations such as AT&T, Bank of America, Citizens Bank, State Street Corporation, Sovereign Bank, Blue Cross Blue Shield, the Red Cross, Liberty Mutual Insurance Company, Bank of New York Mellon, Putman Investments, John Hancock Financial Services, and Verizon as well as Genzyme, Raytheon, the Boston Globe, the Federal Reserve Bank of Boston, NSTAR, EMC, Teradyne, Brown Brothers Harriman, Eastern Bank, Boston Medical Center, Brigham and Women's Hospital, Massachusetts General Hospital, Partners Community Health Care, United Way of Massachusetts Bay, City Year, and the offices of the Governor of Massachusetts and of the Mayor of Boston.[2]

THE EMERGING LEADERS PROGRAM

Before beginning our work with young professionals, we examined the potential need for leadership development efforts and what issues might be significant in the future. Jennifer Deal and her colleagues (2001) note that demographic data indicate that there are too few people in the management population defined as "emerging leaders," or, "rising managers from the generation born between 1964 and 1978." In the past there have been enough individuals from which "organizations could select candidates for managerial and leadership positions," but now there are too few with the appropriate skills for taking on the leadership challenges that our country faces. Similarly, Stuart Crainer and Des Dearlove (1999) predict that organizations will have a hard time finding managers through the year 2050. The need for new leaders is also reaffirmed in a special issue of *Leader to Leader* in 2006. In the introduction the following is noted: "With the pending retirement of nearly 78 million Baby Boomers over the next several years, the potential for a huge gap in leadership is a significant threat to this nation's ability to remain a global leader." The leadership gap also is hitting the nonprofit sector. A recent headline in the *Chronicle of Philanthropy* is "A Growing Leadership Crisis." The article says that despite many recent layoffs, at least 24,000 senior-level nonprofit positions will be available in 2009. This theme of a leadership gap is confirmed again in studies from the European Foundation for Management Development, IMB executive studies, and Hewitt Associates reports. All cite a concern over the pending leadership gap, both in the United States and internationally. In a recent Hewitt report, Indraneel Roy, from Hewitt's Global Leadership Consulting Practice, states:

> Leadership talent is in short supply around the world, yet a handful of companies are able to consistently groom and grow great leaders through the ranks, even in the most demanding talent markets and in the most volatile economic and financial climate.

The good news is that leading companies have developed systematic approaches to identify leaders and understand that leadership development is not only for the CEO and executive staff but must be part of every organization's strategic plan.[3]

In addition to a concern about the leadership gap mentioned above, there is concern about the changing business climate not only in our region but in many other regions of our country. Extensive mergers and acquisitions, the growth of new technologies, and many entrepreneurial business startups are producing major shifts in the local as well as the national business environment. With mergers and acquisitions come the loss of formerly prominent business organizations and their leaders as corporate headquarters become consolidated in new locales. Sadly their former executives who often served as major civic leaders also are now lost through retirement or transfer. To replace them, new leadership is needed and much will come from new business sectors: high technology, biotechnology, and green technology. All these are changing the face of corporate America. Moreover, small entrepreneurial businesses are also growing as well as some nonprofits. Leadership of the future should reflect this changing business environment and be representative of these business realities. New leaders will need to be in place as change continues to dominate in corporate, governmental, and nonprofit sectors and as power shifts into new patterns.

We also see that the kind of leaders we will need in the future will differ from those in the past. For some years in the middle of the twentieth century, a predominate business influence in the greater Boston region was an organization of leading businessmen who met in the Boston Safe Deposit Bank and hence came to be called the Vault. They, in large part, determined the direction of many business and political decisions for the city and under their leadership Boston as a city improved considerably. The Vault was a powerful but not a diverse group. Business, civic and political leaders determined that a small group of leaders making decisions for the community was not the way to go for the future and other organizations began to play a role. The Vault ceased to operate and several of its members subsequently became members of the Massachusetts Business Roundtable when it was formed in the 1970s. Leadership is now more diverse and more dispersed and new models are emerging. In addition to the Roundtable there are now also the Massachusetts Taxpayers Association, the Associated Industries of Massachusetts and several industry specific groups in addition to Chambers of Commerce in many regions of the Commonwealth. Many of these associations focus on statewide issues rather than primarily the city of Boston. From conversations with current business and nonprofit leaders as well as young professionals, a return to the days of the Vault or something similar is not predicted although a few individuals in our community think some variation of the Vault might again be useful. The young professionals, however, look to more inclusive models. They are moving into leadership positions with more respect and desire for collaboration and for making followers part of leadership.[4]

Moreover, leaders for the future must reflect the populations in their geographical regions. The demographics of our city cited in the 2000 census show 49.5 percent of the city as Caucasian, with Blacks at 23.8 percent, Latinos at 14.4 percent, Asians at 7.5 percent, multiracial at 3.1 percent, and other single race at 1.4 percent. Persons of color are now the majority, and as a city Boston is more diverse by race and ethnicity than at any time in the past. Although the Commonwealth has its first African American governor, overall the current leaders do not reflect the new demographic reality. A 2009 study by the Commonwealth Compact at the University of Massachusetts Boston notes that of the companies surveyed, minorities continue to be underrepresented at the executive level, with 23 percent reporting that they have no people of color on their leadership team. Most reported, however, that overall workplace diversity has improved.[5] So now and in the future a more diverse leadership structure is needed.

As we looked at the leadership gap, the changing model of leadership, the new business climate, and the demographic reality, it was clear that an effort to encourage more young professionals to take on leadership roles and subsequently to promote a collaborative model might be welcome. We were aware of the many outstanding community and other leadership development programs that exist throughout the country, but also saw a need for a program in our region based in a business school that would stress collaboration, inclusion, and teamwork as well as the need for civic engagement. This model of collaborative and inclusive leadership probably would not have been popular in the previous decades, but change is in the air.

In the late 1990s business and civic leaders from Boston began an initiative (City to City) to visit other cities to learn about how other areas were facing various urban issues. On trips that began with visits to Seattle and Atlanta, Sherry and Hubie Jones, a prominent civic leader and also assistant to the chancellor for Urban Affairs at U Mass Boston, discussed the need for new leaders and new leadership models. Subsequent conversations took place with the Mayor of Boston and other leaders about what to do about future leadership for our region and the Commonwealth. One of the business leaders supported the idea of a new initiative and concurred with the concept of developing a new leadership cadre for our region. In his role as CEO of one of the major financial organizations, he generously donated $250,000.00 to the Center for Collaborative Leadership upon the occasion of his retirement as CEO so that our efforts could begin. He now is Chair of the New York Stock Exchange Group and in that role remains involved with the program. He has been the opening speaker for each cohort and wrote in the *Boston Business Journal*:

> Our region and our city are poised for significant leadership challenges as more of our current leaders retire and move on. It is critical that outstanding individuals be ready and willing to take their places. But the new leadership will not and should not look like that of old. It must be more inclusive and respond to national and regional demographic changes. It must also be more collaborative—a characteristic not always the norm in Boston.[6]

We then surveyed business and other leaders in the nonprofit and governmental sectors in our region to ascertain their views on the major leadership challenges in the future. Three items topped the list: hiring and retaining talented staff; helping individuals develop an effective leadership style; and fostering teamwork. In addition to the survey, we also interviewed several leaders from the above sectors. They voiced similar concerns. One of those leaders from the telecommunications industry who also speaks regularly in the program expresses the need this way:

> Nourishing the next generation of leadership right here in Boston is critical if we are to remain a world-class hub for the finance, education, technology, communications, and health care industries. As today's business leaders, we must teach the executives of tomorrow how to collaborate effectively with others in an unprecedented fashion. We need to build in them the confidence to infuse their academic learning with their unique personal experiences.[7]

We formed a board of advisors that includes many of the leaders who were interviewed, and then we recruited our first cohort of young professionals to participate in the hands-on program that covers practical as well as theoretical issues in leadership. These individuals are selected by their organizations as potential leaders. In most cases that means that they have an advocate or at least someone in the organization who believes that they have demonstrated leadership potential.

COLLABORATION AS THE THEME

When you work with aspiring leaders, your own leadership philosophy comes into play. What have we learned along the way? What would have been helpful to us at an early stage in our careers? Some of what we have to offer comes from holding leadership positions—our personal experiences. We also have observed leaders in action and we have read and thought about leadership quite extensively. We—Sherry as a university president, and Pat, as a college dean respectively—observed leadership and saw again and again ways in which it could be better.

As a new administrator at Yale in the 1970s, Sherry was privileged to see collaboration and inclusion at work as she watched and learned from the first female provost (and later Acting President) at Yale, Hanna Gray. She was a strong leader and always decisive, but she practiced collaboration and also was inclusive. Her influence made a lasting impression and reinforced Sherry's personal views on leadership. Not only did she like what she saw, but it worked! Gray was a very effective leader and subsequently became the first female president of the University of Chicago.

Early in her career Pat worked as a youth program director for the Young Men's Christian Association (YMCA) of Honolulu. The organization of this metropolitan office consisted of two large comprehensive branches (athletic membership gyms, residence halls, swimming pools, youth programs, cafeteria, etc.) and three community branches that consisted of community outreach and youth programs. Although the resources available to the comprehensive branches were considerably larger than the community branches, the leadership of all five branches that made up this large organization agreed to share resources and facilities so the quality of programs and services provided by all the branches were consistent regardless of the size and budget of the facilities. What she learned from working in an atmosphere of sharing and collaboration was the ability to deliver quality programming across the organization. She learned early on that collaboration works and has continued its practice throughout her career.

Our view that effective leadership is based on collaboration has informed our work, and we believe that collaboration and inclusion is the model needed in the future. Many sources contributed to our thinking. Asian cultures are known to place value on collective effort rather than individual accomplishment. Many years ago Chinese philosophers stressed the importance of collaboration and those views were practiced in Eastern societies before they caught on in Western cultures. Chinese philosophers call for leaders who are team players and who know how to work with others. Individuals who do not need to take credit for every action and who know how to give others credit follow the advice of Lao Tsu in the familiar Chinese proverb: "The wise leader settles for good work and does not take all the credit for what happens. When the work is done, let them say with pride, we have done this together." The sense of interconnectedness and the internalizing of the concept *okage sama de,* which means that we are extensions of one another and we are all connected, also go a long way to explain and illuminate the intensely collaborative nature of the Japanese. W. Edward Deming is associated with quality practices and kaizen approaches that started in the 1950s and became a revolution in Japan. The key elements of kaizen or continuous improvement are quality, effort, involvement of all employees, willingness to change, and communication. Initially, when American companies tried to adopt these best practices in quality from Japan, they were unsuccessful because the cultural context in the United States was quite different from Japan. The approach in Japan traditionally has been collective, while in the United States the focus is more on individual contribution. More recently, some American companies such as Callaway Golf Company, Raytheon, and Beth Israel Hospital are incorporating these collaborative leadership efforts with success. In 2009, Chao C. Chen and Yueh-Ting Lee combined major ideas from Chinese philosophy with some Western ideas as they looked at leadership and management in China and they outline how both Eastern and Western approaches continue to be important.[8]

In addition to looking at Eastern models, other studies have been helpful in gaining a broad perspective on leadership including James M. Burns (1978), John Gardner (1990), Daniel Goleman (1995), James Austin (2000), Warren Bennis (2003; 1990), Joseph Raelin (2003), Scott Quatro (2007), and Edwin Hollander (2009). Concepts from the earlier works were useful as we made the decision to establish a Center for Collaborative Leadership in 2001, and others have been helpful as development went forward. The word collaborative was a deliberate choice. As Bennis and others argue, leadership strength comes from blending many ideas.[9]

Along with Jay Conger (1999), we realize that collaboration as a leadership strategy is not a given, and that it is not embraced by all who practice leadership. Other competing ideas for leadership models such as the trait and contingency models have supporters, and there may still be a few who support the Great Man theory according to Hollander's (2009) overview. In fact, in our own leadership journeys, both of us observe some who continue to subscribe to the heroic and Great Man theory of leadership. However, collaboration is the model recommended by many scholars and practitioners who also see that power is shifting to this newer paradigm.

As we noted above, a collaborative model is not all that new. In the United States Mary Follett advocated collaboration and teams early in the twentieth century and these ideas came to the fore again in the 1960s. And in 1961, W. C. H. Prentice argued that a major task of a leader is to help move others toward goals. What works best is for the leader to know well the individuals with whom he works so that he can help develop and guide them. "The man who successfully marshals his human collaborators to achieve particular ends is a leader."[10] This sounds "new" but he made these points over 50 years ago. His work reinforces the concept of leadership that involves relationships among leaders and followers who operate within a given context. What is needed is an integrative model.

But as Conger notes, collaborative strategy recommended in the 1960s did not fare as well in the 1970s and 1980s. By the 1990s we again saw a more favorable view of collaboration as a leadership model as knowledge became the currency for successful organizations. And collaboration is viewed as the best strategy for the twenty-first century. How to achieve structural change based on collaborative models will not be easy. Hollander argues for collaboration and inclusion and provides a model for these challenging times as he notes the importance of the reciprocal leader-follower relationship.[11] That the upcoming generation of leaders will move in the direction of collaboration is our hope.

We also agree with the concept that much about leadership can be learned. Leaders are not "born" that way. Young professionals should also understand the roles of transformational and transactional leadership and how each style may impact their own leadership development (Burns 1978; Bass 1985). As Cynthia McCauley and colleagues report (2006), "... although transactional leadership can be effective for motivating followers, transformational leadership is more strongly related to numerous leadership outcomes such as follower satisfaction and group productivity." And we agree with Quatro (2007) and others about the need to develop holistic leaders.[12] So our goal in working with young professionals is to expose them to various models and theories and to engage them in developing models that work for them and that will address twenty- first-century needs.

CURRENT RESEARCH

In the last decade several works that look to the future and provide advice to future leaders and the organizations where they work have become available. Studies such as Bruce Tulgan's *Managing Generation X* (2000), *Managing the Generation Mix* (2006), and *Not Everyone Gets A Trophy* (2009) along with Claire Raines, Ron Zemke, and Bob Filipczak's "Generations at Work" (2000) and Raines *Beyond Generation X: A Practical Guide for Managers* (1997), J. Jennifer Deal, Karen Peterson, and Heidi Gailor-Loflin *Emerging Leaders: An Annotated Bibliography* (2001), Warren Bennis, Gretchen Spreitzer, and Thomas Cummings (eds.) *The Future of Leadership* (2001) provide helpful insights on the topic of future leadership.

Tulgan's focus is on the workplace and about how best to bridge the generation gap there. He stresses how members of Gen X deal with multiple forms of information and how much they value flexibility and collaboration. Tulgan also provides examples of Gen X, particularly women and persons of color, who still face discrimination in spite of legislative victories and organizational statements promoting diversity. Helpful advice on dealing with the multigenerational mix also is mentioned. Following in that vein, Raines provides practical advice for those working with Generation X and discusses qualities that she finds in Xers such as embracing technology, independence, creativity and wanting lifestyles with more balance. The structure of the work environment also is the focus of the Zemke, Raines, and Filipczak study. They, like Tulgan, provide helpful insights. Xers, they note, like flexibility and are at ease with multitasking. Successful organizations learn how to realize the potential of workforces that are diverse in age ranges as well as other dimensions. The Deal (2001) bibliography follows up on the workplace theme and lists several sources that discuss Generation X and the challenges they present in the workforce, especially how to retain them.[13]

In their book of essays, editors Warren Bennis, Gretchen Spreitzer, and Thomas Cummings pay particular attention to how the organization of the future will need to change, and they discuss leadership lessons of the past that are important for the next generation. Several of the essays in their book offer important insights related to the next generation of leaders and have informed our thinking on the topic. The importance to leaders of building relationships, especially one's relationship to subordinates, is the theme of the essay by James Kouzes and Barry Posner in the Bennis book. In line with the Zemke study, they also describe the challenges presented by leading across generations. The youth culture in the modern high-tech and knowledge-based organization often is in conflict with the skills and habits of many older workers. The Baby Boomers (numbering some 80 million) and Generation X (about 50 million) have different value systems and work habits.

The Bennis collection also features insights by two "young" leaders in which they express their hopes that discussions of leadership will include thoughts from young and emerging leaders. Tara Church in her essay "Where the Leaders Are: The Promise of Youth Leadership," discusses the importance of wanting to make a difference and she argues for leadership development programs for youth. In " Seeking a Newer World," Edward Headington points out that Generation Xers want "more direct action" and ways to practice their ideals. He says that this new vision of leadership involves working with others to offer "our services directly" and "reaching out to others from diverse backgrounds to find new solutions." The author states that (this was written before Barack Obama obtained the Democratic Party nomination and then was selected as President in 2008) the focus of Generation X is on "community service and away from conventional politics." Both young authors stress that Generation X will seek new definitions and ways of doing leadership.[14]

Generational differences are also discussed by Jay Conger (1998), Pam Withers (1998), Joanne Cole (1999), Jim Rapp (1999), Jeffrey Cufaude (2000), and Mark Murphy (2009). Generation Xers want real balance between work and private life according to Conger who also notes their desire for a workplace that feels like a community. Withers addresses what managers need to know to work with Generation X. He notes that employers need to focus on making work more meaningful and also may need to provide more autonomy such as flexible work hours. Rapp (1999) advises managers to provide constant feedback to Generation X. Cole notes that Xers like teams, and want to know that their work is important to the organization. They also want to participate in planning processes for their units. Cufaude suggests that executives need to spend more time talking with and listening to the younger generation. He believes that older leaders need to rethink their strategies for engaging younger generations. Mark Murphy (2008) focuses on Generation Y and their need to know "why" certain tasks are to be performed. They need to have reasons for what they do and they like to see the big picture.[15]

Similar to many of the essays in Bennis, the authors Paul Rodriguez, Mark Green and Malcolm Ree (2003) discuss the challenges of managing a workforce that includes both Baby Boomers and younger workers. They surveyed workers at a major telecommunications company, both Boomers and Xers, and found significant differences. Their study draws some preliminary conclusions and cites, among other issues, that Xers prefer a challenging task that can be accomplished in a short period of time while the Boomer's time frame is longer. Xers like using the Internet and Boomers prefer the telephone. Boomers like regularly scheduled hours while Xers like flexible hours.[16]

In her survey of recent studies, Pixie Anne Mosley (2005) notes that Xers are seeking balance and personal enjoyment during their younger years and are not willing to defer personal interests until retirement. She also points out that Xers are more diverse and are more tolerant of diversity than any previous generation. Xers also seek balance between their work and personal lives, both for themselves and for their employees.[17]

Ron Carucci (2006) agrees with the authors above and notes that many emerging leaders are saying "no" to the leadership patterns of their predecessors and in many cases their mentors. They are looking for new models. He urges all who work with emerging leaders to be generous in displaying gratitude and appreciation and reminds us that to bring out the best in these new leaders, we, the "incumbent" generation, must listen to them and appreciate their passion and their new ways of defining leadership.[18]

Some 150 of Generation X were interviewed by Karl Moore (2006) who finds that they believe that each person's "story is important, not just the dominant story..." of the senior executive. He also highlights the importance to this generation of not eliminating emotions and feelings from business life.[19] And the article, "Leadership's Online Labs," (2008) highlights again the differences of Generation X from Boomers and discusses changes in leadership development efforts in the future as more and more emerging leaders will be communicating online and using online games to develop their leadership skills. Elizabeth Agnvall makes a similar point and describes how Staples and many other companies are using technology for leadership development.[20] Tulgan (2009) confirms these findings and adds that they need regular feedback.[21]

With the exception of Tulgan, Moore, and Carucci's works and the two essays in the Bennis book, most recent studies do not quote heavily from emerging leaders themselves. We believe that these voices are essential since both Generation X and Generation Y have views about organizational structures and about leadership. Additional emphasis on the voices of the emerging leaders themselves, written by them, is needed.

ANOTHER LOOK

Since we want to know more about what these emerging leaders—those of Generation X and Y— think, we solicited their views through essays, surveys, focus groups, individual conversations and observations. We asked them what leaders should strive to be in the future and how organizations should be structured to best support their young professionals. From conversations as well as recent studies cited previously in this chapter, we know that emerging leaders are eager for leadership experiences and not afraid of challenges. As the following chapters demonstrate, the next generation of leaders hopes to modify organizational structures to make them more collaborative and inclusive. Our belief that effective leaders now and in the future must embrace collaboration and inclusion was confirmed in December 2006 when *Time* magazine proclaimed that the Great Man Theory of History "took a serious beating this year," noting that the future is "a story about community and collaboration on a scale never seen before." *Time*, in highlighting collaboration, declared all leaders as the "person of the year."[22]

CHAPTER 2

HOW DO EMERGING LEADERS SEE THEMSELVES AS LEADERS?

HOW MANY OF US WAKE UP EACH DAY AND THINK ABOUT OUR LEADERSHIP style and how it impacts our peers and colleagues? Probably not many, even though we know we should. In our own leadership journeys, more attention to reflective practice would have been helpful. When you are in a leadership position facing many crises on a daily basis, reflection often takes a back seat. Sherry believed strongly in collaborative leadership but did not exercise it appropriately shortly after she became chancellor of UMass Boston. In her first few days on the job she found that the university was facing a daunting budget crisis. She worked closely with the senior staff to design a plan to deal with the crisis. A few of the faculty were consulted but not about the basics of the plan—only on the principles involved such as not to cut across the board. Not surprisingly, when the plan was presented to the university community, it was rejected. All of it! Cuts had to be made anyway, but the experience was painful and all too common for many in leadership positions. Because several more cuts came along, there was a chance to try again and to use a more collaborative approach the next time. This meant having a broad-based group of faculty and staff make a series of very difficult recommendations. None was popular, but there was greater acceptance because of the broader involvement. So reflection took place—a lot of reflection—but after the fact and the reflection had a positive outcome. This experience reinforces the importance of reflection as not only helpful but absolutely necessary.[1]

For Pat, reflection played a major role in deciding between pursuing a more secure position rather than remaining in an administrative position supported by grant monies. Five years into being the director of an academic skills training program for displaced homemakers funded by the Carl Perkins Act, she was encouraged by her supervisor to apply for a faculty position funded by state monies. The faculty position would provide more job security and provide a more flexible work schedule. Her current director position was funded on a year-to-year contract. She applied for the posted faculty position and went through the search process and was one of two finalists. The night before the second round interview with the vice president of academic affairs, she listed the pros and cons of the position and the strengths and weaknesses she would bring to each position. After some soul searching, she decided she would stay with the grant-funded position. Although the funding for the director position was not as secure as the faculty position, it was work that she was passionate about. Providing training for single mothers, divorced and widowed women with no marketable skills was challenging, but the results were very rewarding. When she arrived the next morning for her interview, she withdrew her candidacy and spent the time informing the vice president about her vision for at-risk women at the college. Going through the process of interviewing for the position gave Pat the opportunity to reassess and reflect on her skills and areas of passion and compassion.

REFLECTIVE PRACTICES AS NECESSARY TOOLS

To reflect on what went wrong and could be improved is a valuable exercise, but one that should not be used only in a crisis situation. Many young professionals with strong leadership potential do not devote sufficient time to reflection to evaluate their strengths and shortcomings. So the importance and benefits of reflection need to be stressed early. We encourage reflection in several ways: self-knowledge/awareness, writing essays on leadership and articulating and determining purpose and developing goals that align with that purpose.

SELF-KNOWLEDGE/AWARENESS

The focus needs to be on the person and how she/he can develop into a better leader, and an understanding of one's strengths and weaknesses is an essential first step. Warren Bennis (2003) suggests that self-knowledge is essential, and it includes both what you know and don't know about yourself. And Peter Drucker (1999) advises us that we need to learn to manage ourselves and, "Place ourselves where we can make the greatest contribution."[2] Daniel Goleman (1995), in advocating for the important role of emotional intelligence for leaders, lists self-awareness as the first step. Joseph Raelin (2003) concurs with the need for self-awareness and notes: "...leadership development has more to do with surfacing one's leadership tendencies than with introducing particular skills that constitute someone's list of leadership qualities."[3]

Comments from emerging leaders indicate that they see the importance of self-reflection. The need, as discussed by Chi Huang, a physician, is clear.

My entrance into leadership in medicine was circuitous and unexpected. As a practicing physician, my desire was and still is to provide the very best care to my patients and their family. And yet there were instances in my practice when systems and operations prevented me from delivering the most efficient and effective care. Motivated by this challenge, I cautiously entered into management and leadership with the same singular desire to care for people, but from a different vantage point.... The greatest challenge in my early career in leadership is understanding and managing people. People have different needs and motivations. Paradoxically, I have been challenged to know myself better, my strength and weakness, in order to grow professionally.

Later he credits Goleman (1995) and notes the importance of emotional and social intelligence.

... leaders need the ability to self-identify and self-regulate their emotions and also to understand the social dynamics of various groups of people. It is this specific skill that lends itself to effectively managing people.

A young woman leader from the nonprofit sector, Andrea Hurwitz, also reflects on the need for self-awareness as she outlines her views on what it takes to be a young leader.

... It is the young professional who chooses introspection over apathy, who challenges her own instincts to better understand what lies beneath her decision making, who is a young leader. Young leaders are professionals who translate the information they have absorbed so that they can take life's challenges and turn them into successes.

Reflection is seen as an ongoing process by Mary Tolikas whose work is in the biomedical area. Tolikas also sees the need for looking inside and outside oneself to the broader community.

So my journey in leadership continues. It is a journey within my own self, a continuous commitment toward building self-awareness and self-actualization and finding the strength to be continuously humbled by the learning. And as my experiences multiply and grow, so does my belief that it is the greater human values— such as justice, liberty, equality, freedom, and opportunity—that should underlie all my actions as I strive to achieve happiness for myself and my fellow world citizens. Leadership is also an outward journey, with the continuous commitment to keep looking for and connecting with the people who share similar values and hold on to a similar commitment for collective hope and passion for positive change. In a world seemingly full of complex connections and diminishing boundaries, can we all share and grow with similar human values or will protectionism in the face of intense competition prove to be an unsurpassable challenge?

Leadership is about transforming, transforming the world around you and the world inside you. And in the process, "plan to be surprised."

Other comments from emerging leaders indicate that self-reflection is a necessary but difficult exercise.

Although it's important and necessary, *it's also painful to look inward at your own shortcomings or challenges, both personally and professionally.*

I learned a lot about myself and my innate leadership skills. I stepped outside of myself and really used the time to reflect on my strengths and weaknesses. I really learned a lot about diversity in all of its manifestations and how important it is to take into consideration when leading.

It takes a lot of work... examining your strengths and weaknesses.

I learned that there are many ways in which I can take on more of a leadership role in my current position, despite my role as an individual contributor. I have clarified many areas for personal development and growth. It gave me courage to take more career risks and more confidence to achieve goals.

ESSAYS ON LEADERSHIP

There are many ways to encourage reflection, and we ask young professionals to write an essay describing their leadership style and discussing a challenging leadership experience. These essays provide insights into their issues. Several of these essays were revised by some of the emerging leaders after they returned to their workplaces. Subsequently, we collected and printed these essays. Now excerpts from them appear throughout this book so that the voices of these emerging leaders are heard.[4]

Several themes emerge from their writing. For some the essay was a chance to reflect in ways they had not done before and they benefited from taking time to reflect—to think about leadership and their own style. Some discuss their understanding of the need to be more self-aware. Others write about how they see themselves as leaders and how they might need to change. Almost all stress the need for leaders to find ways to continue to learn. As they write about their experiences, the essay as a reflection tool is confirmed, although some resist doing it at the time. Michael Rawan, a banker, provides an interesting perspective.

[Writing the essay] allowed me to reflect on my experiences, the mentoring I have received, the lessons I have learned, and the legacy I have been building. This essay is both a product of my journey as well as a homage to those that have guided and influenced my career.

Lisa DeAngelis, who at the time worked in a construction company, states her reasons for writing her essay with her friend Deanna Yameen who is in the nonprofit sector and how the essay helped clarify their thoughts.

> *... only recently in my career have I begun to understand that there is a better way of doing it; and by "it" I mean better ways of aligning yourself with your organization, having an active voice in the leadership that translates into the collective momentum of the company. It's my interpretation of synergy where, by having the right people in the right place at the right time with a common vision, the impossible becomes possible. Everywhere we look—sports, school, business—it's a competition, who can be the best. Within the organization it doesn't have to be a competition where there is a winner and there are losers. In fact, better things are accomplished when it isn't. When all persons can bring their whole selves to the table, and fully contribute, the outcome is incredible compared to what even the most talented leader can accomplish on his or her own.*

A lawyer, Christie Getto Young, who works at a major nonproft agency, used the essay as a way to look ahead.

> *My application essay focused on my aspirations to utilize the skills and experiences I would gain from the ELP to transition into a more formal management role. At that time, I was searching to develop more confidence and become more comfortable with my professional authority so that I not only truly functioned as a leader but also moved up the ladder to a more senior supervisory position. I was in my early thirties with a supportive husband and a two-year-old daughter. I lived and worked in Boston, and we owned one car, which we used on weekends. I could leave my office, pick up my daughter from her childcare center and then walk home all in approximately 45 minutes. At no time during the process of drafting my essay, or during my year as an ELP Fellow, was I particularly distressed when trying to balance my work and family lives.*

With a commitment to working in the political arena, David Halbert writes about the benefits of reflection and for the need to move away from the Great Man theory.

> *As someone interested in developing my leadership skills, and of achieving leadership positions of greater influence, I have strived to be both self-aware in my decision-making process, while simultaneously cognizant of how those decisions are assessed by others. By reconciling these two viewpoints, which often stand in stark contrast with one another, I find the final outcome is often of greater value than if I had simply acted from my own perspective, or conversely that of others.*
>
> *My goal is to be an elected official. As I have watched others attempt to lead, I have seen how a lack of understanding of the perspective of others, combined with an overestimation of the value of one's own views, leads to frustration and failure. In order for me to reach my goal, and be the type of leader that I strive to be, I*

know that it will be vital to stay connected to the light in which others see me. This is not so that I can always do what they want, but instead so that I know how to explain what I am doing and I why I feel that it needs to be done.

In times past, success could be achieved by the imposition of a singular world-view and ideology on others. Effective leadership in this context was determined by either brute strength or ruthless guile, often at the detriment of others who were deemed weaker or less cunning. As time has passed, and globalization has become the vanguard of progress, it has become not just preferred, but absolutely necessary, to have the ability to perform self-examination through the prism of others.

Sandra Bailly, from health care, discusses her leadership journey and how it is evolving over time. Her dual-citizen background (Panama and Barbados) plays a major role in her development.

A series of major life milestones shaped and continues to shape my view of myself as a leader. Embracing the view of oneself as a leader is an evolving process that is both a personal and public journey. As one moves through different stages of leadership, the ability to influence others toward a given cause/effort requires transparency (living in the fishbowl) and a willingness to put oneself out there first.

Ron Bell works in the Massachusetts Governor's office. He reflects on the need to learn from mistakes and to build relationships.

. . . leaders are not perfect, but leadership in the twenty-first century is learning from our mistakes and talking about them and passing that knowledge on to other leaders, helping them learn from experiences. That's not being done enough. I've had to search for my mentors. Too many people are holding on to what little influence they have and not sharing their wisdom. As we go into the twenty-first century, there is not going to be another Dr. King—one person in the black community—there is going to be a whole bunch of them. And that's a good thing, because we need to get perspectives from people of different races, ages and genders.

Relationships are key. We've become tense in our society and within ourselves. We've gotten away from the face-to-face, the looking square in the eye and seeing if someone is being truthful. Some of us have hidden behind technology, which is a great thing but it's caused us to become unrelational. We need to get back to the kitchen table, have meals together, congregate and forge relationships. Through my office, I'm trying to build that kind of community. I'm meeting with all kinds of incredible organizations with great programs and encouraging them to talk to each other. Leadership for the twenty-first century needs to have a strong foundation in cultivating our relationships.

DETERMINING PURPOSE AND DEVELOPING GOALS

An additional way to foster reflection is an exercise where the participants are asked to succinctly state their purpose. In dyads they reveal their ideas and then share their thoughts with the larger group. To state your purpose in a sentence or two takes thought and practice, and they struggle. And for most this is not something they have done before in a conscious way. Yet when they share with each other, clarification is easier and the results are positive. Thinking about and then articulating purpose helps to define the kind of leader you want to be and what you need to do to get there. Of course, this is just a starting point. The purpose of the exercise is to stretch one's thinking about the big picture and to put day-to-day activities into a larger context.

Some of the most common goals outlined are expanding networks, particularly across sectors, the desire to learn more about current issues in the region, and to understand the benefits of civic engagement. Young professionals also want access to current prominent leaders to see what challenges they face and how they meet them, and they seek information about different leadership styles to understand what might work best for them.

In interviews individuals who are now alumni/ae think again about their goals and what they hope to accomplish.

> *My primary goal was to take advantage of networking opportunities. However, I have been pleasantly surprised by my own professional growth through developing techniques used in the collaborative process of addressing complex social issues.*

> *My hope was to open up new networks (personal & professional)—to understand and open up connections to the Boston business network.*

> *A couple of my goals were to develop network strategies…and to develop different types of leadership skills…Depending who you are working with you need to learn different ways and one of the goals that I had was to learn different types of leadership, figure out which one you are, and when to adapt it and when to change. So when I deal with my team and co-workers, depending on whom I'm dealing with, I use different types of leadership skills…So those were my two main goals…and they were absolutely met.*

Others describe their goals in quite personal ways, ways in which they discover in themselves the capacity to be leaders. Many had always thought of leadership as someone else, as the person who sits at the top of the organization. Now they begin to see how leadership can be dispersed and practiced in new and expanded ways.

> *…I never really thought myself a leader. I think I'm still a developing leader, but my views of what a leader should be have changed since the program*

> *…The program focused on collaborative leadership, and how there are different types of leaders. And I like the description of what a collaborative leader is. I think I identified with that more than the ones who delegate, or overpower, or whatever.*

> *To be authentic and consistent, always do the right thing. Step up but also step back to let others lead.*

The program helped me conceptualize what being a top leader would be like and figure out what skills I needed to build... to differentiate between management skills and kind of visionary, charismatic leadership skills that a lot of the leaders that came to speak to us spoke about. And so the program just really challenged me to think about how I could develop those skills in myself, because I shy away from that a little bit...

Amanda Trojan, whose work is in the high tech field, writes about her goals and her leadership journey.

I am still at the beginning of my leadership journey. I have a basic understanding of my skills. I know that in the coming years I want to focus on conflict resolution and communication skills to prepare me for leading in a global environment. I want to begin to learn these skills within my next leadership role. I'm ready for the challenges ahead.... Knowing what I want, I can focus on what needs improvement in my day-to-day interactions.

Another young professional from the high tech sector identifies with Goleman's outline of the importance of emotional intelligence for leaders and his call for self-awareness, self-regulation, motivation, empathy, and social skills.[5] In an interview another young leader relates how opening one's mind to consider diverse points of views is important.

...A better sense of my leadership style, and greater awareness of the diverse minds, talent and people that exist and expanded networks that I can leverage outside of my immediate workplace.

Her Haitian upbringing is important to Anne Marie Boursiquot King who is in a health care foundation. Her background gives her unique perspectives as she describes what is important.

Perhaps it is the experience we all shared. Perhaps it is the common understanding that to get to the front of the line you have to actually get in the line behind everyone else. Perhaps it is my Haitian upbringing. The elders in my family and community always reminded us youngsters about working hard today for the rewards of tomorrow. Whatever the common denominator, I feel that many other younger, up-and-coming individuals do not have that sense of "you have to put your time in." I have been called upon many times to coach and mentor young people and I get the sense that once they've made a bit of progress or reached a milestone, they want the big reward.

Trojan also comments: "It's important as leaders to constantly inventory our abilities so that we can utilize the skills when we need them and work to build the skills that we don't have."

Networking across boundaries was a major focus for Pauliina Swartz from financial services. She is pleased with her emerging leader colleagues because of the many areas they represent and the variety of experiences they offer. She is surprised by how much she learns from them.

What impressed me most about the program, though, were my fellow emerging leaders, who were smart, passionate, and often accomplished in many fields. Their diversity was refreshing and enlightening, for they were diverse not only in gender, race, and ethnicity but also in the types of organizations they represented. These ranged from small one- or two-person "startups" to large multinational companies, and included such industries as telecom, media, and financial services as well as government and nonprofit entities. Some of my most memorable discussions were with fellows who, unlike me, had chosen careers in the nonprofit sector and were taking on various social challenges, including HIV/AIDS, teen pregnancy, and the plight of street children. These fellows had already emerged as leaders and have great potential to make an impact in their organizations and communities.

We find that when they look at their goal statements several months after preparing them and reflect upon them further in interviews, they see their own progress and realize that they have achieved many of the things that they hoped to do.

They are also asked to discuss with a peer a leadership experience that did not go well. They discuss what went wrong and why and their colleagues offer suggestions about what to do differently. As the discussion takes place, the process itself helps to clarify one's leadership goals and purpose. We are pleased that some have continued to assist each other with refining their leadership purpose and with professional goals. One group of alumni meets regularly to continue these conversations and to assist each other professionally. They call themselves the South Shore Men's Group and they tell us how beneficial it is to have a group of professional peers with whom to share experiences and from whom to seek advice.

So, finding ways for potential leaders to undertake thoughtful reflection is essential and beneficial. Reflection continues as emerging leaders are asked to be more aware of their strengths and weaknesses, use writing to clarify their thinking and to be mindful of the larger purpose as they formulate their goals.

LEADERSHIP PRACTICES INVENTORY

In addition to engaging in reflective practices, participants complete the Leadership Practices Inventory (LPI). The LPI, developed by James Kouzes and Barry Posner, asks individuals to rate their abilities in areas the authors believe that foster leadership development and also are ones that exemplary leaders possess. There are thirty questions and survey respondents indicate whether they participate in the behavior rarely, sometimes or frequently in five key areas including: (1) modeling the way, (2) inspiring a shared vision, (3) challenging the process, (4) enabling others to act, and (5) encouraging the heart. And the more you demonstrate the trait, the better.[6] The survey questions encourage further reflection and introspection and respondents are informed that they will complete the survey again after a specific period of time.

This exercise helps individuals focus on their current leadership style and what may be working as well as what might need to improve. The LPI pre and post-tests also provide a useful analysis of how, over time, individuals may improve their leadership capacities. This survey was given to the emerging leaders in each of the 2002–2008 cohorts as they began the program and again when they completed it. The LPI results from the 2002–2008 cohorts show encouraging patterns, and interviews confirmed many of these findings. We found positive increases in the scores overall and for each cohort with the completion of the second LPI survey, which was administered several months after the first.

There was an increase in the mean scores across all seven cohorts from LPI-1 to LPI-2 from 215 to 234.[7] (See figure 2.1 and table 2.1 included in the appendix for mean scores and cohort summaries.) Also some 48 percent of respondents achieved LPI survey scores at a level of 240 or higher, meaning that almost half of all ELP participants developed a tendency to "usually," "very frequently" or "always" engage in the identified leadership practices. These increases in scores suggest that being selected for a leadership development experience by an organization and then participating in leadership activities assists individuals to become more attuned to positive leadership behaviors. The period of time between administering LPI-1 and LPI-2 appears to be a time for participants to reflect on, refine and gain confidence in their leadership abilities. Reflection and training make a difference.

As we examined the data further, we also looked at the mean scores of respondents for each of the five separate categories in the survey (see table 2.2 for leadership practices) in addition to the overall cohort scores. There were gains in all areas: inspiring a shared vision, modeling the way, encouraging the heart, challenging the process, and enabling others to act. The level of significance of their gains across each of the categories and subcategories is statistically significant. We are encouraged, in particular, with these increases because participants clearly gained competencies in areas of personal behavior that are important for leaders. These areas of personal behaviors are ones that can be improved, and these young professionals are doing just that. The increase in developing a personal philosophy (see appendix) was especially encouraging as was the increase in encouraging the heart. The goal setting and exercises to define your purpose likely play a role in these gains.

The highest initial LPI ratings are in items that address personal attributes of leadership such as the following:

- testing one's own skills and abilities
- taking initiative to overcome obstacles
- speaking with conviction about meaning and purpose of the organization's work
- treating others with dignity and respect
- developing collaborative relations
- following through on promises and commitments
- setting a personal example
- praising people for a job well done
- giving team members lots of appreciation and support for their contributions

Even though these were rated fairly high at the beginning, the second LPI ratings consistently reflect improvement, indicating that the participants at times engage in the identified activities as at the highest frequencies. We also found lower initial LPI ratings scores on leadership traits such as:

- testing boundaries
- influencing others to envision the future
- having a clear philosophy of leadership
- recognizing and rewarding positive collaboration by others
- facilitating colleagues' skills acquisition
- holding others accountable for shared principles and standards

In each instance, however, the second LPI scores demonstrate improvement, indicating that the emerging leaders developed more enhanced skills in these areas. From conversations with them, it appears that some of these areas improve as they assume more responsibility in their organizations and have more confidence in themselves. One notes, "I hope to take more risks and really challenge myself to grow." Another writes: "I will become more confident, resourceful, thoughtful and adaptive." And another, "The possibilities are endless." A good summary: "I did not believe you could learn so much about yourself." Another strikes a positive note of being allowed to step outside of "our comfort zone." Others report how difficult it is to absorb feedback that may be negative, but that it is an important part of developing one's style. This is not surprising as Kouzes and Posner report that of the 30-item behavior assessment, they find that the "statement that ranks lowest from the observers' perspective, and next to lowest from the leaders' perspective is this one: 16. (He or she) asks for feedback on how his/her actions affect other people's performance."[8] Overall participants note continued personal and professional development augmented by increased self-knowledge and finding new approaches and perspectives about leadership.

GENDER DIFFERENCES

When we look at gender, we find that female participants initially self-assessed themselves as having higher levels of leadership abilities than men at the time of LPI-1. However, while both male and female participants registered significant gains across all LPI categories, males make greater gains than females. In fact, by LPI-2, the mean male and female scores are both 234. This represents a gain of 8 percent for male participants and a gain of 6 percent for female participants between LPI-1 and LPI-2. (In chapter 4 on gender we will look in greater detail at some of the issues for women leaders.) In conversations with males, we learned that they saw themselves as having less of the "soft power" attributes of leadership skills when they entered the program. They believe themselves strong on the "harder" and more technical skills so it is encouraging that they see gains in the "softer" areas.

Since almost all the participants have strong technical skills, a great deal of focus is on the less technical side: communication including both speaking and listening, negotiation, networking, inclusion, teamwork and the like. Many who study leadership now agree with Goleman that these softer areas need attention and practice. We do not ignore technical skills and believe that both are important. However, we do agree that sometimes the softer skills have not received as much attention as is desirable. We read with great interest Joseph Nye's (2008) call for "smart power" in which he recommends a blending of soft and hard power to "smart" power.[9] Nye's advice, although focusing primarily on diplomacy and related areas, also has broader meaning.

The LPI helps individuals focus on positive leadership behaviors and since the positive traits in the survey are also ones that are addressed in the program, it is not surprising that improvement occurs. Interviews with participants also provided further evidence. Young professionals, especially males, become more aware of the need to develop the more personal leadership skills and they do so. They also see these as essential skills for effective leaders and no longer view them as peripheral areas.

ALUMNI SURVEY

To better understand what emerging leaders have to say about leadership for the future and about their leadership styles, we surveyed the alumni. Surveys were administered in 2007 and again in 2008, and respondents were drawn from the total group, 2002–2008. Similar to the total group, they are racially and ethnically diverse with over a third people of color. They are well educated, the majority having obtained a BA or MA. Ages range from 24 to 58 with an average age of 37. This is not a group of Baby Boomers. (See tables 2.3 and 2.4 in the appendix for the demographic and organizational details.)

For those in the corporate sector, the largest segment works in an organization engaged in finance or banking. But areas such as telecommunications, high technology, insurance, and communications are also well represented. However, in the survey responses there are some different career choices for the two racial groups. Whites are much more likely to be in the corporate sector, with non-whites more likely to work for a nonprofit organization or the government.

Although respondents work in different fields, a majority of them have attained a leadership position in their organization. Nearly three-quarters of respondents (73 percent) directly supervise other people, which is similar for men (76 percent) and women (71 percent) with some differences for whites (76 percent) and non-whites (69 percent). The number of people they supervise ranges from one to 150, with a mean of ten and a median of four. The mean was eleven for men and nine for women, eleven for whites and eight for non-whites. In addition, over half the respondents (54 percent) manage a budget, most of which (83 percent) are over $100,000 per year. That difference does not vary by gender and 53 percent of men and 54 percent of women manage a budget, but there is a bigger difference by race, with 60 percent of whites reporting that they manage a budget but only 43 percent of non-whites so reporting. These young professionals are well positioned to assume even greater responsibilities in their organizations in the near future. These surveys, which were completed after they returned to their workplaces, also provide another chance for personal reflection. The individuals report on which leadership styles they think they possess, how satisfied they are with their current leadership style, and whether they would like to change their leadership style.[10]

The self-reported leadership styles (table 2.5 in appendix) cited most frequently were collaborative (99 percent), adaptive (97 percent), and authentic (95 percent). The least self reported style was charismatic (64 percent). That collaboration was ranked at the top is not surprising. Young leaders stress the importance of collaboration in interviews and in focus groups and those conversations are supported by the data. They also talk about the definition of a leader being separate from the title that one holds. They see themselves as more attuned to collaborative styles than some of their older colleagues, some of whom prefer more hierarchal approaches. They are less enthusiastic about charismatic leaders as they have seen many such leaders fall from grace so it is not surprising that this is ranked somewhat lower.

Several excerpts from their essays support the survey results. Lisa DeAngelis and Deanna Yameen in the introduction to their joint essay state:

> Many people encourage potential leaders to become independent, and the one person who runs out ahead of the pack is often rewarded. Collaborative leadership points the way toward moving everyone forward together. It not only respects, but actually fosters and promotes, diversity. Although everyone needs to move toward the same goal, success rests on each person bringing his or her talents and viewpoints to the table. The role of a formal leader in such a system is completely redefined. In a world of competition, technological advances, and an increasing need for social responsibility, interdependence is the key to true success.

Yameen also comments:

> My thoughts are that regardless of organizational design, collaborative leadership recognizes, values, and even celebrates that fact that everyone is a leader in the role that they play.

In his essay, information technology specialist David Dance, who is in health care, also highlights the importance of collaboration. "Effective leaders must be willing to collaborate by listening to others, especially those that may not agree with them."

And another emerging leader, Hugh Drummond, from the field of communication, applauds teamwork and sees it this way:

> I have found the best leaders to be those who recognize and welcome the contribution of the entire team. They do not fear contrary opinions or suppress differing styles. Applying these principles in my life, I work hard to always build a collaborative structure that fosters shared success and teamwork and inspires my team to believe in themselves and their objective. Doing this establishes a firm foundation that will weather even the stiffest adversity when it inevitably comes. Today a leader must lead with less control and more openness than ever before. Think about the power of the individual today.

Armindo Gonçalves works at the Boston Redevelopment Authority (BRA). He outlines why he believes that leaders must give of themselves and that they need to make a difference.

> From my perspective, leadership requires personal sacrifice and taking positions on matters that may be right but not very popular. This type of leadership is lacking in nearly every facet of our society, because personal sacrifice requires selflessness: giving something of oneself in order to make a difference. Sadly, in Western society, where self-preservation and individuality are of utmost importance, personal sacrifice is almost nonexistent.

There were some differences between genders, with men more likely than women to report that they are strategic and charismatic and women more likely than men to report that they are authentic and inclusive. There were fewer race differences, though the non-white group was more likely to see themselves as strategic and charismatic. As we will discuss in a later chapter, the commitment to collaboration sometimes presents problems for young leaders whose organizations have not adopted a collaborative model.

When respondents critiqued their current leadership style (summarized in table 2.6 in the appendix), almost all respondents are quite positive about their leadership style, with 4 percent reporting that they are extremely satisfied, and the vast majority reporting that they are very satisfied (44 percent) or somewhat satisfied (47 percent) with their leadership style. Only 5 percent said they were a little satisfied with their leadership style and no one said they were not at all satisfied. Yet, the majority of respondents (75 percent) said that there were things about their leadership style that they wanted to change. Clearly the reflection process has an impact. There were almost no differences between the two gender groups in their satisfaction with their leadership styles. There was some difference between the two race groups (white and non-white), and whites were more likely to say that they wanted to change something in their leadership style.

DECISION MAKING

Respondents had many ideas for changing their leadership styles (table 2.7 in appendix). Nearly one in five (19 percent) said they wanted to improve decision making, including improving decision-making skills in general and being more decisive. Some respondents report that they want to have more confidence (15 percent). Here we note that women rated this higher than men and whites more than non-whites. This gender finding is confirmed in conversations with young women and with their comments made in focus groups. More men than women selected the need to be more inclusive. They become more aware of the importance of this issue as they meet and work with a more diverse group of individuals. Improving communication by being "more direct," "being a better listener," "improving public speaking," or "developing better networking and [public relations] skills" is also mentioned frequently (14 percent). These findings again are in line with conversations with emerging leaders and focus group discussions.

ROLE OF SUPERVISORS

Respondents were also asked about how each of their leadership styles developed. We want to know the three strongest influences on them (table 2.8 in appendix). Over half (58 percent) report that a former boss or supervisor has been one of the top influences on their leadership style. This is an interesting finding and coincides with Kouzes' and Posner's observation that studies of corporate executives show that the "single best predictor of career success is the relationship (they) had with their first supervisor." And over half (53 percent) report that observing other leaders has been influential. We know from conversations that many report favorably on interactions with supervisors at their current organizations. In many cases, these may be the same individuals who select them for participation in leadership development. This is a positive sign and shows that many organizations understand the need to develop talented individuals and continue to experiment with the best ways to retain them. Joanne Cole (1999) in her article "The Art of Wooing Gen Xers" stresses how important it is for organizations to assist employees with career development options. She sees these actions as positive steps in retaining the best of the Generation X.[11]

There were only small differences between the two gender groups, with the notable differences being reports of fathers' influence (53 percent for males and 35 percent for females) and former boss or supervisor (64 percent for females and 51 percent for males). For the race comparison, the big difference is, again, the influence of fathers, which were reported much more by white respondents than the other race group (51 percent versus 31 percent, respectively).

We also learned from their essays about what makes a difference to them. Rawan comments on the strong influence his family had on him. This is in line with Kouzes' and Posner's observation that when asked about leadership role models, young people select family member as the number one choice.[12]

> My parents have been most influential, and I have watched them each enjoy success in their professional careers. More important, though, they have taught me that professional success should only be there to enhance success in personal life and not replace or compete with it. They have encouraged me to know no limits but yet be grounded by considering the impact your actions have on others. They have also taught me the value in building relationships with many people and the power that can be gained by bringing these people together.

Sandra Bailly's story also addresses her family influence, particularly as it relates to the role of siblings.

> Gender…Another defining aspect of early childhood that shaped my view of self as a leader was simply growing up with a brother. Although I instinctively gravitated toward nurturing and caring for others, I recall being fiercely determined to keep up with the physical and intellectual pace of a slightly older brother. There was nothing that he could do that I could not do too, and possibly do better. There

was plenty of healthy competition and self-awareness, and an unwillingness to settle for double standards imposed by gender seemed rooted in my core. It also helped to have a mother who promoted the idea of female independence through education and employment. In her mind, femaleness should not limit my potential or myself as a leader. As a result, I became that black woman who tends to see the glass as half full rather than half empty.

MENTORS

Four of ten young leaders (42 percent) report having a mentor in their organization. There was a difference between men (38 percent) and women (44 percent) but no difference between the two race groups (42 percent for whites and 41 percent for non-whites). There are many ways in which mentors assist emerging leaders (see table 2.9 in the appendix on mentors). For almost everyone with a mentor, their mentors give advice and feedback. The majority of mentors also open doors for future opportunities, point out the respondent's strengths and weaknesses, and meet with the respondent on a regular basis.

Hurwitz describes the importance of mentors.

Young leaders are also able to grow their networks by one or a few very important people whom they can call mentors. It is a great blessing for young leaders to build this type of relationship with someone who can offer career-related or other advice and also connect with other professionals. I have been fortunate to get to know one particular person, outside of my family, who stands out as a mentor to me. One of the greatest joys I have experienced as his mentee is that I know he is truly an advocate for my career advancement and well-being. As a young leader, I have observed how my mentor has interacted with me, and I hope to use these lessons as a mentor to a young leader in the future. Having a mentor is a rare gift, and it is my hope that young leaders will continue to hone and treasure these relationships.

Bailly also sees benefits for young leaders and has now assumed the role of mentor herself to many of them.

I enjoy being around those who can laugh (especially at themselves), those who understand that life is too short (an insight gained from caring for and losing my mother to breast cancer in January 2000), and those who acknowledge that everyone is a very important person. In contributing through others and reinforcing the development of others, I hope to reflect the following core values to a relatively young professional team: diversity, determination, dedication, and resiliency. As a midlevel leader immersed in a corporate setting for the last twelve years, I am comfortable growing and developing young, professional talent. I spend a great deal of time nurturing and caring for others, and I have enjoyed watching them bid their capacity and achieve goals, but I force myself to balance my desire to help others grow by devoting adequate time and effort toward growing and advancing myself, too.

She also sees a role for "upward" coaching.

> *In supporting the development and advancement of superiors, I also expanded my own self-awareness about how my diverse background, pursuit of learning, and need to nurture others collectively come together in my leadership style. Upward coaching without a personal agenda permits one to explore one's own strengths and weaknesses...*

The data also suggest some gender and race differences, though the number of respondents on which these comparisons are based is relatively small, since the total number of respondents who reported having a mentor is 55. Males are more likely than females to report that their mentors meet with them on a regular basis and enhance their networks. In the comparison of the two race groups, whites are more likely to report that their mentors point out their strengths and weaknesses, while the other race group is more likely to report that their mentor enhances their network.

In focus groups the topic of mentors and the importance of having mentors or personal advisors is discussed frequently. Several discuss the various roles that mentors play. Some define mentorship broadly as encompassing the entire network that is developed. Others note that rather than having a single mentor, several people can fill that role. Some like the concept of a personal board of advisors. Others focus more on the concept of personal coaching and many now see that as the way to go. Many also indicate, like Bailly, that they plan to be mentors to young leaders in their organizations. Believing that they have a role to play in mentoring the generations that follow them, several are already working with schools and other nonprofit organizations. They see this is an important contribution for the future.

We also find that focus group discussions for alumni provide an opportunity for young professionals to continue to define their leadership style and to reexamine their purpose. The conversations, like the LPI and goal setting, provide an opportunity for continuing self-reflection and hence improvement. In addition to the South Shore Men's Group mentioned previously, other less formal groups have also formed and many individuals assist each other in a variety of ways. These expanded and diverse professional networks are becoming important mechanisms for further growth.

CONCLUSIONS: ORGANIZATIONS CAN ASSIST YOUNG PROFESSIONALS

These young leaders are anxious to move ahead in their paths to leadership. Reflection followed by positive action steps works for most of them. As they become more aware of positive leadership behaviors, they strive to improve in those areas. They value networking and understand its importance beyond social situations. Many have mentors, supportive supervisors and helpful family members and find those associations valuable.

Data from essays, surveys, LPI results, interviews and reflection exercises demonstrate that providing opportunities for reflection on various leadership behaviors makes a difference. When followed with discussions and exercises dealing with leadership, individuals show significant improvement. Most of these changes involve being conscious of certain behavior patterns and making efforts to change or alter these patterns. When young professionals reflect on some of their gaps in soft skills, they become more aware of areas where they can improve. And when leaders have this information early in their careers, they have a better chance of making the changes, hence the need to focus on young professionals—emerging leaders.

If organizations are willing to make the investments in young leaders, the payoff will be long lasting. In fact, Jeffrey Cohn, Rakesh Khurana, and Laura Reeves's article (2005) "Growing Talent as if Your Business Depended On It," emphasizes that companies that do not prioritize leadership development end up "either experiencing a steady attrition in talent or retaining people with out-dated skills." These firms, they note, become extremely vulnerable when they have to cope with the many changes in the current business climate.[13] As a first step, organizations need to support and assist young professionals in reflective practice.

CHAPTER 3

WHAT QUALITIES MAKE EFFECTIVE LEADERS?

AS WE HAVE WORKED WITH EMERGING LEADERS AND OBSERVED ESTABLISHED leaders, we find that certain qualities and behaviors help leaders be success-ful. We do not subscribe to the trait theory of leadership, but rather find that successful leaders exhibit some fairly consistent behaviors. We agree with Kouzes and Posner that "leadership is an observable set of skills and abilities than are useful whether one in the executive suite…or on Main Street."[1] Many of these qualities have also been useful in our own careers.

Sherry's list includes all the behaviors described in this chapter, but she elaborates on three areas from personal experience and discusses these in more detail when meeting emerging leaders; they are communication, net-working, and collaboration. From experience she advocates frequent and transparent communication in a variety of means for anyone in a leadership position. Each person has a special gift—her/his voice. Use it to share your vision and to help people understand who you are and what motivates you. For Sherry, numerous presentations to faculty and others in higher education as well as the wider community means that where and how you commu-nicate must be carefully evaluated. Each presentation is important to that group so always be prepared and aware of the particular setting and of your role. Speaking provides a unique opportunity to clarify what is important to you and your organization and to share those thoughts with others. Enjoy it and use it every chance you can.

Networking also works and is essential. Some of Sherry's networking efforts are instructive and show that sometimes you can develop a network for par-ticular needs where one does not exist. As a university president, she worked with Zee Gamson at the New England Resource Center for Higher Education to develop a network of women college presidents in Massachusetts. In the late 1980s, women presidents were still small in numbers, some 8 percent nationally, but there were several in Massachusetts so we invited them to lunch. Many then became part of an ongoing conversation and provided support to each other in a variety of ways. In addition to discussions of common concerns on the campuses, the group also found its voice in the policy arena. Six of the women presidents (including those of UMass Boston, Wellesley, Regis College, and three from community colleges) and two female trustees met with the Governor of Massachusetts in 1991 to oppose new regulations that would cut the welfare benefits of recipients attending college, by limiting their benefits to attending a two year (not a four year) college. The meeting garnered a headline in the Boston Globe "College Presidents Meet with Weld on Welfare Cuts," and at the meeting members of the group outlined the problem with a state proposal that would seriously impact many students, including large numbers of female students.[2]

This network stayed in place for several years and was useful to the presidents but also found a role regarding policy implications for students. While at Yale as associate provost, Sherry also benefited from a small network of three women including Mary Rowe at MIT and Eileen Shapiro at Harvard. In the 1970s, all found support in each other in dealing with gender and racial issues as universities began to change their policies and practices. Sherry's external network in the business community was also forged while she was a university president and provided many advantages to the university and also gave leaders in the business community a better understanding of the role of public universities. That network continues to this day and is the source for many of the outstanding speakers for the program. So there is no doubt about the importance of networking and of making it part of all you do.

Collaboration also has been a major part of leadership activities for both of us in our professional lives. We both resist the temptation to take charge although admit that sometimes it is necessary when you are in a leadership position. Overall, however, better decisions occur when collaboration takes place and all points of view are heard. This is true not only for the college setting but also for business organizations as well as nonprofit ones. As a female university president, it was part of Sherry's agenda and some may have attributed that to a female style. But collaboration works with both male and female colleagues. As a management strategy having a diverse group involved brings about better recommendations and decisions. Adding doctoral programs and achieving doctoral university status was an effort that involved many—a dedicated and hard working team. And when the university embarked on its first capital campaign, it was a team effort, a collaborative one that made it successful. All on the team could take pride in what was accomplished. None of these initiatives could have been achieved with a top down set of orders, so the more collaboration worked, the more it became the norm.

Always important for Pat were risk-taking, being entrepreneurial, and supporting diversity and inclusion. Pat's career began in the nonprofit sector and the first organization she worked for was the YMCA of Honolulu, Hawaii, first as an outreach drug abuse youth worker, then a youth program director responsible for teenage leadership development programs. After nearly a decade of youth work, she pursued her dream of becoming an entrepreneur. With profits made from the sale of some real estate, she opened a children's boutique. Influenced by children's stores she had shopped at in New York and San Francisco, she leased space next to an upscale women's clothing store, and within a month with the help of her family and an interior decorator, renovated the space, filled the store with merchandise, and opened for the Christmas season. Handcrafted clothing and toys became the hallmark of this specialty store. Then five years into the business, a large community-based organization in Honolulu recruited Pat to return to community work as the director of programs and volunteer services. She accepted the position and hired a manager to oversee the store. During the seventh year of business, Pat's husband was offered a position in Massachusetts, and they moved to the mainland with their three children. Her husband's position was secure, but Pat was uncertain about her career choices.

She embarked on another entrepreneurial endeavor. She set up a wholesale business of importing tropical flowers and foliage and made arrangements to have a wide array of tropical plants sent by air to Massachusetts on a weekly basis. Once Pat and her family were settled in a home and the children were in school, she ordered the first shipment of flowers and started her business. With the "yellow pages" that covered a 50-mile radius, she visited flower shops and sold her goods. During the same time period she was sending out resumes responding to postings in the classified ads. (The Internet was not widely used at the time.) After three weeks, she was interviewed at North Shore Community College (NSCC). After her second round interview was over, she brought in a bundle of orchids for each of the search committee members because she had completed the deliveries earlier and she had a surplus of flowers. She was hired, and her boss later told her that in addition to being the most qualified for the position, he was impressed with her spirit and resourcefulness.

While at NSCC Pat served as the director of the displaced homemaker program (an academic skill training program for women), coordinator of human service training, and the dean of the division of human services. Her division had the best representation and retention of faculty of color, but the college faculty, administration, and staff did not reflect the diversity of the student enrollment of the college, so Pat took an active role in the college-wide diversity committee. This committee had oversight of hiring searches and diversity programming for the college. Pat was one of the co-founders and trainers of the National Coalition Building Institute (NCBI) chapter at NSCC. In her various positions she reaffirmed her values in collaboration, entrepreneurship, and risk-taking and the need for inclusive structures.

Hence our work on leadership development focuses on areas that we believe will benefit leaders of the future: collaboration (including teamwork and networking), communication, context, authenticity, empathy, ethical behavior, innovation, creativity and entrepreneurship, inclusion, and gray thinking. Those are stressed in the major components of the program, which involves meeting with and learning from established leaders, participating in specific skill sessions, and engaging in collaborative efforts through teams. These areas are also identified in surveys and in conversations as ones the young professionals themselves cite as most useful in their personal journeys. At the top of their list we always see the big three: collaboration, networking, and communication.

As noted in the previous chapter, potential leaders need to begin with honest reflection and evaluation. We discussed how we use the LPI categories of modeling the way, inspiring a shared vision, challenging the process, enabling others to act, and encouraging the heart as an important initial step of reflection. Reflection is followed by focusing on skills and behaviors that leaders need to consider if they are to improve.

COLLABORATION

Young professionals applaud collaborative approaches and like the idea of moving away from command and control structures. They see the benefits of engaging people with different viewpoints, and they also argue that collaboration helps produce buy in. It is important for the people you collaborate with to believe it was their idea. They advocate building alliances and partnerships. Breaking away from a leader centric model and seeing the need for participation by followers in shared decision making is the way to go. Hollander bemoans the fact that in some quarters the "Great Man" theory, supporting the view that the leader is the main actor, continues.[3] We concur and do not support the Great Man theory, and believe that the next generation of leaders will change organizations to make them more collaborative and inclusive.

We like these comments from alums.

Effective leadership is effective listening—question asking... to find out what's behind it; [n]ot the "John Wayne style of leadership"—seen as a collaborator versus an opponent—as a consultant, inviting others to "tell me more."

I give credit to others, recognizing their ideas—I live it.

At work I have a team of 16 people—collaboration is important—I need to recognize ideas listen and not shoot down opposition—otherwise I could be missing out on a great opportunity. I have to examine the merit of the ideas and be open to changing direction.

Unfortunately in some organizations collaboration is more of an idea than a reality. A McKinsey study on the value of employee collaboration finds that nearly 80 percent of the senior executives surveyed said that "effective coordination across product, functional and geographic lines was crucial for growth, yet only 25 percent of the respondents described their organizations as 'effective' at sharing knowledge across boundaries."[4] We hear this same concern expressed by many emerging leaders who sometimes become discouraged when they advocate for collaborative strategies. On a more positive side, many organizations are moving toward more collaborative structures and support our view that emerging leaders should have opportunities to practice a variety of collaborative activities.[5]

Surveys and essays support the conclusions reached in focus groups about the value of collaboration. Learning about and practicing collaboration consistently comes near the top of the benefits cited. These young professionals see leadership in a more inclusive way than do some Boomers. They do not favor the old "top-down" capital "L" leadership model. They believe that everyone can be a leader and that it is important to enhance leadership qualities in everyone. One of them notes, "it is hard to make change on your own." Another explains that everyone "needs to be brought to the table" and that communication is needed at all levels of an organization. They highlight the importance of making everyone feel a part of the team and they emphasize how important it is to share the credit and help people take ownership of the group's ideas. Their vision of a new collaborative leadership model is encouraging. Again, in their words: "It takes a team that works together to be successful." And, "Collaboration with both internal /external partners is key to reaching lasting and effective solutions to complex business challenges." ... "true leadership requires collaboration—for some people who may not be on board with your mission, it takes empathy and long term understanding of where you need to be." It also requires, "Remembering that nobody did it alone!"

Yameen's thoughts follow prior observations of John Kotter (1996)[6] on Leadership (capital L) and leadership (small l) that indicate both are important but that small "l" leadership is absolutely necessary.

I'd prefer to draw a line between Leadership and leadership. To me capital "L" Leadership is about your position within an organization. On the other hand, leadership with a small "l" is what we all need to exercise. Collaborative leadership

does not mean we are all doing the same thing or have the same amount of author-
ity. I consider small "l" leadership to refer to the fact that we are all leaders in
our roles. I may have an organizational position near the top of an organization
chart, but I may not be able to do the jobs of many other people who appear to be
placed on a lower rung. Let's put it this way: If you put me in charge of benefits or
payroll, you'd have a revolt on your hands. No one would be getting paid. Am I
more important? No. I need people in those jobs in the same way they need me. A
truly collaborative leader recognizes this and makes sure people are supported in
their roles and that they have a voice and, again, that they are challenged to act on
the shared values of the organization or institution. Ultimately, everyone should
feel as if it is his or her duty to constantly challenge themselves and everyone else
to do the same. That responsibility should be shared within the organization and
probably outside of the organization as well.[7]

This theme is expressed again in focus groups where several raise concerns
about the role of leaders versus the title of leader. They see individuals
who are named leaders but who do not display positive leadership qualities. Leadership is a characteristic, they say, not a title and they distinguish
between leaders and bosses, noting that not all bosses make good leaders.
Leaders, however, can be found in any position and are often identified as
leaders because of their behavior.

Young follows up on these themes as she discusses the importance of leading from the middle and of collaboration.

During my year as an ELP Fellow, I learned a great deal about leading from
the middle and collaboration. All of this helped me to see that success need not
be defined by how high one can rise and that extremely innovative and effec-
tive accomplishments are often achieved collaboratively—rarely by one great leader
shepherding a team of followers.

Hugh Drummond makes a strong plea for collaboration among leaders as
well as in organizations.

Technology and the Internet give voice to everybody, even the least among us. In
an instant, one can touch the world. It empowers everyone, amplifies a cause, and
builds awareness. Effectively used, the Internet can foster discussion and creativ-
ity, build community, and provide freedom. Used differently, it can attack, tear
down, and even spread hate.

In previous paradigms, leadership for some meant control. Theirs was a top-
down world. Validity came through experience, pedigree, connections, and fame.
Information and communication went from top to bottom and, only when desired
and deemed appropriate, from bottom to top. Today that sort of control is virtually
impossible and leaders who think in these terms will not succeed. New generations
of workers approach the work world differently. They know that information is

accessible. Jobs are not permanent. Change is definite. Diversity is expected. The next generation of leaders must effectively embrace collaboration and openness in their drive to find success.

The importance of collaboration is also highlighted by Dance.

"My-way-or-the-highway" leaders will not survive the twenty-first century. Effective leaders must be willing to collaborate by listening to others, especially those who may not agree with them. The skills to network effectively are a must-have for this century. Having a small and limited group of peers will not work in the long run and there is no excuse for shy leaders. They must be open, honest, engaging, and personable at all times.

In her essay a working mother and banker who prefers to remain anonymous discusses how collaboration has helped her through difficult times.

Having experienced various leadership roles in my business career before mother-hood, I have surprised myself with the leadership qualities I have developed as a special-needs parent. The particular values that have been critical to my leader-ship development are diversity, networking, and a commitment to working col-laboratively. Moreover, true leaders need to find their passion and develop both confidence and courage to become effective advocates for their cause. As I work to carry over these skills into my professional life, I've found that they have allowed me to become more effective as a leader and have driven me to take on more leadership roles.

The emerging leaders practice collaboration primarily through work in teams. Each participates in a team project for an eight-month period. A general area of activity, which is important to the region, is selected each year. In 2007, they examined the topic: why do young professionals stay in the greater Boston region? They are very positive about the city and region and made a series of recommendations on how to strengthen activities in some areas to encourage more young professionals to make their professional lives here. Subsequently they were invited on a local television show to outline their recommendations. The topic caught the attention of many stakeholders because it addressed an ongoing issue in our community.

Many men and women who come to the greater Boston area to study do not remain to work after graduation. The team suggested that a possible strategy for retaining more young professionals is to institute something they term *webternships*. This plan does not utilize the Internet or the Web initially. Instead these young professionals suggest creating a new personal network—a web—of all the college students who participate in summer internships in companies in the area. Why not bring them together for a two-day summer retreat/workshop? This would be an opportunity to tell them more directly about the benefits the area has to offer (maybe including a Red Sox game!). The workshop time could also be used to do some focused leadership training, and then these interns would have a cohort—a network—that might encourage them to stay and work in the area after graduation. The common experience would help them remain connected. The idea has caught the attention of many in the business community. Recently the Greater Boston Chamber of Commerce listed as a primary goal for the region that of enhancing internships including an annual internship summit in line with many of the recommendations of this team. And in July 2009 the Chamber and the Federal Reserve Bank of Boston jointly hosted more than 300 summer interns at the Bank to highlight the city as a good place to work and live. This effort is part of an expanded effort of the Chamber and the Bank to retain talent and is in line with the innovative thinking of the 2007 team.

In 2008, the team focus was on the role of young professionals in philanthropy. Research from this project revealed that young professionals want to work in companies that practice corporate social responsibility (CSR). One team worked with the Massachusetts Business Roundtable to look at company practices around CSR. Members of the team interviewed several employers, representing a cross-section of industries, and compiled findings from nine of those companies. The five key findings about effective CSR are: create and maintain a clear link to the company's mission and secure executive endorsement, engage employees at all levels as the decision makers and leaders for CSR targets and activities, leverage employees' skills to make positive contributions to the community, provide opportunities for employees to develop new skills, and encourage teamwork through group volunteer programs. With greater competition for customers and for talented individuals, CSR is seen as an excellent recruitment and retention tool for businesses. Because all areas in the country are struggling to attract and retain young professionals, corporate philanthropy can be used to help get those individuals and keep them. Even in these difficult economic times, organizations need to focus on the long term and CSR needs to be part of their strategic planning.[8]

In 2009 the teams worked with Boston World Partnerships, a new nonprofit organization created by the Mayor of Boston to raise global awareness of Boston as one of the world's leading centers of intellectual capital and innovation. The plan is to use cutting edge technology to enhance an understanding of the advantages of this area. These young leaders are highly skilled in a variety of new technologies so their input is particularly beneficial to the organizers of the project. Once again team members are involved in significant issues and can apply and practice team skills in a real world situation—one in which their findings make important contributions.

This intense effort also helps young professionals learn first hand that collaboration isn't always easy and that teamwork, although productive, can be difficult. Teamwork requires defining the goals and the scope of a project in ways that all can accept so that there can be a meaningful end product in a reasonable time frame. It also means figuring out what each person on the team is responsible for and who will do what. The issues that arose as the team projects went forward are ones that are similar to those found in the workplace as discussed by Anne Field (2009).[9] How to establish trust? What to do about colleagues who do not participate fully? How best to define goals in a meaningful way and get results in a reasonable time frame? How to make sure that everyone's point of view is heard and respected? How to agree to disagree with respect? The teams are assisted in their work by a coach who helps them through the various hurdles.

The team members come from diverse corporate and organizational settings, which add to the richness of the conversations. One of the major long-term benefits includes building new networks and strong collaborative relationships. This experience creates special bonds among team members with their colleagues and some of the teams continue to meet to share professional experiences long after their specific project has been completed. They become consultants to each other. In addition to the enhanced networking that occurs, the team experience also fosters creativity, innovation, and out-of-the-box thinking. Another benefit is that participants gain an understanding of the many issues society faces. For example in previous years, one team looked at the role of pilot/charter schools and whether their numbers should be expanded. Another team examined whether legal immigrants should be allowed to pay in-state tuition at state universities and what affect this might have on economic development. Individuals learn first hand how difficult many policy decisions are, what factors determine how policy is set, and the role that citizens can play in these complex issues. When completed, the team projects are presented to the president of the Federal Reserve Bank of Boston, the Mayor of Boston, and other interested stakeholders. These are real teams, working on real projects, with deadlines and deliverables. This experience highlights in a practical way the benefits of collaboration, and the end result is often better because it was not one person's idea but came from blending and refining many ideas.

Many commented favorably during interviews about the team experience and the benefits of collaboration. The team project helped these young professionals learn how to deal with strong personalities and how to work through difficult problems and challenging time frames. These are issues that they face in the workplace on a regular basis.

It was a good way to build relationships with people from different sectors/ industries; opportunity to see different leadership styles; appreciate "strengths and weaknesses" of each person.

I can now look at issues through several lenses. I see the importance of bringing everyone to the table.

[The team project] was where the real leadership played out. We took turns in our group being leader; sometimes someone had to back-off a little bit and another person took charge—planned the meeting, planned the notes and all that. So our group worked really well together, I was very pleased and those are the people I mainly keep in touch with.

Several others note that they see how successful collaboration can be helpful in their workplaces and that they have a "better understanding of how to go about organizing a business initiative by identifying the people one needs to talk with inside and outside the company." Others note that they have moved from "taking charge to allowing the conversation to flow and trying to lead from the back." And another discusses the benefits from "accepting the difference in approaches and styles among colleagues." And finally, "we learned...not simply management skills, but collaborative leadership skills so that you could work with a diverse group of people."

It...focuses on learning collaborative leadership techniques through working with your cohort as well as meeting with various existing leaders in the community, and in addition to that it helps you to develop an amazing network of people through-out the city of Boston who work in a variety of different fields whether it's public sector or private sector.

In her essay, Yameen also comments on some additional benefits of collabo-ration and teamwork as facilitators of change.

The choice of a dialogue is very important. The very root of the word reflects our values. I used to think that the word began with "di," meaning two—such as two people talking. It actually stems from "dia," meaning through. This means that a dialogue involves people, on equal footing, going through something together. It is a joint experience that affects all involved. That's true collaboration. As leaders, we are trying to bring about positive change. Making change is difficult, since our old habits exert a fairly strong influence. Actually writing in a different format and continuing to do things differently when appropriate sends a strong message.

Drummond explains his personal first-hand experiences with the Bill Bradley presidential campaign and the benefits of working as part of a team.

As you can imagine, watching the months of unbelievable dedication end in ago-nizing defeat was difficult for all involved. As a campaign leader, I was deeply concerned about the lasting impact defeat would have on my team, most of whom were involved in their first public service experiences. Over my two years with this group, we worked hard to create an environment that fostered success and team-work, and we inspired each other to always believe in self and the mission, thereby establishing a supportive foundation should critical incidents of crisis arise. Our days tested our reach and our stamina. We were grateful for our shared ability to remain balanced, even during the tensest circumstances. The emotions of victory or defeat could not interfere with the tasks at hand. My team knew that I respected their commitment in all that they did.

We strove to be approachable in everything. We were a close team, yet we understood how we fit into the world around us. We encouraged each other to take ownership when one of us saw a void, and to do whatever was necessary and appropriate to get the job done. As in any charged environment, confrontation and conflict struck frequently. I approached each day with quiet good humor, even when I had nothing to laugh at. As the department head, I . . . believed in our com-bined talents, and when challenged, stood up for what was right. I was stubborn at times so as to push the edge, I confronted difficult personalities with patience and good spirit, and I never allowed troubling issues to fester too long and detract from our goal. After all, campaigns never have time on their side. No matter the gripe, we were on the same team.

. . . For me, I learned a lot about leadership and the style of collaborative lead-ership that I would take forward from this experience and apply to my personal and professional life. The campaign team left that effort filled with the noble spirit of public service, a firm belief in the power of teamwork, and an eye on the future.

The working mother and banker (anonymous) outline how important collaboration is in the business world as well as in her advocacy work.

Most important, I have learned that the collaborative style of leadership promi-nent in today's business world is clearly applicable to my advocacy role. . . . I have come to realize wholeheartedly that a collaborative approach is entirely more effec-tive in achieving [the] desired outcome.

I was fortunate to have been exposed to a collaborative management style very early in my career. When I was an assistant manager in my office at age twenty-three, my manager was a role model for the collaborative approach by fostering team decision making, valuing input from coworkers at all levels, and building group consensus. For instance, when we needed to hire a new officer for our group, each of us interviewed the candidate and we made a group deci-sion to extend the job offer. Not only did this set the stage for the new hire's smooth transition, it also made each member of the team a stakeholder who was committed to the employee's success. When I was promoted to my first manage-ment position several years later, I modeled this collaborative style with my own employees and found it to be a tremendously powerful ingredient of my career success.

A nominator also praises the collaborative team experience:

> *The participants learn how you sometimes have to sharpen your focus to come up with a manageable project. They start off with a topic of affordable housing, and they have to whittle it down to something much more specific in order to get something done in the time that they have, and that is something that you often have to do on the job, particularly if you have a leadership role. Although they don't necessarily realize that they are going to learn that, they do learn it before they are through. Nominator KK*

Their efforts in collaboration also lead to improved project management on the job.

> *They come back to the bank better able to manage their time and set priorities, which eventually will help them in leadership positions. Another one [benefit] is project management—one specific individual I was talking with said that when she did the project with her team, she learned a lot of project management skills, and when she came back to the bank, we put her in a project-kind of role which she hadn't thought she was ready for before. Nominator KK*

By providing them with ways to see the benefits of collaboration with an actual team experience, these emerging leaders are better prepared to work in teams in their organizations and to become experienced collaborative leaders. Our hope is that they will also assist their organizations in becoming places where collaboration happens on a regular basis.

NETWORKING

In our own experiences networking has been a driving force. This is not lost on the emerging leaders. In focus groups and survey responses, they applaud the benefits of building strong networks professionally and personally, and we continue to give them examples of how very helpful networks are. They cite as an enormous opportunity meeting individuals they would never meet otherwise. Effective networking is a business imperative rather than simply a social skill. In a session on networking techniques, we stress that networking takes place in a variety of settings and that it should focus, in part, on what you can do to assist other individuals—how to be helpful. We practice everything from the placement of a nametag (right shoulder) to the handshake and how to eat (don't) while networking. They are eager to know how to do it more effectively and how to keep a network current.[10]

These young leaders initially become acquainted with some fifty other young professionals from a variety of businesses and other organizations. Immediately new professional and social networks develop. Later their network expands further when they also have opportunities to meet the 400 alumni/ae all of whom have had a similar leadership development experience. When we ask them about the impact, they note that their networks become wider and deeper and that they have more diverse contacts and they cite enhanced networking as a major professional and personal benefit. Because we create a network for them by bringing together some 50 talented young professionals, each individual does not have to find new contacts on a person-to-person basis.

An especially important facet, and one frequently noted by alumni, is the benefit of networking across and among business and organizational sectors. They call this cross sector networking. For example, financial services individuals meet those from real estate, higher education, telecommunications, nonprofits, technology, biotechnology, and the like. The connections with people in a variety of areas present enormous business and philanthropic opportunities. A banker meets someone from the Boston Children's Chorus and becomes its treasurer. A teacher whose charter school stresses careers in health meets several individuals from hospitals and others in the health care industry and outstanding speakers for her classes become available and new connections are formed. Another individual from a nonprofit organization finds a banker who is sympathetic to the role of that organization and assists with fund raising. A banker with a degree in engineering hears about a nonprofit board that works for school improvement, focusing on math and science, and joins it. The participants consistently emphasize the value of the networking opportunities that includes building or enhancing personal and/ or professional networks often in fields unrelated to their professional work. The traditional "old boys network" is transformed by these young professionals, and now it includes several females and many persons of color. Yet it works in ways similar to the networks of old. The concept is reinforced when established leaders relate to them how important a variety of connections are. These connections, they note, help leaders achieve their desired leadership roles from managerial positions to board memberships. The team experience gives participants another way to hone their networking skills since they have regular contact with five to six individuals from a variety of organizations over an extended period of time.

Comments from participants describe the benefits of networking.

Collaborative leaders appreciate the power of networking and that's something that I hadn't given any credence to prior to my involvement in the program... how to involve people would be another.

I wanted to gain an opportunity to network with other professionals... I also wanted a chance to hear what the current leadership felt the next generation had to do in order to move the city forward. We talk about collaboration and... that's what I wanted to hear—hear what the message was as to what emerging leaders need to do or should be thinking about in order to help the city move forward, but also what their thoughts were about collaboration . . . how to make it work.

. . . my goals were to develop network strategies . . . and to develop different types of leadership skills . . .

Georgianna Meléndez, who is co-director of a university project aimed at promoting minority representation in organizations and on boards, describes the importance of networking and how it helped her. At the time she was executive director of a nonprofit organization focusing on domestic violence.

It [the Emerging Leaders Program] allowed me to develop strong relationships with professionals from diverse sectors, backgrounds, and ways of thinking. Those relationships carried over to professional success. Fellows became committee members on the board, helped facilitate funding opportunities, fundraised for the cause, led to other connections that did the same . . . and it goes on. I have access to a network of leaders that have been open, helpful, and strong. We all do for each other and we open the door to as many people as we can.

Nominators and supervisors also see focused networking as an opportunity for young leaders to "make connections for those whose jobs do not expose them to the outside community" and that working with participants from other organizations helps them gain an external perspective, which in turn helps them do a better job. A sponsor from one organization mentions the importance of networking across sectors:

Leadership training is always helpful . . . However, for an agency like this one where we serve the public and we really want to understand perspectives, to have our emerging leaders connecting to the wide-range of leaders that are emerging through all of the different sectors, that's a great networking opportunity. And my sense is that those connections will last for life, and they will provide a broad prospective to issues and that's very important to people who work here . . . Nominator R

COMMUNICATION

The importance of communication became quite apparent in the months leading up to the 2008 election. Barack Obama was not only a strong speaker but also was adept at using electronic media in a variety of forms. The communication strategy worked and many were able to see first hand how those in leadership positions benefit from communicating effectively. And very few individuals in leadership positions can stay there if they are not influential communicators. Young professionals recognize the need to hone communication skills, and they mention that in every conversation as well as in surveys. They see it as one of the main functions of an effective leader.

Communication is not only key for leaders, they tell us, but leaders also set the tone and leaders need to communicate with every level in the organization. Because part of leadership is having an understanding of your audience and how your message may be perceived, leaders should be empathetic and put themselves in others shoes. Leaders also need to be open and transparent. They worry about what happens in organizations where there is a lack of reliable information, and they see that the rumor mill flourishes and fills a vacuum. Good leaders keep the doors open for communication, they argue, and this also builds confidence in the organization. They want to be skilled at building relationships and in communication and see the need for mastering all forms of communication—electronic, paper, and oral.

They benefit from meeting established leaders who are excellent storytellers. And using stories to help young professionals understand leadership is proving to be an excellent strategy. Stephen Denning (2007) describes how leaders can inspire action through communication and he equates strong communication skills with transformational leadership. "If leaders' inner commitment to change is to have any effect, they have to communicate it to the people they aspire to lead."[11] These experienced speakers have exceptional skills in framing the issues effectively.[12] Each of our speaker/leaders has a distinctive and quite different style, which also demonstrates that there is not a single model to be an effective communicator. But each communicates her/his goals clearly and forcefully and stresses that you can't lead if you can't make clear what you are committed to and passionate about. They tell stories about their lives and these have lasting benefit. One of the alums relates how he remembers one speaker, currently in a major role in the financial sector but formerly a Vietnam veteran, discussing that in Vietnam the bullets were real, but in the business world, the only bullets are "paper bullets." "The concept of 'what's the worst thing that could happen' encourages me to take risks...I bring this perspective into work each day."

We see immediate benefits as young professionals observe effective communicators in action. One speaker almost wears out the carpet as he marches back and forth while he speaks of his personal experiences as a Latino college student in Ohio and his support of inclusion. Another speaks in a quiet voice with no gestures and the room is silent—individuals listen intently for every word. She describes the courts and law and the impact on individual rights. Another lists lessons learned from several years as a CEO. His strong commitment to diversity and inclusion is evident and can be seen throughout the company he headed. One who was raised by a single parent, a policeman in New York, describes running for and winning elective office as the first African American district attorney and the leadership lessons he learned along the way. Some use slides and other visual aids to make their points about what makes for successful leaders, but most simply tell their story. All are effective and their impact on young professionals is a lasting one.

An emerging leader notes:

The leader talks really stood out for me. To hear…something and ask "what did you do wrong and what did you do right?" And at the level that these leaders were, very rarely would they open up and have that type of conversation outside of this program…The leader talks were really influential and some of the speakers talked about what they would do differently. I think about that now, and I am very aware of it.

Another writes:

Getting to know some really talented and inspiring emerging leaders at the same time that we are being exposed to wise words from prominent area leaders has been an amazing experience.

Andrea Hurwitz found comfort in hearing about experiences, many of them difficult, that senior leaders endured to arrive at their current jobs.

I was initially shocked by one attribute that was present in so many…the leaders' careers were a series of unplanned events. I had assumed that the most successful leaders had embarked on a predetermined path, that they had had a vision from a young age that guided their journey. In fact, it was quite the opposite; many of the leaders' choices were part of a series of organic steps that had never been anticipated. I was inspired by the risks that so many of the leaders took as their careers progressed. So often, it was these moments that yielded their greatest growth.

As I think of the leaders of the future, one of my hopes is that they will take the time to ask both types of questions—the clarifying and the "pathway to leadership" ones. The latter are critical for broader professional growth and introspection. In a world where "Googling" someone could be mistaken for getting to know another person, or where it is easy to get caught up in the deadline-driven assignments that are critical today, it is my hope that young leaders will continue to ask about others' stories—about the professional and personal choices that guided their careers. The wisdom they will garner from these discussions may not necessarily help to complete today's "to do" list, but it will join the broader fabric of one's leadership understanding and growth.

King notes the strong effect of hearing an established and authentic leader discuss what matters.

She did not speak about being a leader, but clearly she was one. She spoke about the skills of listening and making the commitment to listen; the dynamic of being in a position of power –perceived or real; and being proactive in bringing different voices together.

. . . But in terms of leadership—a word she never used in her presentation—it was clear to me that she was a leader in philanthropy, in her community, and seen as one among her peers. There was neither hype nor the sense of I did this or that. . . . she was a leader in how she listened to the different parties with whom she was engaged. She did not come across as having told anyone what to do or how to do it just because she knew the answers. . . . Like the other leaders I've met and heard, she listened, worked with people, paid her dues, and gained respect and recognition for her contributions.

Meeting and hearing such individuals reminds me that I have much more to learn, experience, and contribute before I can call myself a leader. Leadership is the embodiment of various components [such as] listening [and] understanding that you have to work hard. . .

Huang, the medical doctor, notes how important it is for him to hear from established leaders and how that experience influenced him.

The opportunity to listen to and learn from world-class leaders was invaluable. It was at this point in my career that I comprehended that leaders are created and not born.

After hearing and interacting with these leaders there is no doubt in anyone's mind of the importance of being an effective communicator. The importance of an open style of communication is a lesson well learned.

We provide guidance and practice to enhance public speaking skills, partially by building on the strengths of the speakers. The young professionals learn how important it is to have a clear and concise message and how to frame issues correctly. They also are given examples of the importance of presence and of how effective speakers exude confidence. We stress that practice is necessary even for the shortest speech. In one exercise they make public presentations based on their research from their team findings. The presentations are critiqued, and they receive instant feedback on areas where they need to revise their approach. We also discuss how to prepare for being a member of a panel or other situations in which you are not giving a major address. How to deal with the media is covered, and several of our young professionals have been featured on local television panels. Strong communication skills are an important part of leadership and these young leaders are now better prepared in that area.

Communication nowadays is also through social networks using electronic media—LinkedIn, Facebook, MySpace, and the like. They see benefits and new ways of staying connected but they also understand the possible drawbacks. In spite of the variety of ways to communicate electronically, most indicate that face-to-face interaction remains important and necessary to them. At a recent event several spoke about how important it is to see each other and to talk and to listen. They want to have personal contact in addition to email and other electronic sources.

Improving communication skills also means learning how to have difficult conversations and how to be a good listener. One describes how what he learned was immediately helpful on the job. "The first day I came back to the office, I scheduled a lunch with someone I had had a difficult conversation with. I told them how I would handle it if there is another one in the future, I asked them to hold me accountable...I used the skills in the first week." The importance of two-way communication, including listening and how listening facilitates communication and thereby effective leadership is stressed. In addition to difficult conversations over specific issues, they also tell us how problems arise when someone, perhaps a superior, tells you to be honest and tell me what you think. But when one engages with them, one finds that they don't actually want honesty. Honesty is the last thing they really want, and "you are doomed." They argue that you need to move carefully in such circumstances and get to know your manager or supervisor and determine the best way to get your message heard.

Their comments at the end of the program demonstrate that learning about and practicing communication has a direct impact in the immediate workplace. One of the alumni recently made a point of telling the current cohort that he had failed to take our advice to always practice—even for the shortest speech—and that he regretted that he had not done so. Listen to that advice, he said.

CONTEXT

Young leaders tell us how important it is to understand the context and culture of organizations. One notes that how the company is "supposed to work is never typically how the company actually works." They benefit from Ronald Heifetz's (1994) analysis that reminds us of the need to "get on the balcony" to try to understand what is really happening. Leaders, he says, who stand on the balcony gain new insights into difficult situations. We remind them that this concept helps one understand the nuances and complexity of a situation because it forces one to consider all aspects and all possible alternatives. Don't make assumptions that because something worked one way before that it will follow the same path. It also is a helpful tool in thinking about your role as a leader. How do others perceive you? What messages are you sending? How do others see you? What new approaches might be used to address a problem?

Understanding culture and context are also an important part of being on a team. An appreciation for the complexity of situations and the surrounding environment is essential. Anthony Mayo and Nitin Nohria (2005) agree that understanding a given context is an important skill as is the need for the leader to be able to adapt to a given context. Heifetz also discusses the differences between technical problems and adaptive problems, and these young professionals apply some of these principles in their team projects where they practice problem solving and active listening.[13] They analyze various stakeholders' points of view and figure out how to deal with conflicting interests. Understanding the issues from many vantage points and taking the time to analyze the possible complications is an important step in developing an action plan for a team or for an organization. The team experience provides valuable training for managing difficult situations in the workplace.

In conversations and focus groups, these young leaders also tell us of their struggles with the dilemma presented by whether to modify your behavior in a given context and how that may relate to your values. They see the need to be adaptable depending on the type of organization, for example, differences in profit and nonprofit. But they ask what do you do when what appears to make one successful in a particular organization is in conflict with your core values? Do you go out drinking with the boys if that is expected behavior for getting ahead, even if it is not what you prefer to do personally? They agree that you can make some compromises, but that you also should stay authentic to your own values. One notes, "corporations that are successful are ones that stick to their values" and they believe that it is important for individuals to do the same. Another comments that there is a balance to be struck between what we believe and realizing that we have to work with many different kinds of people to get things done. Overall, they advise that one's values must be considered because they are an important part of who you are. As you understand and adjust to the culture, do not compromise your values. One comments that "who you are and how you display yourself as a person sends a message." Retain your core values and strengthen "your belief in yourself."

One emerging leader writes about how important it is to gain an overall understanding of the context of a business situation.

> *Now when I implement certain initiatives…when I am looking to open new markets, I have a better understanding of how to go about not only organizing the initiative but about the people we need to talk to both inside and outside [the company] for perspective…that perspective has allowed me to be more effective when it comes to reaching out to constituencies that before I may not have reached out to for feedback…that's more of a holistic approach to leadership as opposed to just get the job done and do it successfully…*

Another relates his experience with how to figure out the relevant context.

> *It was interesting because I know that had I not attended the program I would have gone to a [specific] task force with an internal agenda and that would be to make sure we got what we needed and not necessarily view it as a collaborative*

effort to address the issue. . . . I was able to go into those meetings and not only look
to information that would be of value to us but also to fully listen to some of the
concerns that others were having.

One notes how the experience helped subsequently in the home
organization.

I believe that one of the reasons I was asked to participate in a multifunctional
task force [at work] was because I had just finished [ELP] where we were work-
ing with people outside of the organization. The learning that I got from dealing
with people who are not within our organization and trying to get a cohesive
group together really was a remarkable benefit that I then had the opportunity to
practice in my workplace.

Valuable learning occurs by discussing and practicing the actual components
of a successful project. The experience is of benefit to the participant in the
work situation because this particular individual had not had project management experience.

A nominator also discusses how important it is to understand context.

It takes a long time to develop a sense of how the pieces fit together. Some of it is
as simple as continuing to develop empathy and understanding where people are
coming from . . . like who is fitting where, how do decisions get made, where are the
major influences coming from and what is motivating them . . . in terms of being
an effective participant in those kinds of discussions, you have to really hone those
skills, give them a landscape—who is interested in being carried where and why,
what's the long range outcome that the folks are looking for. Those are things that
are developed over time but if you can speed it along, that would really be an asset.
Nominator Q

When leaders understand the context, they are better able to handle conflict
and to learn from it. Follow up exercises in negotiation focus on being respectful of the points of view of others and understanding the underlying reasons
for conflict in order to develop various strategies for resolving it. Developing
empathy is useful as is not being stuck in your position. What does the other
party need to have to move forward? Win-win situations where both parties
get something of value are the goal. Practice in "getting on the balcony" to
enhance an understanding of a situation and skills in conflict resolution and
negotiation also are particularly useful in a variety of workplace settings.

AUTHENTICITY AND ETHICAL BEHAVIOR

Young professionals want to be authentic and ethical leaders. Leaders, they
say, need to be absolutely committed to something and be passionate, sincere,

and ethical to play a leadership role. No one wants to follow someone or work with someone who appears to have no core belief system and who changes from day to day. They see being consistent as a part of authenticity and value that in leaders. Bill George (2007) describes these characteristics as authentic leadership.[14] Prior to our discussions, young professionals had not given much direct thought to the concept of authenticity, but came to see that authentic leadership encompasses efforts in modeling the way, inspiring a shared vision and encouraging the heart—concepts that are part of reflection. They quickly recognize and praise the authenticity of leaders whom they respect.

Daniel Goleman's (1995) concept of emotional intelligence (EI) also speaks to authenticity and young professionals find it useful to evaluate their own efforts accordingly. Authentic leaders are empathic and self-aware. Stephanie Cote and Christopher Miners (2006) as well as Kevin Groves (2008) have offered additional supporting data that such behavior benefits organizations. Young professionals come to realize that emotional intelligence is a necessary component of leadership development and a strong indicator of organizational success. Since structured interventions can increase EI levels, an understanding of EI is part of the reflection process.[15]

One of the more productive ways to learn about authenticity and observe emotional intelligence is for emerging leaders to meet authentic leaders and hear their stories. One speaker discusses how his ethical values came from his family, particularly his grandmother. The values she instilled in him remain and are a major part of the leadership model he describes. Although she is over 100 years old now, he continues to seek her guidance. Other speakers also discuss the importance of strong ethical values, and many note how their individual family backgrounds and early experiences contributed to their values. Other insights are that each person needs to find her/his own path to leadership because that is what makes one authentic. Speakers also mention how important it is to continually learn and that leaders should give back to their communities.

Another credited his success as a CEO to having strong empathy and to understanding where others were coming from and using those insights on a daily basis. That approach also was put in place with customers and it worked. Speakers also discuss overcoming obstacles and how leaders create their own opportunities in many cases. Most are able to bounce back from difficult circumstances as stronger and more clearly focused leaders. Difficult experiences become ones for learning and for improving as they learn from mistakes and from overcoming obstacles. These conversations make a deep and lasting impression. When reflecting on hearing the speakers, several note the impact of the strong moral compass of these individuals and how important that is to being a successful leader. These presentations again help young professionals reflect on desirable leadership behaviors, and they are able see themselves and their leadership style in new ways.

Authenticity is key to Meléndez who writes about how she has followed her heart:

> I have had friends and colleagues ask about why I made certain moves, why some so short and why so long in others, and how do I make a decision to take a chance? My response is simple and consistent. I follow my heart. If I can believe in the mission and I think that I will be challenged and grow in some way, AND I believe that the work will have a positive impact, then it is a no-brainer. Not all of my risks have panned out. I have learned some hard lessons. I have reflected on mistakes I have made and have had to revisit my strategies, but I have always learned something.
>
> I also have learned lessons from my peers along the way. Some were good and some were really challenging. In our fear of taking risks, we can sometimes hold each other back.

Others commented further on what was gained from hearing from established and authentic speakers, especially when they discuss how they might handle something differently. "It was important to have conversations with leaders who were willing to talk about what they did right as well as what they did wrong, and how they might have acted differently. The current leaders offered skill tips that were invaluable."

Closely tied into conversations on authentic leadership are exercises and discussions on ethical dilemmas. Honesty and integrity is the number one quality that young leaders want to see in their leaders and they, too, desire to be leaders of integrity. As ethical challenges appear more often in the business and nonprofit sectors (Enron, Tyco, Bernie Madoff, the Catholic Church), sessions on ethics have become increasingly important. Central to the conversation is a discussion about why so many ethical lapses have occurred in recent years. Deborah Rhode and Amanda Packel (2009) remind us that only a quarter of Americans think that executives are honest and that "employee surveys suggest that many American workplaces do not support" a culture of integrity. Yet individuals perform better when "they believe their workplace is treating them with dignity and is rewarding ethical conduct." And young professionals tell us that frequently that they confront ethical questions in their organizations.

We discuss the Parable of the Sadhu (Harvard Business School case, 1997) and ask them to wrestle with the ethical dilemma raised here. The author of the article faces such a dilemma when he encounters an ailing Sadhu on the mountain he is climbing as he is fulfilling a long awaited dream to climb the peaks in the Nepal region. Providing assistance to the Sadhu would impede his own progress, and he faces difficult decisions as he contemplates what to do and how to behave in this challenging situation.[16] In processing the story participants are able to recognize many parallel circumstances that they face every day and feel better prepared to deal with them. In comments and written evaluations they tell us that ethics discussions and decisions are difficult and that they benefit from having intense discussions of these issues in a setting where trust has been established and various viewpoints can be shared and debated.

Entrepreneurship, Creativity, and Innovation

Leaders need to be innovative thinkers and entrepreneurs who are risk takers and creative. These qualities are needed in both the corporate and nonprofit sectors. Our young leaders meet both business entrepreneurs and those whose creativity is demonstrated in the social sector. These individuals thrive on innovative out-of-the-box thinking and seizing opportunities. One woman created her own high tech company, an academic established an online learning company, and another woman heads a unique business that makes specialized candies. Still another has created a Hispanic news service. And at a major hospital in our city, social entrepreneurship from pediatrician Dr. Barry Zuckerman resulted in a national program Reach Out and Read to engage doctors to encourage reading and provide books to their young patients.

As emerging leaders hear these stories, they learn about creativity, innovation, and risk-taking and again see authentic leaders who follow their passion. They also identify the challenges that are present when one moves outside the boundaries as an innovator, but the rewards are evident too. We see much of this creativity and innovation manifest itself in the work of the teams as new ideas emerge. The end result is enhanced because of the collaboration that occurs.

In addition, some of these young professionals have become entrepreneurs themselves. Paul Francisco came to the United States from Honduras and began his career as a professional football player (Miami Dolphins, New England Patriots, and Cleveland Browns). Recently, with a colleague, he launched his own business and discusses his path to becoming an entrepreneur.

My outlook was shaped by watching men and women of different races work and live together harmoniously as I grew up. I learned that people have more that unites them than differentiates them. All of us are born inherently good; some acquire racial biases as the result of upbringing and cultural experiences. I know that prejudice can be overcome as long as people are willing to understand where their biases come from and are willing to change.

That was the philosophy I adhered to as diversity sourcing specialist. I enjoyed bringing diverse people to Boston, despite the challenges. I was helping to build leadership skills among professionals of color as well as fill a need in the city. Diversity recruitment was an area I felt passionate about and one that I wanted to explore.

Workforce diversity in America no longer had the same meaning it did thirty years before. Gone were outdated conversations about quotas and affirmative action. Workplace diversity was now about developing businesses, strengthening management teams, and showcasing leadership. It was about helping individuals and companies achieve their personal and corporate best. I knew it was only a question of time before I would launch my own business focused on diversity recruitment. I had found a niche for myself.

In addition to Francisco, several others have established their own businesses in areas such as communication, public relations, and technology.

INCLUSION

Francisco's business is in line with what is needed now and in the future. Leaders must be inclusive and understand and appreciate cultural differences. The demographic data for our region and the nation indicate that a more diverse leadership structure will be essential. The new global economy and its rapid pace of change mean that a greater appreciation of the benefits of inclusion is occurring and that diversity must be viewed broadly to include race, ethnicity, gender, cultural and religious backgrounds, sexual orientation, disability, age, and organizational identity. In the cohorts of young professionals highlighted throughout this book, over 40 percent are people of color and over half are female. And the organizational variation is enormous. These young professionals represent a wide range of businesses and organizations from major U.S. corporations to smaller companies, governmental agencies, and nonprofits. Bringing together young professionals who are diverse is an important step in creating a pool of future leaders, and it is a necessary first step, but it is not enough. To "teach" inclusion and cultural awareness is not a simple task. Specific discussions and strategies related to inclusion are needed and some of those conversations are difficult. Yet many are affected positively. The importance of seeking out others who see things differently should be common practice.

We know from surveys and interviews that this area is the one that receives both positive and negative comments from young professionals when they reflect on leadership learning experiences. Diversity sessions have a strong impact on most participants and yield positive results in areas such as learning to work across sectors, changing perceptions of individuals who are different, having new experiences of being the "other," and learning about unconscious racism. Almost half of the participants report that they increase their ability to work with diverse groups due to these experiences even though that experience often moves them out of their comfort zone. They also note that as a result of these discussions they think differently and more broadly about the concept of privilege. One notes, "I seldom have an opportunity to work with people of color and while I do have friends of color, often these types of privilege conversations do not come up." Most see the benefits of getting to know and work in a large diverse cohort, and for many the emerging leaders experience was a more diverse setting than their workplace.

Another comments: "I thought we were doing better on diversity than we are, based on the stories shared with me this week." Another statement repeats what we hear time and again.

> *I have always worked in racially diverse environments with mostly women in the nonprofit sector. It was such a rich experience to interact with an equally racially/culturally diverse group of men and women and people from the profit sector. I saw commonalities and gained understanding of business and how to better collaborate across sectors.*

This quote sums it up:

> *This was a fantastic opportunity for me to interface with MANY different races, ethnicities, and cultures. I recognized how privileged I really am, and at the same time, how deprived of the value of all these other cultures, races, and most importantly, people, I have been.*

The emphasis on inclusion and diversity is generally viewed as helpful by most, but we also are aware that for some moving to an inclusive stance is difficult. The conversations produced a level of discomfort in some of the participants, which is understandable. One stated, "I am diversified out."

Others help us understand how they reach their levels of comfort with diversity and inclusion. Early in her life Bailly, an African American woman, developed an understanding of the need for cultural awareness and outlines the benefits of inclusion as a leadership strategy.

> *As I embarked on my first journey through Europe in 1985, I recall absorbing the message that "nothing is right or wrong…just different" as I approached another new culture and family. This message resonated with me then and resonates with me now as I approach diverse groups in everyday life as a leader. I am passionately connected to cross-cultural experiences and exchanges and seek out opportunities to travel and learn new languages (my most recent trip was to India in November 2007). Again, this was a growth experience that shaped my view of self as a leader, and it has reinforced my willingness to remain open, take risks, recognize*

differences, and influence others through diplomacy and engagement. Inclusive collaborative leadership is understood.

Other comments indicate a broader sense of diversity. "Diversity as a race issue is so prominent in the [United States] but much more broader than that—now I have a different skill set for diversity—it's much broader. Now I am understanding and accepting diversity and how it contributes to productivity." Another writes, "I changed my definition of diversity—its expanded to discipline and thought—it's the way I look now to define creative solutions—it changed the way I look at other organizations—I know I need more input."

Our conversations indicate that they welcome diverse points of view and believe that honest and straightforward discourse is needed. The next two chapters address issues related to gender and race and the benefits of inclusion in more detail.

CONFIDENCE

Rosabeth Moss Kanter's book *Confidence* (2004) outlines in some detail how important confidence is to building successful organizations and winning sports teams and how it helps people achieve high levels of performance.[17] Having confidence and using it in positive ways to move an agenda forward is an important lesson. We are pleased to find that these young leaders gain confidence in themselves and their organizations in them. Confidence is enhanced initially when the person is nominated because the nomination is a way for the sponsor to confirm leadership potential. The organization recognizes that person's achievements and hence the selection for further leadership development. Moreover, we find that a substantial number of participants report a change in job responsibilities afterward.

Organizations also find that when participants return to the workplace, they demonstrate more self-confidence in addition to having developed expanded and productive networks. One sponsor puts it this way:

I think the greatest benefit is increase in confidence. . . . in the world today confidence is the biggest impediment to leadership . . . I have incredibly talented people who don't often feel like they are as talented as they are, therefore hold themselves back, don't always express themselves freely and are a little bit uncertain, because the world is made up of people who are uncertain to exert their power and influence. Nominator R.

Another comments on the boost in confidence:

It [leadership development] was positive reinforcement because it gives them a boost in their confidence and their visibility. It motivates them to try harder and do more and be more career-focused. Nominator KK

Other comments from sponsors concur and discuss seeing young leaders reenergized and more civically conscious.

I can tell you that they all have been very energized, they've all come back to me...and said "Thank you, I'm loving this program."...So, the way I would see the change is just becoming much more civically aware. That...and being proud of themselves for putting themselves out there, being involved on teams, what they are learning, what they are contributing. I could see a lot of pride. Nominator RR

What I've been able to observe of a colleague here who was in the program is that I think there has been a growing sense of competence and willingness to lead here within our group...Nominator Q

Trojan expresses the value of confidence to her as she grew as a leader.

...demonstrating confidence can get you far in life....in many cases, acting as if you are in charge, especially in a leadership situation, will propel those around you to trust you as their leader. As a result, you will also feel that strength...Not only does acting confident get people to believe in you, but it can also result in great strides in learning...When you're put into a situation that stretches your ability, you learn more than if you are always at ease in your role....The more difficult the situation and the more you manage your way through something, the more the learning sticks.

Another writes about finding a new sense of confidence.

The ELP helped give me the confidence to accept a new position that was not only a challenging career move, but also one that helped me to attain my personal goals to achieve a better work/life balance.

GRAY THINKING

Another concept that is important for leaders and one that resonates with young leaders is the idea of "gray thinking."[18] So often leaders believe that they must move quickly to make the right decision and find the right answer or they will be perceived as weak. Their decisions are black or white; they take pride in being clear with no nuance. Yet more thoughtful deliberation would have been beneficial and a better strategy. When Ellen Zane, president and CEO of Tufts Medical Center, speaks she emphasizes how often she uses this concept in her own work and the young professionals relate to the idea positively. The concept supports not making every decision instantaneously and being able to hold two opposing concepts in one's mind as more data are gathered and critical thinking occurs. Some tell us that they had not thought about this as a productive leadership technique before the discussion, and one mentions that he knows a specific case in his organization where "gray thinking" would have led to a more productive direction.

Conclusions

From essays, interviews, and focus group discussions, we find many positive comments about the impact of a range of positive behaviors for young professionals and also for their organizations. What they value most are enhanced networking opportunities and improved communication skills, which top the list, along with a renewed understanding of the importance of collaboration and teamwork. For communication, many specifically cite improvement in public-speaking ability and how they have become better listeners. They also have a much better understanding of the need for effective communication throughout the organization. In addition, more inclusive cross sector networks, especially across professional lines, have been forged. The expanded networks mean that they are connected for the long term in new ways. Collaboration is cited and they remember the team experience more fondly in retrospect rather than when actually engaged working on the teams. Better collaboration also leads to more positive interactions between and amongst colleagues. When the emerging leaders return to the workplace, they have increased their appreciation for collaboration and have honed their skills working in teams. Because they are more aware of the difficulties that can emerge in working on teams, they are better prepared to deal with them.

Also high on the list is an increased awareness of the need for cultural awareness. Most now have a more complete understanding of diversity and are better prepared to deal with these issues and help their organizations realize the benefit of an inclusive culture. Equally encouraging is that they are more at ease and more respectful of others' points of view. They had not thought much about authenticity as a necessary component of leadership, but are now aware of how significant it is and how much they value that quality in leaders whom they respect. They use different terms for it in discussions such as following one's passion and having a clear vision. They want to be authentic leaders, and as we saw in chapter 2, many define themselves that way.

Focusing on areas such as communication, collaboration, networking, context, authenticity and ethics, entrepreneurship, inclusiveness, confidence, and gray thinking helps young professionals develop the leadership behaviors that are needed in the twenty-first century. The personal opportunity for growth also enhances their confidence, and the organizations involved also see positive benefits as individuals return to them more confident and with a new set of skills.

Now we turn to issues of gender and race to see what effect they have on young professionals pursing leadership roles.

CHAPTER 4

WOMEN AND LEADERSHIP: PROGRESS AND ROADBLOCKS

WHERE ARE WE? STILL STUCK

Women were hopeful in the 1960s and 1970s as federal legislation favoring women came into place and the opening of new opportunities seemed imminent. We believe it is essential that more women occupy leadership positions, and it has been one of the major forces driving our work. Workplaces of the past, and many in the present, still do not do all they can to support women's advancement. When Sherry started her professional career, there were many barriers. In the early 1960s, she was offered a salary 20 percent less than a man would be offered for the same position and was told that it was easier to hire women so they are paid less. It was perfectly legal since the equal pay act was not in effect at the time. And in a subsequent conversation at the university where she was pursuing a graduate degree with a generous fellowship, she was also told that said university would never hire a woman in the very department where she was a degree candidate. There was no Title IX to prevent such a conversation or such a reality.

A decade later in the 1970s Pat's experience was more positive. With the Equal Pay Act of 1963 in place, her first professional position out of college with the YMCA of Honolulu was at equal pay with her male counterparts. She also was one of only two female directors of 42 directors at the five branches. Training opportunities internal and external to the organization were abundant and encouraged. Seven years into her tenure Pat was offered an opportunity to attend graduate school, was awarded a YMCA national scholarship, and provided a year sabbatical. She was also awarded a fellowship from the Department of Health and Human Services. So there was some improvement from the 1960s to the 1970s but where are we now? And what is next?

In our alumni survey, discussed in chapter 2, we find some differences between the responses of women and men professionals. More women have mentors, but the men report more positively that their mentors meet with them on a regular basis. Both genders are satisfied with their leadership styles, but more men than women indicate that they are making "a lot" of progress toward their career goals. Men also are more likely to say their values match their organizations, while for women, their values match "somewhat." In addition, more women than men see diversity and inclusiveness as an important leadership challenge for organizations in the future, and women give a higher rating to networking than men. As for personal style, men favor strategic and charismatic and women choose authentic and inclusive. Women have more concerns about confidence than men.[1] Although blatant discrimination has decreased, more subtle forms, along with stereotyping, remain in too many instances. One of our colleagues describes the current situation for females as "still stuck."

And when we look at where we are, much has yet to be realized. Recent research on women's progress highlights both the good and the not so good and supports much of what we have observed in young professional women. In *Enlightened Power*, the authors (2005) include essays by current women leaders who tell of their experiences and also delineate the many challenges remaining. In his foreword, David Gergen notes he is convinced that "women are the equals of men in all fields of endeavor, starting with leadership." He also states that, "command-and-control leadership has given way to a new approach, often called an influence model of leadership." The new leader, he says, "persuades, empowers, collaborates and partners," and when we describe the new model, we use terms such as "consensual, relational, Web-based, caring, inclusive, open, transparent—all qualities that we associate with the 'feminine' style of leadership." (Joyce Fletcher expresses concerns about the meaning of this for women. Although more relational styles of leadership are widely praised, to the extent that they become associated with women, they become less valued or as she says "women's 'deficiencies' are redefined as strengths.") Gergen agrees with other authors that we need to "dismantle the emotional and physical barriers that exist for women seeking leadership roles." The remainder of the book of essays highlights stories related to women's leadership and the battles that have been fought and reminds us of the barriers still in place.[2]

In their book *Women and Leadership: The State of Play and Strategies for Change* (2007) Barbara Kellerman, Deborah Rhode, and their colleagues also highlight the many issues that remain for women. They summarize the facts about the progress or lack of it for women. In the political arena, data show that representation by females has increased but remains well behind where one might expect it to be. Although women are a majority in the electorate, they held only a quarter of upper-level state government positions and 16 percent of congressional seats at the time of this publication. Some slight improvement occurred in the 2008 elections. The picture in higher education also is not as positive as it could be. Women make up over half of college graduates, but less then a quarter of full professors and only a fifth of college presidents are female. Women also lag behind in the corporate world both as CEOs and on boards of directors. At the time of their research, women numbered only 2 percent of Fortune 500 CEOs and 16 percent of boards of directors. By 2009, there is some improvement, and there are now fifteen women heading Fortune 500 companies, up from seven in 2003. The appointment of Ursula Burns as head of Xerox in 2009 is an encouraging sign. Yet as Kellerman and her colleagues argue, there has been limited success in moving women into leadership roles traditionally occupied by men and "even less in moving men into domestic roles traditionally occupied by women."[3] And data from Massachusetts show trends similar to the national data. A 2007 study by the Office of Women and Politics and Public Policy at the University of Massachusetts Boston indicates that 87 percent of the board members at the state's largest corporations are male and 94 percent are white.[4]

Other essays in the Kellerman book pick up on the Gergen theme and discuss the conventional wisdom that female leaders are more participatory than males and more likely to be "empathetic, supportive, and collaborative" and that that view is consistent with women's self reports. But other research reveals that when we look at women who are actually in leadership positions "no gender differences, particularly when it involves evaluations of leaders by supervisors, subordinates, and peers in real-world settings" predominate. And others note that those women who do advance "must work harder and negotiate a more challenging path to leadership than men do" Vicki Donlon (2007) concludes from her research that women are held back by a combination of "their different leadership styles," "by each other" and by organizations that have "not kept up with cultural changes" and mandated more family friendly policies.[5] So women continue to face barriers, especially in the top executive suites here in the United States as well as in other industrialized countries.

Alice Eagly and Linda Carli in "Women and the Labyrinth of Leadership" (2007) argue that the prior metaphor of a "glass ceiling" for women does not provide the insight that we need because it implies that "women and men have equal access to entry- and mid-level positions." The authors state, "they do not." A better way to understand what confronts women is the "labyrinth." "For women who aspire to top leadership positions, routes exist but are full of twists and turns, both unexpected and expected." The authors outline several of these barriers, such as that promotions come more slowly for women than for men with equivalent qualifications. And they note "a set of widely shared conscious and unconscious mental associations about women, men, and leaders.... people associate women and men with different traits and link men with more of the traits that connote leadership." Men, they argue are associated with "agentic qualities, which convey assertion and control." Women, however, are associated with "communal qualities, which convey a concern for the compassionate treatment of others."[6] This double bind makes it a struggle for women to find and to exercise their leadership style. We need to better understand the various barriers that exist and how some women do make their way.

And in a survey summarized by Regina Maruca of both men and women executives, it was interesting that the males blamed the glass ceiling on the shortage of women in the corporate pipeline. The women, however, state that their careers are stymied by negative preconceptions and stereotypes about their professional capabilities. And in addition, half of the women queried said exclusion from informal networks was an important factor holding them back. Rebecca Shambaugh (2008) identifies "sticky floors." These, she says, are "self-defeating and unrecognized beliefs, assumptions, and behaviors that hold women back." She alerts women to some of these and suggests that women speak up for themselves more often. In addition, we suggest that there may be some things that need to change in organizational structures and in the culture that creates more obstacles for women than for men.[7]

Clearly the topic of women's leadership remains one of keen interest especially as work toward increasing the number of women in leadership positions in all organizations continues. So overall we note progress, yes, but substantial change, no. We hope that today's young professional women will make greater strides and that they will be among the leaders who will help society move in that direction. As this chapter concludes, they still face many barriers, but they are moving ahead in spite of those. The 192 talented female professionals (along with 150 men) in this study with in leadership development provide us with many insights. We sought their views on the progress women are making and the challenges they face. These young women have the potential and the determination to navigate the labyrinth and the sticky floors but also to bring about the needed changes in organizations that will signal greater progress for individuals regardless of gender.

LEADERSHIP DEVELOPMENT: IS EQUAL ENOUGH?

Who are they? The organizational make-up of female participants compared to males indicates some differences. As noted previously, women outnumber men in our sample (56 percent female) with slightly more men than women coming from the corporate sector. When we look at banking and financial services, we find men and women in almost equal numbers. In government, the numbers of women and men are almost equal. But more women than men come from community services, education, and healthcare. Yet the representation of women in the total group indicates that overall they come from organizations similar to those of their male counterparts. In addition, more women are single, divorced, or separated than men who tend to be married. Some of the men have stay-at-home spouses supporting them and their families; this is less often the case with the women.

Women throughout their careers are "afforded different developmental opportunities" than men ranging from job assignments to more focused activities that could enhance leadership development.[8] We hoped to set up a different pattern. The leadership development activities in which these young women participate are designed to provide men and women with equal leadership experiences. Meeting current leaders, male and female, and hearing their stories is important for both genders. In addition, skill training and extensive networking experiences are essential for both men and women. Topics include issues that are relevant to both: communication skills, dealing with the media, negotiation, and conflict resolution, leading from the middle, ethics in organizations, project development and completion, teamwork and collaboration, and fostering inclusiveness.

It is our intention that women and men receive equal opportunities in the program, and that the training will help them achieve equal footing and be better able to confront workplace barriers and to advocate for needed changes. We observed several indicators in various facets of leadership development opportunities to ascertain if women are actively participating or just bystanders. The following areas were examined: frequency of questions asked of session speakers by males and females, selection of team leaders at sessions on negotiating, the attendance at special networking events, and the extent to which women and men are selected by their peers for positions in the alumni association. Their responses to typical management problems presented as case studies were evaluated, and we also looked at the gender mix in nonprofit board positions. And we noted gender differences in those seeking specific career and advancement advice.

WOMEN SPEAK UP

Prominent women as well as men are guest speakers; one third of the speakers are females, among them have been the president of the Federal Reserve Bank of Boston, the president and executive vice presidents of major banks, the president and founder of a high tech company, the first female chief judge of the Court of Appeals for the First Circuit, female CEOs of two major hospitals, as well as female cabinet secretaries from the Commonwealth of Massachusetts. We know from their comments how very much the young women value the interaction with established female leaders who may serve as role models. They need to see successful women in leadership roles and so do the men because the exposure of men to powerful women also is vital for women's advancement. Women speakers share their own leadership journeys, and each has a powerful story to tell. Many discuss their own experiences with discrimination. One lesson that often derives from these sessions with guest speakers is the need to meet challenges head on and move ahead. Interacting with established women leaders is an important aspect of the leadership development journey for young professionals.

We monitored 23 sessions during 2006, 2007, 2008, and 2009, and found that the women were more active in ten of the sessions than the men, and in others their participation was equal to or only slightly behind the men. They participate and ask questions with both male and female speakers.[9] Cecilia Ridgeway (2001) writing on gender status beliefs notes that "men in mixed groups talk more" and that they use less tentative speech. She reminds us that inequalities can develop depending on how much each individual participates and how influential they are. Those who become influential and respected "speak up often," offer suggestions and defend their views.[10] We see some slight differences in men and women asking questions and entering into discussions, but our findings do not support the more specific differences noted by Ridgeway.

A few sessions stand out. In March 2006, when the program focused on media relations and three major speakers were males (the publisher and the editor of the *Boston Globe* and a male from a regional TV show), the women asked fewer questions than did the men. Similarly, when the speaker was a male executive vice president of a major health care organization, the men asked more questions. But in 2007, when work/life balance was the topic of discussion and the speaker was female, the women far outnumbered the men in asking questions. Also in 2007, at a session at the Globe similar to the one noted above, women directed more questions to the male editor and more questions overall than did the men. In 2009 at the *Globe*, we find women able to hold their own once again. Overall, they asked more questions that day than did the males. We also found that in one instance when the speaker was a female CEO of a hospital, the men's questions outnumbered those from the women. The CEOs remarks were followed by an address from a male medical doctor and the women's questions directed to this speaker far outnumbered the men's.

In 2009, when the speaker was the chair of the New York Stock Exchange, the women asked more questions, which also occurred again when a male

AT&T vice president presented a case study along with a male colleague from The Bank of New York Mellon. And in another recent session where two speakers were male and two were female, the women asked more questions of both male and female speakers. So clearly women hold their own as active participants and in many situations they predominate. We are pleased that these young professional women are equal participants in asking questions and in participating in the substantive discussions that occur. In addition, one of the women reported, "changing [her] interaction style in a male-dominated setting to ensure being heard." They are learning important lessons about speaking up and being recognized.

WOMEN AS NEGOTIATORS AND TEAM LEADERS

We did find differences in behavior and responses in three recent sessions that dealt with negotiation skills where the young professionals, men and women, engage in an intensive negotiation exercise. As part of that exercise, they work in assigned teams and each team picks its own leader—a negotiator. In three different years, 2006, 2008, and 2009, more men were chosen initially to represent these teams than women, and in all the sessions the men were clearly more active participants. When the team leaders were chosen initially in 2008 and again in 2009 with mainly men in that role, we heard from the back of the room comments, primarily from male participants, such as, "Where are the women?" When team leaders were chosen in 2008 for the second set of exercises, half of the teams selected men and half selected women for the leaders. In 2009, two women were selected initially to head the negotiation teams, but when the second round occurred, no women were selected. Yet when team leaders were selected in 2009 to make presentations to the Mayor, three women were selected along with three men. So awareness exists that women as well as men should play leading roles, and the group responds accordingly although on occasion males continue to predominate.

We also notice that during the exercise in all three years, men ask more questions overall and the numbers for men hold up whether viewed as raw numbers or weighted averages. Overall, the men more than the women, seem to relish the game of negotiation and outlining strategies to win. The women participate, but the men are more active in negotiation sessions that they see as a highly competitive game. We find this quite interesting because at the beginning of the exercise participants are told that the goal is to maximize profit for your company (your team), and several women have told us they learn a lot that is immediately beneficial and relevant to their own work environments from these sessions.

After the game is over, another difference is observed. The men are comfortable with the outcome whereas a few of the women mention that they are uncomfortable and feel that this exercise weakens their trust in some of their colleagues. This finding is consistent with differences in communication and interaction styles noted by Deborah Tannen about how boys and girls play differently. Boys tend to play games with rules and referees, and let it go when the game is over. Girls tend to play relational games in which hurt feelings may linger. (Now that many more girls play competitive soccer, there may be a shift in this gender difference.) We discussed this observation with some of the women and not all shared the view that women continue to harbor concerns about the negotiation game. Some were very positive about the experience and called it productive. We are reminded of Deborah Kolb's findings that women's strategies for negotiation can be equally effective but are often different from those of men.[11]

WOMEN'S PARTICIPATION

We also looked at women's participation in extra events beyond the formal program. Several events are scheduled each year to enhance networking opportunities with other young professionals and to provide opportunities to meet other established leaders. We found no major differences in women's participation over time although at some events women's numbers were larger than men's, but with weighted averages, those differences are small. One surprise was that at an event featuring one of the few female executives of a major bank, more men participated than did women.

We have an active alumni association and the alumni officers include both women and men. Females have been elected chair four times and males have held that post three times so both have assumed that leadership role. The current chair is male and the vice chair is female. (She will become the next chair in the future.) Females held more of the alumni board positions with ten of the seventeen officers in 2008, but in 2009 the numbers are reversed with thirteen males and nine females. (There has been an expansion in the number of positions on the alumni board.) So both genders are active in providing advice and planning programs. Serving on the alumni board is a valuable experience in that one learns how to be an effective board member. We ask the alumni chair and past chair to serve on the board of advisors for the program, and that provides additional board and networking experiences.

When we surveyed these young professionals about their civic commitments as displayed by membership on nonprofit boards, we find that 41 men indicate such involvement compared to 32 females. This is a somewhat surprising finding because many nonprofit organizations are headed by women. One explanation for the larger number of males appears to be that the male participants have better established networks, which help them to be noticed and then chosen for board appointments. But we are pleased that many of the young women in addition to the men have asked for assistance gaining board positions, and several males and females have been appointed to nonprofit boards. We encourage all young professionals to become active on nonprofit boards and we also discuss how to get on a board and what it is to be a good board member. We expect board participation for both genders will grow in the future, as participants understand that serving on boards can enhance their own skills while they provide valuable community service.

Women are generally sympathetic to promoting and helping other women, but believe they cannot always be up front about this. Here they differ somewhat from Elizabeth Parks-Stamm and her colleagues who find that the "interpersonal derogation of successful women by other women functions as a self-protective strategy."[12] Yet these young women professionals also believe that women have to be better than males to be successful as they move up career ladders.

MANAGEMENT DECISIONS

We also experiment with some typical management problems to see what actions are preferred. We ask females and males to record their actions to four business case studies to see if differences by gender show up in the ways participants think about the cases. Each case deals with an employee/human relations problem in a typical business setting, and the young professionals are asked to select an appropriate disciplinary action ranging from no action, to verbal or written warning, to probation, suspension, or termination. We used the cases with two different groups of young professionals at two different time frames.[13]

Scenario one deals with finding pornographic material on an employee's computer at work. In 2006, both men and women selected written and verbal warning as the best actions, but slightly more women than men choose the more harsh actions of suspension, termination, or probation. In 2007, reacting to the same case, twice as many men as women picked the disciplinary actions of probation, suspension, or termination although the preferred measures for both genders again were verbal or written warnings. The differences overall were not significant for the genders.

In the second case, a female employee had to be disciplined because she did not abide by parking rules in restricted areas. Because she was sometimes late, she parked in a reserved lot when she had no authority to park. Written and or verbal warnings were the actions selected most frequently by both genders in 2006, with few women or men recommending the harsher actions of termination or suspension. In 2007, again both men and women selected written and verbal warnings as the best actions. But more women than men recommended the harsher actions of probation or suspension. None recommended termination. Again, the differences in responses were slight.

In the third case, participants are asked to deal with a supervisor at a company that has a policy that no supervisor will create a "hostile" work environment. Under one supervisor several females leave the company, and then one female complains about a hostile environment so the question was what action should be taken against the male supervisor. In 2006, the response favored by the largest number of the women was the written warning and more women than men selected probation and suspension. However, more men choose termination than women. In 2007, twice as many women as men choose the harsher penalties of probation, suspension, or termination. These responses show a slight preference among the women for harsh penalties when the case deals with possible sexual discrimination. Here we did find some minor gender differences.

The fourth case deals with a long-term employee who develops problems with productivity. In 2006, the largest number of respondents selected probation, and slightly more women choose this option than men. The genders were nearly even on selecting termination and suspension, but these numbers were small compared to those selecting probation. In 2007, men and women both choose the options of probation, suspension, and termination over those of written and verbal warnings. Again, differences were not significant.

Overall, the actions proposed by the women were not much different from those of the men except when dealing with cases that dealt with possible sexual discrimination. The case results provide evidence that when these women engage in managerial decision making, they can be "tough" and make hard decisions and that their decisions do not differ significantly from males although they are concerned when discrimination may be present.

Participation data in various aspects of the program show little variation by gender, but one area in addition to the negotiation session where we note some gender differences is in seeking career advice. To date, more of the males than females have sought advice on the best ways to network and how to move up the ladder to CEO or other leadership positions. The males exhibit more determination. When we asked some of the females if that pattern could be explained, the answer was that perhaps the women were concerned that they might be imposing. Many women offer assistance to others at work, or are sought out for it, and so have heightened awareness that it requires time and thought. The men are pragmatic. Needing assistance, they figure out how to pursue it. Ron Heifetz (2007) notes differences in how both men and women compete for proximity to people in positions of authority. "They compete for legitimacy and they compete for attention," he states. He notes that men and women do "different dances" in their efforts to draw on referred sources of power.[14] Our experience here is somewhat surprising since we assume that equal numbers of females could benefit from additional input. When women do seek guidance, the conversations are very productive, and as is the case with male participants they discuss ways to have successful and satisfying careers.

We also want to learn about any differences females note concerning the benefits of the program. No significant differences are apparent and items that make the top of the list are similar for males and females. There is general agreement that one of the major benefits for women is the expansive network that is established. In particular, they benefit from working in teams with other young professionals, something that enables them to enlarge substantially their overall networks and to demonstrate their own capabilities. Specifically, they appreciate the opportunity to network across a variety of business, organizational, racial, and ethnic lines, which also is frequently noted by males. Many females have women's networks in the places where they work, but a broader network is needed. Eagly (2007) sees that one of the issues women confront is the lack of time to socialize with colleagues and build professional and social networks that help them in their path to leadership.[15] These women take a step in correcting that problem. They note that their minds have been opened to new ideas and new concepts and that the connections made are invaluable. They appreciate learning about various business groups and also about the nonprofit and governmental sectors. They also state that many of these connections and cross sector networks would not have been possible in the normal course of their work and lives.

The women also see benefit from specific skill development in areas such as communication. Hearing the stories of established leaders about how they advance as well as what challenges they face and how they meet them has a lasting benefit. The women also appreciate learning that they do not have all the answers and that leadership is not "easy." (Males in our surveys also value the practice in communication and hearing from established leaders.) The women indicate that they need to hear women and men talk more about their personal challenges with work/family issues such as raising children while moving to positions of greater responsibility. How do they do it? What are the strategies? They suggest that the male model of a successful man with a stay-at-home wife who manages the home and children while he moves up the career ladder is not helpful to them as they look at their own career and leadership trajectories. Many of them voice support for organizational changes that would be positive for both genders.

Overall we do not find significant differences in the ways in which men and women participate in and benefit from leadership development opportunities. With the exception of some differences in style in negotiation exercises, women are equal participants with men. They speak up and ask questions, they attend additional skill-building and networking session, and they are selected to serve as officers, including chair, in the alumni organization. Women clearly demonstrate that they understand the importance of a variety of networking activities and experiences. They do not shy away from making difficult management decisions when dealing with real-life cases. These young women have the potential to navigate the labyrinth and to fight for the additional changes in organizations that will signal greater progress for women.

BARRIERS REMAIN

ATTITUDES ON GENDER

So can we assume that they will be on a fast track in their organizations and slated for more responsible leadership positions? One of the major goals of working with young women professionals is that they should obtain leadership skills and enhanced social and business networks that will enhance their ability to occupy top leadership positions in the future. But it is also possible that they will have the skills and the networks, and yet we will not see major changes in leadership structures for many of the reasons cited by Kellerman, Rhode and Eagly and others. Unfortunately, we find that men and women do not always receive equal treatment in their organizations and subtle forms of discrimination continue to exist. Barriers remain.

Some males admit that they need to overcome gender bias. Gonçalves, who came to the United States from Angola, describes how he had to overcome sexism in his own leadership development and credited thoughtful mentors and his mother, who had no formal education and could not read or write, for much of his success.[16]

Describing his experience with his mother, Gonçalves writes, "…like many English-speaking children of immigrants, I often accompanied her to doctor appointments so that I could translate instructions and advocate for her."

He then reflects on his early attitudes on gender.

A direct result of being mentored in high school was that I was forced to confront my underlying sexism. As a Cape Verdean male, I grew up with a cultural "machismo," and I viewed women in a somewhat patronizing manner. My mentors picked up on this right away. They explained that if I wanted to succeed in America, I had to abandon my male chauvinism and begin to think about women differently. They explained that chauvinistic beliefs about women were not appropriate for job interviews, social settings, or political environments. So every time I made a disparaging remark about females, I was called on it by my mentors and had to deal with the repercussion: strong-willed women lecturing me on equality. This cultural deconstruction of my personality was a painful process, but I believe it was one of the biggest gifts my mentors gave me. As a leader in my community today, I truly value the contributions of women and I insist on including women in decision-making discussions, because they bring a much-needed perspective.

As he uses what he has learned, he also discusses how gender attitudes can inhibit global initiatives.

... I've developed personal relationships with all of the senior government officials in Cape Verde, and I continue to advise them on long-range planning objectives. One of the biggest issues I've had with the Cape Verdean government is that it's male dominated. Every time I speak with the Prime Minister, I remind him of the importance of involving women in governance, and I'm pleased to say that he recently appointed a female minister of education, a female minister of finance, and a female minister of defense. The response to these appointments has been extremely positive.

His background contributed to his attitudes yet he worked to overcome his bias. Yet for some, gender bias is present without the recognition of its source. Not all gender bias is cultural. Interestingly, we often encounter good "teasing" about gender at our sessions. Remarks like "you shouldn't say that" or "we have women here" are sometimes part of informal conversations. These males are aware of what is happening and take steps to try to curb obvious expressions of bias. That they recognize it and attempt to correct it is positive. They are probably less biased than many males of older generations, but they also realize that underlying attitudes and behaviors are difficult to change.

In focus groups and other conversations the young women are quite vocal about the barriers and stereotyping they continue to face. In describing a variety of business situations, they note that if the female comes across as too passionate (even though she may believe strongly in the issue), this behavior often is seen as a weakness because women are typed as too emotional. Women get labeled as "pushy" when they try too hard to work for their point of view. So women often must control this impulse, which in a man, is viewed positively as demonstrating his commitment and enthusiasm. Men are perceived as stronger and women weaker. We hear that women get in trouble for exhibiting aggressive behaviors that are acceptable in men. In addition, too often they are not offered the same professional development opportunities as male colleagues. Women want those challenging assignments too. Moreover, women regret that they often do not see themselves taken seriously. Many also note how frequently they are the only (or one of a very few) females in a meeting and how they must work to get their voices heard and their presence felt. They cannot help but notice that they are the "other" in the room. They believe that speaking out and being heard in the program has been a positive experience, and they are prepared to do so more often.

Another problem highlighted was that the women believe that they have to be twice as good as their male counterparts to get ahead. They have to prove themselves constantly. They also tell us that men are given more leeway in making mistakes and moving on. Women have to manage a delicate balance. The double bind discussed previously continues to plague women. In addition, some work with individuals, primarily men, who continue to practice a command-and-control kind of leadership, and some note that institutional cultures that are primarily male also often tend to focus on sports and on humor along with business discussions. Some of the women have learned to enter into these conversations about sports and athletic scores so common in the corporate culture. They are finding ways to assimilate, but it is clear that there are some things about the culture that they would like to change. (Many of the concerns we hear articulated are similar to those discussed by Kellerman, Rhode, Eagly, Carli, Fletcher, and others.) As they raise these issues that often persist because of old stereotypes, the group becomes more sensitive to what is happening at their own organization and how to deal with it.

Sherry often tells a personal story that puts the stereotype issue in perspective. Shortly after arriving at UMass Boston as chancellor, she and her husband Jim Livingston were attending a social event and talking with some other couples. A new couple entered the room and was called over to "meet the new chancellor of UMass Boston." The gentlemen from the new couple immediately reached out to shake her husband's hand! College presidents, of course, are usually tall distinguished looking men not small women.

Not only stereotypes but generational differences also may get in the way of the advancement of women. We also hear that some older "bosses" are more autocratic and hierarchical and have less interpersonal approaches than those in Generation X. They may have made it to the top in a more traditional way and are reluctant to make changes toward a more congenial and personal style. It is difficult to conceive of them having the kind of open conversations about possible bias that we have had with our young leaders, male and female.

When women participants discuss their own styles whether via the survey or in conversations, they describe themselves as collaborative and as persons who value teamwork and relating to people on a personal basis. When we ask how women fail as leaders, one answer from the young women themselves is that sometimes women are too emotional in organizations where that is not acceptable. It is not a positive trait to show "feelings" and again, they say, there are generational differences. Older managers seem to have more difficulty with anyone, male or female, who shows too much emotion and is too personal. But the young women believe that one should be able to express oneself without such behavior being seen as negative. They also note that men can disagree about an issue and then leave the room as buddies whereas women have more trouble with honest conversation where there is disagreement. Those "bad" feelings linger. We saw this in the negotiation exercise described previously. They also mention that women are more likely not to want to rock the boat and not to have the hard discussions—although needed—that might generate conflict. (These observations are in line with those discussed previously by Fletcher and Rhode.)

When we asked about women they look up to as global leaders, they mention the female senators Diane Weinstein and Barbara Boxer from California, Oprah Winfrey and Eleanor Roosevelt, and reluctantly Margaret Thatcher (whom they do not want to emulate). They have mixed reactions to Hillary Clinton and note she brought a lot of baggage to her run for president.

Many of the young males are aware of bias and stereotypes and admit that some of this thinking occurs in their organizations, but they also are clear that they would like to see changes. They argue that they support a workforce that includes women and point out that females bring different and helpful points of view to the organization, especially to a team or a working group that may be stuck in old ways of thinking and acting. Some note that women need a brusque style to get ahead and should not be criticized for it when that style is displayed. Others state that we need to move beyond clichés about women and see them as individuals with strengths and weaknesses just like men. That these conversations take place indicates that issues remain, but we applaud the honesty that these young leaders show when dealing with the issues and their willingness to be hopeful about confronting and eliminating biases and stereotypes.

Recent research by Michael Gurian and Barbara Annis (2008) discusses the variation in brain patterns and brain chemistry between males and females that may account for some of the differences in ways they see and deal with these issues. Women appear to be wired for multitasking and men seem to want to "get it done." In addition, women tend to read signals in faces and gestures better than men, and they also report that men tend toward hierarchical structures more than women who are more inclined to work in teams. And in line with some of the comments we pick up, women remember interactions, "including conflicts," longer than men. This research is intended to help organizations become aware that both sexes have important contributions to make and that both are necessary.[17] Understanding these issues can be useful to institutions that are serious about advancing women and reaping the benefits they bring.

ORGANIZATIONAL STRUCTURES

These young leaders see a role for organizations in creating a climate that challenges prevailing stereotypes and provides a more level playing field.

One of our participants, Pauliina Swartz, notes that business organizations need to be more responsive to women's interests in the market and that businesses can help themselves by promoting women's progress. She is aware, as are others, that women are the major consumers in our society.

> ...I find it amazing that more financial service companies, for example, don't ensure the success of women in their organizations, given that women represent half of these companies' target markets and are often the key decision makers for financial issues affecting their families.

By contrast, Paul Francisco, who, as noted previously, established his own firm to deal with more inclusive work environments, comments favorably on his work experience with women and on how his new organization will emphasize ways to overcome bias.

> ...most of the recruiters I managed were women, and through our supervisory relationship, I developed insights and strategies for leading both genders. One of the key differences I found between men and women is that men mislead ourselves into thinking we don't need coaching. Too often we take on challenges without adequate guidance. My female recruiters tended to be more open about the difficulties they were facing, and they communicated with me more than their male counterparts did. My initial impression was that my male recruiters were performing well because they didn't approach me for help, and that my female recruiters needed more support. But what I discovered was that I understood the abilities of my female recruiters much better because I was talking to them. I was able to coach them as well as learn from them because they articulated their challenges.
>
> Overall, I observed that the quality of men's and women's work was comparable, but I employed different communication strategies with the two. Since my male recruiters were not as forthcoming, I devised methods to check in with them without making them feel as though I was restricting their autonomy or attacking their work. The awareness I developed about communication style differences also made me more receptive to constructive criticism, all of which contributed to making me a better leader.

FAMILY FRIENDLY ORGANIZATIONAL POLICIES

Another barrier that remains concerns policies intended to foster family/work balance. How those policies play out in practice is the issue. For young professionals, the absence of work environments conducive to raising families while moving up the organizational ladder remains a serious problem that weighs more heavily on the females. They tell us that when a woman leaves the office to go to her child's school performance, she is leaving work early *again*. When a male leaves to do the same, everyone thinks he is an outstanding Dad! Organizations say that they are "family friendly," and many times have policies in place, but the reality can be quite different. Following the policy may work against you, they argue. Fiona Moore (2005) finds that the policies often are not useful to those in senior management positions because women are reluctant to take advantage of such policies. We encourage young leaders, men and women, to read *Womenomics* (2009) in which many examples are provided where organizations are responsive to more flexible work practices and find that those arrangements are helpful to both males and females. In many cases it is the females who propose such changes, and they are successful in these efforts.[18]

What also concerns many young professional women is that they continue to be viewed as the caretakers for children and the elderly and hence, if they have responsibility for young children or elderly parents, are viewed as less serious about their work. They worry that women who become pregnant are often treated differently, and it is hard for them to get back on track. Again, there is some sentiment that there are generational differences and that the younger managers are more understanding of family issues. However, their concern for different treatment of married women with children has recently been confirmed in a new study that shows that some employers discriminate against mothers as job candidates. So overall, our conversations support the view expressed by Carolyn Clark (1999) and others that women still have to pay a price for moving aggressively in their careers.[19] What is evident from their stories and experience is that individual women figure out how to navigate and manage their own career paths to obtain leadership positions, but it is the individual effort and not changes in the organizational structures that make such progress possible for most women. The organizational changes described in *Womenomics* need to be realized more broadly and women and men need to promote such changes.

We also are encouraged that many young women have developed their own leadership lifelines and have figured out the best ways to give time to their families and how to balance that with advancing into leadership positions. Most admit that this is difficult and that the choices are hard, but they are finding ways to do it. However, they would like to see more organizational support and recognition of these issues.

The young women also discuss work balance issues in their essays. Writing again anonymously, this female outlines how she deals with the challenges. She is grateful for the opportunities she has received but also sees the limitations and she is quite honest about the difficult choices she has to make.

...I am a 41-year-old woman who has worked in the financial services industry since graduating from college with a bachelor's degree in economics. The youngest of four children, I was born in Illinois of American-born parents, and raised in central Massachusetts in a white, middle-class family. I've lived and worked in the

San Francisco Bay Area, New York City, and Atlanta, Georgia, and now reside in a suburb of Boston with my husband of fifteen years, who also works in finance, and Henry, who attends public school and is in the fourth grade.

I would describe myself as a moderately successful but rather overwhelmed working mother who is continually striving to balance often-competing responsibilities to my family, home, career, and community. I had a number of years of work experience before becoming a mother at age 31, and while parenthood has most certainly escalated the issue of work/family balance in my life, this challenge has been present throughout my entire professional career. As the years have progressed, I have made a series of life decisions that have extensively influenced my career, and career decisions that have significantly impacted my lifestyle and family. These include postponing/forgoing my goal of attaining a master's degree, my decision to continue working full-time after my son was born, decisions on childcare, and choices on where to live, including twice leaving good jobs to relocate out-of-state for family reasons. I can attest to the fact that I've had to make many sacrifices on a day-to-day basis that have impacted both my career and my family, but I certainly do not feel that I am unique in this regard. I realize that my life today is indeed a culmination of the choices that I've made, and I consider myself fortunate to have had the opportunity to make these choices.

I often think of the societal changes that have allowed me to thrive professionally and to succeed in ways that women of prior generations, different cultural backgrounds, or different career paths may not have been afforded. For instance, while my mother never attended college and was a full-time homemaker until I was in high school, I grew up always having had the expectation that I would attend college and have a career. I do wonder how my life and family would have been different had I remained childless or unmarried, if I had had more than one child, or if I had chosen to discontinue working full-time after my son was born, as the majority of my peers did. I remain curious about the broad range of choices other women have made with respect to their families and careers, and I value the fact that our culture and society are evolving in such a way as to make these options more prevalent and acceptable. I also wonder how my professional path would have been different if I had been a man, if my husband had not been as supportive, or if my employers had not been as progressive as they were.

This banker and mother faces challenges, but is meeting them head on, and she values the culture at her organization that makes it feasible for her to deal with these issues.

Another of our participants, Bailly, sees the work/life balance as a particular challenge for younger women and suggests how one can manage.

The work/life balance is a challenge for young leaders, particularly for women. The price of assuming leadership during this stage can be daunting without strong social supports. Strategizing work/life balance requires realistic expectations of self and others. It requires sacrifice and careful planning around the execution and timing for vertical moves in the organization. And it requires constant level-setting with oneself to affirm that wanting to do and have it all is noble but may not be realistic. I learned that it may take longer to achieve my goals, which required patience, and that staging them in parallel with the family needs works best. In the meantime, I focused on producing results/strong performance, developing and managing relationships, and maintaining a personal and professional develop-ment plan. Life Lesson: Superwoman I am not. Mastering the art of strategy and negotiations begins at home.

DeAngelis, whose essay was noted previously, takes a slightly different approach to issues of work/life balance.

In my mind, the work/life balance meant that I would be spending equal amounts of time at both. The image I had was that of a seesaw. There is no way to get to a place where you are spending equal amounts of time at work and in life, nor is that what it's really about. A different approach is to look at time as a pie. At different points in your life/career you will have bigger slices dedicated to work and, at oth-ers, to family. The really important thing is to figure out what makes you happy, what you are passionate about—and then carry that into all parts of your life.

Yameen too makes interesting observations about balance and wants both sexes to achieve balance.

... "balance" does not mean equal. I completely agree that what we're doing is about bringing the best of ourselves and our core beliefs to what we do within a community—whether that community is work, family, or neighborhood. That is where the balance comes in for me. I agree that we need to become happy, but we can very easily lose sight of what that means if we are not committed to a com-munity that challenges us to create value for ourselves and others. Without that counterbalance, or sounding board, or mirror, I know that I can easily, with the best of intentions, do something that seems to make me happy but might actually be destructive in some way. It's easy to lose perspective. I think there are two ways of looking at this. First, every part of our lives needs to be about expressing what we believe to be important to us. If we have decided from necessity or choice the work we are doing, it needs to be a place of self-reflection and self-renewal—as all parts of our lives need to be. Also, I worry that the work/life balance is a fallacy, since it might suggest working a ridiculous amount of hours to the detriment of my health, my family, and ultimately the workplace. Working a ridiculous number of hours sends messages such as: I am indispensable (talk about non-collaborative leadership!); I care more about the company than others do; More time means more value; I need to be here; Others don't (they are less valuable); Sacrifice equals loyalty. I fell into this early in my career.

Swartz agrees with her other colleagues that family friendly work environ-ments are important. Her analysis is in line with the themes discussed in *Womenomics*.

Growing up, I was exposed to people who were more focused on their families, homes, and hobbies than on their careers. This has led me to focus on achieving a work-life balance in my career. Does my insistence on a balance set me back from work opportunities that are deemed to require a full-time commitment? I strongly believe that balance makes me a more productive employee (not to mention happier in general), but face time on the job continues to be a factor in the way people are managed and assessed in many organizations. Organizations looking to promote diverse talent would benefit from providing a work environment and culture where employees can bring their whole selves to the workplace with them. Such a culture would probably make most organizations more interesting places to work as well.

The anonymous banker further expresses her concern about assuming additional leadership roles and what that may mean.

I certainly worry about the costs of assuming additional leadership roles. For many years I have been working to improve upon my work/family balance, and admit that this has been a continuing challenge and source of angst in my life. I take to heart the following advice given by Suzy Welch, wife of business icon Jack Welch. "You can have it all, just not all at once." I did recently make a job change one year ago, primarily because I thought that it would afford me a higher degree of job flexibility and life balance. This change represented a significant career risk, but strongly inspired by the curriculum of the Emerging Leaders Program, I mustered the confidence and courage to make the switch.

But males also face these issues. Ron Bell who holds a major position in the Office of the Governor of Massachusetts also expresses his concern about how to find time for family. Recently when he spoke in one of our afternoon sessions, the first thing he said was that he needed to leave by 3 p.m. to pick up his son. He writes:

Someone like me, who's so consumed with his work, has to set aside time to find balance in life. After all, if you can't take care of yourself, you can't take care of anyone else. So I make sure I work out at the gym, pray for myself, and do things I enjoy. I've learned to make time for my son, because he's a priority. Scheduling time with my family—that's something I had to learn.

Gonçalves also helps us understand that work/life balance is a concern of both men and women.

The commitment that is needed to take on substantive issues puts a great deal of pressure on my personal life, but I never undermine the importance of family. I don't sleep enough and I don't have much leisure time, but the time I do have is spent with my son and daughter. We go fishing and hiking and play baseball, and

I attend as many school functions as possible. I'm grateful that my family understands and respects my commitment to helping underprivileged people improve their quality of life.

Rawan notes how his parents encouraged him to value both work and family.

... they taught me the value in sharing the work environment with family life. I have great memories of annual summer outings my father would host for his staff when he had his CPA firm. I can also think back to my mother bringing me into her office environment when she was spending much of her time in New York. My parents went to great lengths to make sure that my two sisters and I knew whom they worked with and also that the people they worked with knew us. These relationships have remained strong over the years as a testament to the pride my parents had in their work environments. They enjoyed their work relationships so much that they felt they wanted their own family to be a part of them. This has encouraged me to strive to be proud of my work environment, build strong relationships, and enjoy the people I work with on a daily basis.

Young examines her own development as it relates to balancing work and family and how she sees her leadership role going forward and how it has changed from her original expectations. Her open and honest analysis of the issues demonstrates how women wrestle with the challenges.

I was, no doubt, a working mother who at times felt what every working mother feels: guilt, fear, ambivalence, resentment, and even desperation. But for the most part I felt satisfied and successful in my job and at home and thus was ready for what I believed was the next phase in my career: becoming the boss.

The year is 2008. I am now in my late thirties with a still-supportive husband, seven-year-old daughter, and four-year-old son. I live in a suburb of Boston. We own two cars that we use every day. It takes me approximately one and a half hours to leave my office, pick up both kids, and get home. Not long ago, I had the opportunity to be the interim "boss" for a period of six months. The entire time I felt torn between work and home and never felt like I was doing quite enough in either position. That said, I realize that I am not alone and that, as an educated, professional woman, I am privileged to have choices. I realize that I am lucky to have a flexible workplace with supportive supervisors. I realize that nobody expects me to do everything at a higher-than-average standard and "have it all." I realize, however, that I expected all of these things of myself and am now mourning the loss of those expectations.

Shortly after the ELP year ended I was promoted at work. How perfectly timed, how well choreographed this felt to me. I was moving right along as planned and was newly equipped with the skills and tools I felt I needed to excel in my new position. I had already had my second child, and while the juggling of schedules had become more difficult, working outside the home still felt right and fulfilling in many ways. I worked a four-day week and left my office by 4:30 p.m. every day, checking email and finishing projects on an as-needed basis after the children were in bed. My husband and I are equal partners in parenting so I never felt overly burdened at home. While having children changed me in many fundamental ways, it seemingly did not slow down my advancement at work.

What changed between the time I received this promotion and 2008 that has slowed down my advancement? I'm not really sure I know—writing this essay is my first foray into exploring this journey, and I am learning as I live and write it. Here are a few of the changes that I am investigating. First and foremost, I think simply that my children have gotten older and more complicated—in a good way. While their babyhoods were physically challenging, their budding childhoods are emotionally challenging. We actually have conversations now, and they ask me questions that I cannot answer, or sometimes pretend I cannot answer, since I have absolutely no idea how to handle them. The questions usually fall into the categories of God, death, crime, and sex. I realize that this is only going to become more complicated as they age. I want to spend more "quality" time with them, because now it feels like that type of time matters to them (and to me) in a way that it didn't when they were babies and toddlers. It was enough before to simply be with them while I did the laundry or ran errands or even played games. Now there is a presence that I need in order to meaningfully converse with them, to understand them, and even play games with them. There are subtleties that I don't want to miss, patterns that I want to find, and moments that I know are slipping away too fast. Time is precious to me now in a way that I never dreamed it would be.

Second, the satisfaction I get from work does not sustain me the way it used to. I hope that this is not a career-limiting declaration, but work is no longer the place where I primarily derive value and fulfillment. I still like my job and care deeply about the mission of my organization. I generally look forward to going to work and leave at the end of the day with a sense of accomplishment and the feeling that I have helped to make a life better in some small way. I am particularly fond of my colleagues, who are smart, inspiring, and supportive, and make me laugh every day. But my heart soars when I am leaving work and thinking about my children, seeing their faces, and hearing about their days. I feel fulfilled when I hear them play with abandon and I feel valued when I dry their tears and help them solve a problem. My job will never hug me back the way my children do.

This leads me to change number three: My priorities have altered dramatically. Not only do my kids need more time and demand more time, I simply want to give them more time. I want to spend less time at work and more time with my children. An opportunity arose at work when my immediate supervisor was promoted, leaving his position open. I suppose I should have been flattered when everyone assumed I would apply for and likely receive his old job. I was embarrassed when I realized that I did not want this job. Part of the reason was that it would have somewhat steered my career path away from my primary function in the organization. The more uncomfortable part of the reason was that I did not want to work the kind of hours that it required or deal with the stress it would create. It has taken a great deal of courage on my part to admit that I really did not want to work longer hours and expand my job duties (as opposed to not being able to do it). I struggle with this the most, because if I simply cannot work the hours because the demands of my home life are too great, then all responsibility is taken off me and I can still tell myself (and others) that the timing was just off. But this is not true. If I really wanted to, I could have put in more hours and challenged myself to become more creative and efficient with my time. I didn't want to. So what does that say about my ambition, my drive, and my career goals—not to mention my pay scale and 401(k)? By not applying, had I put myself on the "mommy track," depriving myself of ever being taken seriously by this organization again?

I have no idea. I'm not used to being this person and I'm not yet comfortable in her skin. I have spent my life moving ahead to the next logical stepping-stone, so settling in one place for the foreseeable future feels somewhat limiting and, dare I say, dangerous. Perhaps I overstate my situation, because clearly I am not sacrificing my career as a whole for my children or vice versa. I feel fortunate to live in an age and society where mothers are offered more than just two choices: stay home or go to work. Most of the people I choose to spend time with take for granted that this dichotomy is false. But if that is the case, then why do I feel like I'm failing myself and my graduate degrees? I used to think that moving forward necessarily meant moving up the career ladder. I realize now that I am moving forward and moving ahead even if I am not moving "up" in a formal way.

There are no easy or quick answers to work/life balance issues, but these women are recognizing them and finding a variety of ways for dealing with them. It is also encouraging to note that U.S. workers list work/life balance as the top career priority but equally discouraging is that some 81 percent believe that employers do not have programs that actually help them balance work and life.[20] These are issues for both men and women demonstrate that achieving balance requires ongoing realignment and adjusting and has major workplace implications.

WOMEN AND THEIR STRENGTHS

What patterns might emerge, we ask, with this group of young professional women? Leadership is often equated with having a vision, and Herminia Ibarra and Otilia Obodaru (2009) write about the concern that women "are judged to be less visionary than men in 360-degree feedback. It may be a matter of perception, but it stops women from getting to the top."[21] In our discussions with young women professionals we hear something more positive from their own experiences. Most are not yet in CEO positions, but they tell us that from what they see women tend to take a more holistic view of workplace challenges and issues than their male counterparts. They find that female colleagues do focus on vision, on the big picture. They are concerned with how to make things better for their organizations in the future. They also note their impression that males are more likely to focus on the tasks at hand—"let's get it done." One of the women stated that she was a big picture person, but that the males in her group help keep her on task so the combination is positive. One participant who had worked primarily with women in recent years also cautioned that women can spend too much time on big pictures, on vision and on "discussing" and not getting enough done. She believes that they also need to focus on task orientation as well as vision, so balance is needed.

They also believe that women demonstrate particular strength in interpersonal skills and that they care more about the development of their employees than many males and that this is a positive trend for the future. Some also mention that they themselves are playing two roles. As a senior manager one has to be very task oriented and robotic, but when working with individual staff, one can mentor and be more personal. They worry that sometimes women need to hide their personal and relationship side and behave in a more traditional managerial way to make it in today's business climate although ironically it is the relationship building that helps the organization move ahead.

There is no doubt that young women want to and do work hard. They ask for challenging tasks and they thrive on such work. They meet timelines and they travel. They brag about securing new customers and are gratified when their work is recognized. Many have been promoted along the way and see that as validation of their efforts. These are women of vision, energy, passion, empathy, and determination. They have the qualities we seek in leaders.

WHERE DO WE GO FROM HERE?

When asked how they would change policies if they were members of a board of directors, the CEO or a senior manager, the suggestions are many. Overall they want more opportunities to demonstrate their skills. Give them a hard job and they will do it. And they do not want to be passed over because someone worries that they cannot do the job due to family responsibilities. Although some suggest flexible work policies that allow working from home along with flexible hours built into regular schedules, they also state that women will definitely put in the same or more effort if they can have more flexibility. They value the experiences they have had working with males in leadership development because it strengthened they confidence in themselves and their abilities. They like being surrounded by other ambitious and successful young women. They also believe that it is beneficial to the males to be in a group where half are successful women.

They also want to see more recognition of the benefits that occur when organizations have women in major roles. They also expect that more women will be promoted to senior positions in their organizations and the presence of more female role models at the top will benefit the organization and its employees. They hope that with more women on boards and in senior management positions, the discussions will be different and they suggest more comprehensive and fruitful. They welcome the news from Norway that requires gender diversity in the boardroom. Boards there now are required to have 40 percent female representation.

Rebecca Tuhus-Durrow (2009) reminds us that women's advancement for some time was seen as an issue of "fairness and equality." Now evidence seems to demonstrate another advantage—a business advantage. Companies that are visionary and that promote women are also the ones that yield higher profits. A positive link between higher levels of female leadership and profits can be found although studies caution that the correlation does not mean "causation." It may be that these companies are more forward-looking in a variety of ways, the author notes. The issue now changes the discussion beyond a legal one into a business one, and women want companies to realize the many advantages they bring to the organization. Women argue that they have a unique understanding of customers and markets and women are not afraid to pose tough questions in discussions. Tuhus-Durrow also posits that some experts note that women might have been able to "temper the excesses that led to the current financial crisis." The National Council for Research on Women has also responded to this issue and repeats the need for more women in leadership positions in the corporate sector.[22] Also recent research shows that the overall quality of decisions improves when the decision making supports diverse perspectives.[23] There are many reasons to hire and promote women and young professionals women want to make their mark. They want major roles in their organizations, and they want to see their strengths utilized to the fullest extent.

On the policy level, they stress that additional legislative changes in line with the family medical leave act would be helpful. For example, they suggest that organizations find more positive ways of supporting maternity leaves and of easing the return to the workplace. The policy may be realistic and fair, but when there also is a view that the women won't return to their positions, the stereotype emerges again and some began to think that they must be careful about hiring and promoting women. They do admit that a problem can occur when women don't return from pregnancy leave, which makes it difficult for the organization. One notes, "how can you advocate for women when they let you down." Others suggest that more help be provided so that women have access to the same networks as their male colleagues. They know and understand how important such networks are. Most believe that their organizations are trying to do the right thing, but that organizational structures and ingrained behaviors still limit the extent to which family friendly workplaces and structures that support women's development are the norm. Subtle but real barriers remain.

In the overall observations, conversations, and data analysis focusing on young women and leadership, we thought we might hear more about progress that has been made for the advancement of women and some do admit that their lives have improved considerably over those of their mothers. However, what we learned was that subtle discrimination and stereotypes remain in too many instances. We did not hear a lot of whining, but we also did not hear enough about supportive work environments as the norm. Overall they continue to believe that women must work harder to get ahead and that the business atmosphere in many organizations continues to be more top down than collaborative. The newer leadership model that is discussed and advocated by many leadership scholars has not yet arrived in some organizations. The women also worry that for those with children, raising a family makes it difficult to move up the ladder in many organizations. Women work through many issues on their own, and for these women true support is sporadic. They are still left to figure it out and to do so individually. They are alone in the labyrinth. As a society we need to work more productively to help more women obtain and thrive in leadership positions at all levels of organizations. We cannot afford to waste talent. Providing an equal program and activities may not be enough to prepare women for leadership positions. If organizations can identify these issues and figure out how to provide a positive climate that overcomes the barriers, the talent of both genders will be available and utilized.

Yet we are pleased that so many women have been selected by their organizations as potential leaders and this is a very positive step. These young female professionals have been singled out; they are finding mentors and they are building important networks. And the young professional women believe that if more women are in leadership positions, some of the barriers will be reversed. Some also note that male colleagues from Generations X and Y will work with them to bring about positive change. Some see themselves as change agents going forth and one strategy that is emerging is that of women themselves calling for organizational changes and at the same time pointing out the benefits women bring to organizations. So it appears that change will occur as many more individuals recognize the need for change and affirm the need to utilize all the talent available regardless of gender. These young professional women and the men who have come to know them will be part of that movement.

CHAPTER 5

INCLUSIVE LEADERSHIP

CULTURAL AWARENESS: WHAT DOES IT MEAN?

A projected wave of CEO and presidential retirements combined with a national push to diversify leadership within the profit, nonprofit, education, and governmental sectors affords an unprecedented opportunity for promising young professionals to fill these leadership roles. This window of opportunity is opening as the graying of senior managers in all sectors of the workplace takes place. It is time for a new generation of leaders who reflect the changing demographics of the United States to assume these leadership positions. But are they in the pipeline and how will they lead?

We have discussed the issues faced by women and now we address what it is like for individuals of color to pursue leadership opportunities. The United States, in particular, is seeing major demographic shifts. The 2000 census indicated that 31 percent of the American population were members of a racial or ethnic minority group, and projections for 2030 show that 40 percent of the U.S. population will be members of racial or ethnic minority groups.[1] These facts are catching the attention of many in the business and nonprofit communities as they prepare their organizations for future possibilities and challenges. Young professionals are aware of the changing demographic picture and, in general, are more receptive to discussions about diversity and inclusiveness than earlier generations. Many also work in organizational environments that are diverse.

Understanding the many facets of diversity and creating a sense of cultural awareness are important parts of our work. But we agree with Holly Dolezalek (2008) that, "you can't send employees to a diversity car wash or sprinkle them with diversity dust."[2] We also concur with Ellen Foster Curtis and her colleagues (2007) that the focus should be on creating awareness, on helping individuals recognize their biases and prejudices, and recognizing diversity as an asset in organizations. Training in cultural competency also must be part of the ongoing work of an organization and supported by that organization's leadership.[3] It cannot be treated as an add-on. Our approach is to have a focus on diversity issues embedded in many of our activities and to return to those discussions frequently. Focusing on cultural awareness can change attitudes.

In the first year of the program (2002), we learned the hard way. A description of an incident in the first week of the program is helpful. Early in the week, participants identified six options for team projects: financial literacy, access to health care, access to economic opportunity, affordable housing, life after the Central Artery project in Boston, and corporate citizenship. A voting method was initiated in which participants were to decide with whom they would collaborate and on which topic. They also were asked to rank order their topics of choice, and a selection process took place and individuals joined various teams. At the end of the process, teams were announced. The task seemed finished when a female African American participant addressed the group.

> I'm the only person that didn't get to work on my topic of choice—the only one who didn't get to have her vote count is a black woman and that bothers me. When I brought it up [to the group facilitators], I was told I should go to a team that needed an underrepresented group member... When the people in power pull an underrepresented group member to the side and say "how can we fit you in?"... I feel passionate about bringing transparency to that... I thought it was supposed to be different here.

In response to his fellow participant's expressed concern, a white male in the group asked her, "How can I get you through this so you feel good?" The woman replied "Don't patronize me..." At this point other participants joined in, alternately sharing their perceptions of each person's comments, and their own reactions to the process. Individuals in the group addressed the dynamics that were occurring among them, and the ways that the same diversity challenges they faced in the workplace were being played out.

The faculty who designed the process for selecting teams took responsibility for the unintended impact. One noted, "we neglected to address diversity issues in the process because we mistakenly thought week one would be too soon to address diversity issues..." This was followed by a discussion regarding how to proceed. Participants agreed on two changes. First, the team-selection process would be done again. Second, that afternoon the group would engage in in-depth introductions focused more specifically on everyone's experiences related to cultural awareness and diversity issues.

At that time, individuals disclosed various personal and painful experiences. Some of the disclosures included fears and experiences of discrimination on the basis of race, gender, sexual orientation, and socioeconomic status.

A few of the white males in the group also shared concerns that they would be presumed to be prejudiced because of their demographic characteristics.

We learned a lot about "teaching" diversity from this incident. As a result we modified the timing and approach to the diversity sessions and discussions. In fact, the experience gave us pause to reexamine the entire curriculum. Discussions on race and discrimination are difficult conversations to have, so an atmosphere of trust and respect needs to be established for genuine exchange to happen. When the group is diverse, discussions about diversity cannot wait, especially when some individuals may be uneasy in such a situation. Our experience is in line with Anne Donnellon and Deborah Kolb's research (1994) that shows that as new social groups enter the workforce, conflicts and misunderstandings dealing with race, class, gender, and the like have become more frequent and strategies for dealing with such conflicts need to be put in place. And Lynn Weber reminds us of the "interconnected nature of race, class, gender, and sexuality..." and that these issues become more significant to "those who face oppression along more than one dimension."[4] It is encouraging to hear from one participant that the program "helps clear up misperceptions. It helps to connect with people you may not have known existed in those positions."

The first step in creating a safe environment is to begin with a low-risk exercise. The young leaders are asked to think about the meaning and origin of their name and why it was given to them. Then everyone takes a turn to share her/his thoughts. Peter Kiang's (2003) research demonstrates the importance of providing an opportunity for this kind of personal reflection. "By sharing stories... about both the meaning and pronunciation of their names, students learn to recognize and refer to each other in ways that only their closest friends and family members have practiced in the past." Such an exercise consistently results in deep engagement and rich conversations. The individual voices offer compelling insights and important lessons.[5] Such has been the experience of each group over the eight years.

The rich and varied cultural diversity in each group is noteworthy. Many have origins outside the continental United States. Participants list the following countries in their heritage: Angola, Armenia, Barbados, Canada, China, Egypt, Finland, Greece, Haiti, Honduras, India, Italy, Ireland, Kenya, Korea, Malaysia, Poland, Romania, Syria, and Venezuela. Some had grandparents who came to the Boston region from Italy or Ireland. Others had great-great-grandparents who were slaves. In addition to each telling an interesting story, the variety of names and backgrounds is striking. Individuals gain an enhanced understanding of diversity and inclusion from the naming exercise, and conversations about what they learned continue for several days. By appreciating the power of names, we learn much about the similarities and differences in language, culture, family, and society in profound and personal ways.[6] The naming experience is an important first step in creating a climate of trust and respect among participants. One of the alums remembers this experience as a particularly valuable one. "Our cohort began with naming ourselves—we discussed what's in a name—so many things come of that experience...how you tell your own story, name and claim your own path—the image of exposure, your style—these are gems that stay with you."

Ron Bell describes an experience where he was asked to discuss his ancestry while traveling to Israel with many Jewish colleagues. It is similar to what we do early in the leadership development program. It reinforces the importance of understanding people's various backgrounds and origins.

> *We began with everyone sharing a bit about his or her ancestry. I noticed that all the members of the Jewish community knew their family history: They knew where their grandparents, great-grandparents, and sometimes even great-great-grandparents came from. When it was my turn, the farthest I could go back was my maternal grandmother in South Carolina. I never knew my maternal grandfather or my grandmother and grandfather on my father's side. When it was Larry's [another African American] turn, all he could say was, "My grandmother is from down south and she is Cherokee."*
>
> *Afterward, Larry and I spoke about what a shame it was that we didn't know our family history. It reminded me that I had more work to do. Since I didn't know my history, I figured there were many more African Americans who didn't know their histories either. One of the reasons we don't know our history is that it's too painful. But how can we move forward if we don't know where we come from?*

We then ask individuals to discuss meanings of diversity to them. Generations X and Y provide a variety of definitions and their thoughts contain many insights about how such issues are viewed now and will be construed in the future. Many in these generations think about diversity in quite broad terms.[7]

> *...it's people of varying races, genders, ethnicities, religions and professional and educational backgrounds...all of those things that create peoples' life experience—that they bring to the table...that sit around any team...whatever contributes to one's life experience that gives them the perspective that they have.*
>
> *Diversity is...[a] very broad term in my mind, so it's hard to define it. It's a combination of many different things, including: culture, language, ethnicity, race, age, sexual orientation, and I'm just naming a few...before I would think diversity and I would say "well diversity is..." and there would be this boxed definition. Right now what I would say is that diversity is not that simple. And what I mean by that is anything that can be thought of differently by somebody else—anything that I do can be done in a different way by someone else. Diversity doesn't*

necessarily have to do with color of skin, doesn't have to do with your race, your sex, and doesn't have to do with anything other than respecting things that are not you and being open to them, being thought of differently by somebody else...

The collection of life experiences, and skills and any differences... Diversity to me is just working for an environment of many different cultures, different races, different classes, different... all brought together and ideally in a situation that allows each to be what they are in the best possible way...

I didn't really have an opportunity to work with a really diverse group...—plus at work you can't talk openly about certain things, for example the lady [who] said she was bisexual, that's not something I would hear openly in the [company] and for me it was the first time to hear that and think yeah you do have the right to say that, I don't see why not—everybody else here is saying what their orientation is, that's what your preference is and you should be able to say that.

Where all thoughts, actions, and perspectives are welcome... we found very early on the importance of really taking the time to understand the different perspectives both emotionally and spiritually that people brought to this program.

I think diversity can be defined multiple ways—It can be cultural, it can be age, male/female... I thought I was aware of diversity, I think I am open to kind of everything, but this program really focuses on not only you being diversified but understanding when others aren't, and how to deal with that—not taking it personally.

In my mind, multicultural, multigender, multiethnic backgrounds, just a mix of different cultures, genders, ethnic backgrounds—so that people can... get a sense of having an open view of not offending people... of [seeing] that in their culture that might be ok, and having a respect for other people's beliefs, even if you don't agree with them, and you may not live that way—having an open mind about other people and what they do... without judging or being judgmental.

... it's that melting pot that the country we live in is made of...

I think diversity for me is having representation from as many possible walks of life, whether it be ethnicity, gender, sexual preference, dog lover, cat lover. I mean single, married, whatever... I think it's just important to have as many different factors as possible...

Diversity is the differences among people regardless of the race/color thing, the accepting of the backgrounds, histories, and what makes a person who they are... I might have to look that up in a book—what is diversity.

... having a mix of people by genders, different nationalities, different races, different socioeconomic backgrounds that in itself is diversity—it's a diverse group of people.

When I look at it and think about diversity, it's really all those elements: your background, not necessarily your race or ethnicity, but in terms of where you worked, maybe where you went to school, where you grew up, all those elements and then... how do you think about things.

We need even more time to discuss race and racism and cultural differences...had to question my own philosophy/actions based on my culture which I've actually never done before.

These young professionals understand the complexity of issues related to diversity and see diversity as encompassing issues of race, national origin, gender, sexual orientation, age, ethnicity, and other aspects of individual difference. They are aware that a given individual may have a different definition from that of a colleague and peer.

In addition to the variety of perspectives cited above, diversity of opinion is essential for effective leadership and bringing many voices to the table makes for better decisions. The words of folk singer Pete Seeger, "These days my purpose is in trying to get people to realize that there may be no human race by the end of the century unless we find ways to talk to people we deeply disagree with," are instructive.[8] He expands the meaning of the term diversity in ways that help us broaden our definition of it and also provide guidance to leaders about increasing their effectiveness by being inclusive. Some of the young leaders also see it in expanded terms.

"The power and ability that can come from diverse thinking while working on the same project or problem..." "The diversity gathering was also important—prior to that I looked at it [diversity] very narrowly—now I understand that there are all kinds of diversity and that is great." "The significance of diversity—what companies need to do, what the pipeline needs to look like—it all informs day-to-day practice..." Viewing diversity in this expanded way is helpful to organizations, and most young professionals respond favorably.

MOVING THE CONVERSATION FORWARD

Conversations about inclusion and awareness of issues surrounding diversity, as discussed in chapter 3, are not easy. Some welcome the discussions and benefit from them. Others are not so sure. Some individuals have difficulty dealing with issues related to racism and subtle forms of discrimination. When we introduce the concept of "white privilege" and how it affects organizations and the individuals in them, we often sense a negative reaction from some. Many who are white do not see themselves as having privilege because, as they state, they also have had to work their way up to where they are. However, the discussion gives them new insights into what kind of privileges they may have, even though they may not be aware of them. Individuals of color welcome the conversation because most of them have witnessed white privilege in action. Our experience also corresponds with that described by Oluremi Ayoko and Charlene Hartel (2006) who argue that discussions surrounding diversity can be a double-edged sword, increasing the opportunity for creativity and innovative thinking and understanding while at the same time enhancing the likelihood of dissatisfaction and difficulties within the workplace.[9]

Comments from young professionals demonstrate some of the difficulties.

"The talk on diversity that first day was hard but helped the group get to know each other while addressing complex, multilayered issues of race." But one notes, "The diversity issue was a heavy topic that should have had more time." Another describes it this way:

> Diversity for me was...a subject that I was never...comfortable with—talking about it...I don't really perceive myself as Asian, so that whole thing...the fact that we had such an open conversation in the beginning struck me and made me think that it makes you see things in a different light, and it's ok—so you become comfortable with it. So there are people here of different backgrounds, and you really have to think and stretch yourself in a way that you probably didn't think was possible.

> I hate that word...It's like everyone uses the word diversity and everyone sort of hates it now...People don't even know what it means...I think our group is pretty diverse because people come from different ethnic and cultural backgrounds, different genders, different sexual orientations, people are native to Boston, non-native to Boston...

In another interview the individual expressed his/her concern that many continue to avoid discussions of diversity:

> ...How much people avoid the subject of diversity, we deny it. We believe it does not exist. But it was so evident that it is still very alive in different organizations. I learned that there is so much that we need to do, and being aware of "white" privilege is just the first step.

Other comments, when asked what was learned, are also instructive. Individuals admit to cultural biases and how they need to try enlarging their thinking. One admits, "My own cultural biases and how I can have an open mind to learn from others and be inclusive." Another notes substantial learning:

> Opening myself up to the importance of diversity. I do not consider myself to be racist; however, I always felt a little bitter about how much importance is placed on diversity. This week helped me to understand what others experience that I don't. I have also learned so much from the diverse group here.

Overall when we consider the variety of responses, it is evident that the benefits outweigh the difficulties.

My participation in the program has affected my ability to work in diverse groups... there are aspects of the program that I didn't see as diversity but, after going through the program, they definitely did add to that definition. Sometimes you don't even see diversity between profit and not-for-profit, and there is a huge difference on how they approach problems, how they solve problems... In a very collaborative way, you just got to see it right in front of your eyes—different ages, different experience level, nonprofit/[not-]for-profit views, gender, ethnicity— most of the aspects that one would consider part of diversity, the program had the benefit to bring to the table and have people come from so many different angles in similar situations or problems, and you get to see... that people just look at problems very differently, just because of the way they think, because of the way they were culturally brought up... or what ever it is, but they look at it very differently.

I would say in general I am a... liberal person and that diversity is important to me and that the program helped reaffirm my belief of how I view working with people that are diverse, and it helped me understand better how to do that.

When it comes to working on a project team, I would say diversity of... color and gender, but... diversity of age is really important, especially when [working] in the city and you know, there is a disconnect between those in their twenties and thirties, and the rest of the city, so I think a diversity of age is also really important and diversity of perspectives from different organizations.

My workplace is largely white and American (people don't identify with other cultural heritages). The largest impact for me was a strong desire to interact with the type of people I met in this program because of the quality and the depth of the interactions with everyone went far beyond what I am used to.

This program is very helpful in expanding the definition of diversity for me, and that before the program diversity might have just been viewed as race and ethnicity, but now it's viewed in a much broader sense of where these people come from, what are their backgrounds, what are their work experiences, and if anything it's much broader—it goes beyond race and ethnicity.

I used to work in high tech and to some extent it wasn't that diverse. It was more male dominated... I [also] worked in dot.com so there are lots of young people, [but not] a lot of older, more senior people.... [the ELP] has increased my ability to work in diverse groups.... because Boston is so racially divided I just think it is fantastic the outreach that's done and the number of up and coming African Americans in the group. Then of course I came to find out that much work needs to be done in the woman side... here in the city—very white, male dominated... so it's good to have as many women as possible too...... [the ELP] was probably the most diverse setting I had been in, so it was a great experience in itself... I think it gave me an appreciation for experiences people had in their lives, in their work environment and their personal environment. I think the makeup of the group... that [diversity] was an obvious goal—to have a diverse group.... I don't think it was blatant; it was very subtle in terms of diversity.

My department was mainly all male except for me, and for a few months when we had two more females; and so to me now we are a little more diverse because we have that gender balance and a lot of times people here seem to think that diversity is just color or ethnicity and I say No, it's men and women that's diversity too... because it's just not color, and it can also be age too. Because a lot of people in my department are a lot older, so we didn't have the balance of age or gender, so now my department is much (more) diverse.

I think [the ELP experience] probably enhanced [my ability to work in diverse groups]. This, working at the [organization] and the city in general, is one most diverse places I've worked... It's very diverse culturally, ethnically. Since we don't have like a ton of immigrants working here, I shouldn't say that, and we don't have the diversity of non-natives to natives... I think a lot of the people who work for the city were born and raised in the city so that part of it is not diverse.

An alumna describes how the increased awareness affected her in a very personal way. "It changed how I think about diversity. I thought I'm the most open person... but now I am selling my home and the realtor is not someone I would choose to associate with and I challenged myself—thinking my response was not good enough—we had our first meeting last week and I would not have gone that far. I now know that I wasn't going deep enough and can challenge my bias."

We are grateful that the experience works well for many, because these issues will be present in most workplaces in the future and biases will continue to get in the way of performance. In addition, businesses and other organizations must respond more to international pressures and need to support an understanding of other cultures and an appreciation of cultural differences. Ayoko reminds us that collectivist cultures such as Asian, Middle Eastern, and Latin American tend to "adopt a harmony perspective of conflict." A confrontational perspective is more common for English-speaking countries.[10] Emerging leaders need to be aware of these differences and adept in dealing with them. We find great receptivity among them when we focus on understanding other cultures and how one interacts in such situations. They are eager for such experiences.

It is easier to discuss cultural differences than the possibility of continued racism and discrimination. But gradually individuals begin to understand that they may have some bias and they become more aware of subtle forms of discrimination that remain in place. For those who have a more limited idea of diversity, their concepts broaden as a result of being part of a very diverse group. When diversity is viewed as encompassing characteristics that differentiate one person or group from others, young professionals gain an understanding of the concept that goes well beyond examining more traditional differences between blacks and whites.

YOUNG PROFESSIONALS CONFRONT RACISM

As noted previously, slightly over 40 percent of participants are persons of color and over half are female, and they represent many different national origins and backgrounds as cited at the beginning of the chapter. And one goal of the program is to create a learning environment that reflects the demographic profile of the region. For some young professionals, meeting and then working with such a diverse group is an enlightening experience in itself because this provides their first opportunity to participate in a truly diverse setting. Some now articulate an expanded concept of diversity and inclusion and want those discussions to explore issues of inclusion in greater depth. When they hear from their peers about direct evidence of racism, it has a profound effect. Others have worked in diverse settings, and it is a significant part of their professional and/or private lives and working in a diverse group strengthens their awareness and capacity to deal with these issues.[11]

Gonçalves describes his childhood in Angola and the abrupt move that he and his family made to Cape Verde as political refugees as a result of civil war.

In 1975, when I was five years old, violent civil war erupted in my country. Angolan nationalists had formed political coalitions and were fighting for their independence from Portugal. Early one morning, a guerilla militia attacked my village and my family fled our coffee farm. We had no time to gather our belongings before running to the mountains. For three days we traveled on rough terrain, subsisting on manioc roots and water collected on banana leaves. When we reached Luanda, the capitol of Angola, we were protected by the Angolan government. They housed my family in a high-rise building where we stayed for four months.

The conditions in Luanda were extremely difficult, since Angola's struggle for independence contributed to severe food shortages. Along with my siblings, I stood in bread lines for hours each morning, often to find that by the time my turn had come, all of the bread had been distributed. The same was true for the soup kitchen lines in the evening. Many times, I walked home hungry. The pressure of being a child in survival mode is something that breaks you down or makes you strong. At an early age, I learned the meaning of "hard times." Forced to flee our lush and prosperous coffee farm, we became impoverished overnight, without a foreseeable way to improve our situation.

One evening, a bus arrived to bring us to the airport. We boarded a plane destined for Cape Verde, where my grandmother still lived. After the ten-hour flight, we stepped off the plane and saw that Cape Verde was nothing but rocks and gravel. We were transported by an open dump truck to Mosteiros, a small town by the sea. There we settled in a house built from stones gathered from a quarry. The recurring drought and heat waves made it impossible to grow most foods. We spent our days searching for sweet potatoes at the foot of the mountains or fishing for octopus and eels in the ocean. Our neighbors and relatives referred to us as "refugados"; though Cape Verde was the native land of my family, we returned as political refugees.

Hardship of a different sort continued for Gonçalves when he arrived in the United States from Cape Verde. He became a victim of the busing crisis in Boston and had a difficult time understanding what was happening.

After four years of malnutrition, despair, and hardship, my family had the opportunity to immigrate to the United States. I was nine years old and my new home was a crowded apartment in the inner city of Boston, Massachusetts. Within days of arriving in Boston, I began attending school. I was fluent in Portuguese and Cape Verdean Kriolu, but I knew no English. I was put in a bilingual program for six months and then I entered an English-speaking class.

While I quickly learned how to communicate in my new language, I was caught in the firestorm of a federally mandated integration policy of forced busing. As we were marched into the Condon Elementary School in South Boston, white kids stood alongside us, jeering and spitting and throwing raw eggs. I couldn't understand what was happening. In Angola, I lived in a village of twenty houses and in Cape Verde, there were no more than thirty houses. Everyone in my village knew each other and we faced the same difficulties—namely providing for one's family and gathering enough food each day. There was no talk about race or color. So when I found myself in the midst of the busing era, I was stunned and confused. Why did those white people hate us so much?

Slowly, I began to understand that the rage they were expressing went deeper than their anger at having people of color invading their neighborhoods. Most of the white children in South Boston had much in common with my socioeconomic background. Like me, they were children from poor families with few opportunities. It dawned on me that school integration was based more on politics than on race, although race was the focal point. Looking around, I saw that we were all victimized by economic discrimination. The white folks in South Boston were just as marginalized as the people of color in Harbor Point. Through their racist attacks, these white families were voicing their anger with government systems that had failed them. The American Dream was a broken promise for them and they were looking for a scapegoat to communicate this betrayal.

As I started to distinguish between ignorance and facts surrounding the busing conflict, I began to bond with some of the white students in my class. In fact, my ability to engage with white students and white teachers on the issue of busing marked the beginning of my leadership journey. The questions I posed were uncomfortable ones. I asked, "How is it possible that you are a white American struggling for quality education and public housing—doesn't that make you equal to the people of color in this country?" Being able to recognize such harsh social, economic, and political realities at an early age fueled my leadership drive: I spoke the truth even when it meant making people around me uneasy. Understanding the ignorance I was exposed to during the busing era helped me see that the power to forgive is a critical part of achieving change.

Gonçalves recounts how he had to deal with these issues as he pursued his education. His goal is to help others who experience racism and the challenges that go with it.

I chose to continue my studies at UMass Boston, and from there I earned a bachelor's degree in urban planning and economics. To develop further expertise in my field, with the goal of improving the quality of life for disenfranchised people in this country and abroad, I decided to pursue a master's degree in international development and regional planning. I applied to a few graduate schools, including MIT, and was accepted. I debated back and forth which school to attend and I settled on MIT. Another hurdle surfaced: although MIT accepted me, they didn't offer me any funding. I decided to visit the administrators at the university and inquire about scholarships.

I jumped on my bicycle and biked through Dorchester, an area dominated by people of color, and crossed the Mass Ave Bridge into Cambridge, which is predominately white. I arrived at MIT and was eventually directed to the dean of the College of Planning, who agreed to have a brief meeting with me. I explained my situation, that I wouldn't be able to attend MIT without financial support. This dean nodded his head and responded that many students had similar circumstances, but the university was facing hard times and wasn't able to provide funding. When I heard him say "hard times," I looked around his beautifully furnished office and I glanced out the window at the well-dressed students walking on the manicured grounds of the campus. Well, I knew what "hard times" meant. Fleeing a civil war, standing on food lines as a child, living as a refugee without rights, coming to America and dealing with racism and discrimination on a daily basis, and watching the Boston Public School system fail hundreds of black youth.

I slammed my fist on his table and shouted, don't talk to me about "hard times" until you cross that bridge into Dorchester and Roxbury and see children who have inadequate education, substandard housing, lack of nutritious food, and no opportunities. MIT owns half of Cambridge but you don't have enough money to educate an immigrant you've accepted into your program? You're perpetrating a system of economic and social oppression. Don't talk to me about "hard times!" I stormed out of his office and biked home. A week later, I received a letter stating I was awarded a full scholarship.

Others, like Gonçalves, have experienced significant racism. They identify with the Keith Caver and Ancella Livers' (2002) article "Dear White Boss" that discusses the incidents that occur in organizations every day that are offensive to people of color and how those making comments often appear not to understand "what the problem is." Writing to the boss, the authors observe, "…I believe you are in some ways blind to what is happening outside your office door. I truly believe you don't know how frustrated I often am—by the lack of acknowledgment or apparent understanding of how our experience in the workplace differs from yours, and how it affects not just our own morale but the health of the organization overall."[12] These stories from the young professionals are powerful especially when they are related by one of the young leaders to another. As they relate their experiences, new understandings emerge.

In conversations with young professionals who are people of color, we hear about problems that continue. Many of them continue to believe that to be successful in obtaining a leadership position it is necessary to conform to a white male culture. They also argue that as one moves up the ladder, the barriers increase.

David Halbert, who was an aide to City Councilor Sam Yoon and previously worked for Deval Patrick, the Commonwealth's first African American governor, writes:

> As a member of the African American community, my own perspective is of someone from a segment of the population that the late author Lorraine Hansberry categorized as, "young, gifted, and Black." Being a part of this demographic has provided me with advantages and obstacles as I have tried to develop as both a person and a leader.
>
> ... The feelings that I had at this time were compounded by the fact that the community to which we moved and, accordingly, the school system, were overwhelmingly white. Though I had had some experience dealing with a majority white environment as a student in Cincinnati, this was always culturally balanced by the fact that each day I came home to a community where people on the street looked more or less like me. In this new Boston environment I realized very quickly that, whether at school or in the neighborhood, I was always going to stick out.
>
> This sense of isolation was intensified by the fact that, while not much of a student, I was intellectually gifted and often found myself in academic situations where I was one of few students of color, sometimes the only one. Because my friends were often those in my classes, and because most of those students were white, there was a perception among some other students that I was not "really" African American. This raised my sensitivities to the difficulties others face when dealing with the stereotypes against which they are compared. It also gave me reason to be introspective about what I felt it meant to be an African American.
>
> As we begin the twenty-first century, a new generation of African American leaders is emerging and is dealing with a question that goes hand in hand with the idea of double consciousness—namely, how to balance being "black enough" for the world at large, while simultaneously trying to create an environment that is genuinely egalitarian and truly color-blind.
>
> ... This constant struggle to view and comport myself so as to feel proud of who I was and what I was doing, while at the same time trying not to disassociate

myself from my cultural and ethnic heritage, is one that I still find myself in to this day. My thoughts on the use of "nigger," and the criticism I have faced from some as a result, are merely one example where double consciousness has influenced the leadership stance that I have had to take.

. . . What double consciousness creates, more than anything, is a space for an honest discussion. Utilizing the concept in this way, as a tool for promoting a better dialogue and ultimately achieving higher-quality conclusions, is critical as a crucible for leadership. Being willing to engage in these often uncomfortable conversations, as a means to achieving lasting positive change, will play a crucial role in how I express myself as a leader in the future and, accordingly, how I am regarded as one. I believe that when a political figure is willing to engage in frank conversations on uncomfortable topics, in a manner that is not accusatory or incendiary, but rather honest and collaborative, he will be embraced.

Halbert identifies with the problem that many white managers are unaware of how the experience of African Americans in a company may differ from that of their white colleagues. He calls for more open and honest conversations about these issues so that they can be resolved.

Gonçalves describes what may account for lack of progress for persons of color:

As a person of color, I have to stay one step ahead of my mainstream counterparts, despite the fact that I am just as qualified and competent. I have the tasks not only of performing my functions and responsibilities, but also of managing people around me who undermine my professional judgment and intellect. This is commonly referred to as the "Black Tax," or the extra penalty that people of color experience on a daily basis for not being a part of the mainstream club. This type of tax raises our survival instincts to a whole new level.

Common gospel in communities of color, African Americans are taught from an early age that in order to succeed, we must learn to "play the game." I have always refused to play the game, because every game is played to advance one group's agenda, and too often the result is devastating to those in the lower social strata. Also, when a person of color aggressively tries to "play the game" at the workplace, he or she is at risk for being seen as a non–team player. The point is that the rules of engagement for people of color within any given organization are unwritten, and the minute we get close to those rules, they are apt to change.

Bell, an African American, also has had painful experiences with racism:

While my mother was fighting to save our neighborhoods, I was fighting another form of injustice. Every Wednesday when I was nine years old, I was cornered on Tremont Street by a group of white teenagers who spat on me and called me names. After that, I'd go to Cub Scouts, where I'd recite the Pledge of Allegiance smelling like liquor and spit. I endured the experience of busing in the Boston pub-lic school system and learned how to get along with children in different cultural groups. In seventh grade, I attended Boston Latin, a predominantly white school located across the street from Boston English, where my friends went. It was tough being the outsider in school, but being an athlete helped me wherever I went, because sports crossed color lines. On the court, every player on the team worked together to reach the same goal: winning the game.

He reflects on a particularly disturbing incident that took place in Boston later in his career:

A couple of months after my promotion, Roxbury was assaulted by one of the worst racial profiling cases publicized in the country. It was the Charles Stuart tragedy, a story picked up by every major news station and televised across the nation. Charles Stuart was a fur store manager who claimed that he and his pregnant white wife were driving back from childbirth classes when they were robbed by a black man at gunpoint in Mission Hill. He testified that the gunman, who wore a running suit and had a raspy voice, shot his pregnant wife in the head and him in the stomach. As soon as the news broke, Roxbury was under siege. Police swarmed the city searching for that black man in the running suit. Every one of us was a suspect.

In the mornings, I would walk to work and find rows of black men leaning against the Community Center, their hands in the air, getting searched by police. These were good men in the neighborhood, thrown against the wall like criminals. It was the most humiliating thing I'd ever seen, and I was outraged by how power-less we were. These policemen didn't know I was the director of the Community Center, and I didn't want to be lined up and searched, so the first time I saw this happening, I turned around and walked away. I was on Tremont Street, the same street where I used to get spat on as a child.

Walking down Tremont Street, turning away from those men getting searched, was a pivotal moment for me. Anger from all of the discrimination I had endured in childhood and young adulthood was welling up in me, rushing to the surface like a volcano about to erupt. I set my briefcase down and decided right then that things had to change. I realized the best way to exact punishment on those elected officials who didn't stand up for our rights was to hold voter registration drives. We would register every possible voter in the city of Boston and vote those officials out of power.

Bailly describes her experience and her determination to move ahead:

As a first-generation, dual-citizen African American, born to naturalized U.S. citi-zens in Boston (mother born in Panama, Canal Zone, and father born in Barbados, West Indies), I was raised with a rich cross-cultural appreciation and the belief that I can do anything that I make up my mind to do. To my parents, hard work and a good education were the keys to success in America. To them, knowledge was something that "no one can take away." When they reflected on my future as a child of the 1970s, surrounded by the turmoil of busing and racial divides in the city of Boston, they often said: "Whatever you decide to do or be, Do and Be the Best."

Georgianna Meléndez who is of Irish and Puerto Rican heritage discusses a distressing encounter when she went against what might be expected of her as a Puerto Rican:

...I remember being in a boardroom during a leadership transition. The interim executive director was looking for management to step up and do some extra work to carry the agency through until a permanent replacement was hired. I "naturally" volunteered to take on something I had never done before and was immediately challenged by one of my colleagues. Her rationale for challenging me was that I was too "green" (too young and inexperienced). I defended my ability to get the task done despite its being a new task for me. In leaving the meeting, another Puerto Rican manager pulled me aside and scolded me. She asked me what made me so bold. She asked if I realize that if I failed, then we (Puerto Ricans) all fail. My response to her was simple confusion.... Fail? What if I succeed? Do we all then also succeed? I succeeded with flying colors. I think about this incident throughout the years. It reminds me of the importance of trying and of going outside of your comfort zone. It is how we grow. And yes, we do sometimes fail, but we get up again. Sometimes we even succeed...

One of the external speakers, who was the first Asian American on the Boston City Council, reports a recent and troubling experience. As a member of the City Council, he marched in the St. Patrick's Day parade in Boston. While marching, he was verbally attacked by an older gentleman who was observing the parade and yelled at him, "I remember World War II and what you Japs did." Our speaker stopped and talked with the man and his family to point out that he was Korean and the Koreans were not involved in World War II. The man's family apologized to the Korean leader. The story had a profound effect on the young leaders. And that speaker later became one of the candidates for mayor of our city.

Many people of color believe that racism continues to be an issue and see that many barriers remain. In conversations, some black males describe what it is like to be the only black male in a situation and how the non-blacks tend to see an "angry black male" whenever the black male raises an objection or a question about an issue. Race gets in the way and perceptions make these circumstances more uncomfortable than they should be. This conception of continual racial bias and stereotypes was heightened in the summer of 2009 as this chapter was in preparation. During the Sonia Sotomajor hearings, in advance of the vote to confirm her for the Supreme Court, issues regarding race and gender became evident. She was eventually confirmed and is now the first Hispanic Woman to be appointed to the Court.

And then in the middle of July (July 16) the Skip Gates incident occurred. Henry Louis Gates, Jr., who is a prominent African American professor at Harvard, was arrested for disorderly conduct by the Cambridge police after someone reported a possible break-in at his house. Gates was trying to gain access to his own residence after returning from an international trip and had trouble opening his front door. Tensions were high as he and a white police officer from Cambridge met in Gates' home. Words were exchanged and Gates was arrested although later the charges were dropped. The incident became a major news story not just in the Boston area but across the nation and charges as well as denials of racism came forth.

One of the alums, Georgianna Meléndez, co-authored an opinion editorial for the *Boston Globe* on July 22 stating:

> *But a confrontation on Ware Street in Cambridge on Thursday—and vociferous public reaction to it—betray a stark truth: that the election of a black governor and president have hardly put Massachusetts and America "beyond race."*

The city of Cambridge has set up a high-level commission to review the incident and make recommendations for the future; President Obama, who also commented on the case, invited both men to the White House for discussions. The parties seem now to agree to turn this unfortunate incident into a broader conversation about race. The incident had a personal impact on Sherry who has known Gates for some 30 years and worked closely with him at Yale in the late 1970s. As a white woman who also has confronted sexism and gender stereotyping, she notes a sense of disappointment that issues of race, its history, and the complexity involved continue to surface. She also had just reread the essays of Bell, Halbert, Gonçalves, Bailly, Francisco, and Meléndez and their personal experiences with racism when this event took place. Yet we remain hopeful that this unfortunate encounter eventually will have a positive outcome and that productive conversations about racism followed by positive action will take place.[13]

Young professionals are more comfortable discussing diversity and inclusiveness than some others are and we believe that they will make progress on these issues. As they recognize the effects of subtle and not so subtle discrimination, many of them have thought more clearly about their own biases. Overall they seek inclusive workplaces and they want to move beyond racial divides. And when fellow young professionals such as Armindo Gonçalves, David Halbert, Ron Bell, Georgianna Meléndez, Paul Francisco, and Sandra Bailly relate their personal experiences, young professionals who are not persons of color gain new understandings.

One fellow comments on his work setting and how he became more attuned to issues of race and of prejudice:

I wouldn't call banks diverse—it's heavily white male...I think I am more attuned to making sure that as the dominant white male, that I would...go out of my way to try and deal with some colleagues, and include those who don't have similar interests... (I)t feels like coming out of the program and listening to people talk, and listening to their stories, that maybe that is not enough... Talk to me before the program and I would have said, jeez I've never been exclusionary, and then hearing people talk about issues they've had, [that] has raised the bar a little bit for me.

Another describes the advantages of diversity:

When I think of my team and how diverse my team may or may not be—you know I have 15 direct reports: 13 of them are women, 2 are men, 1 is black, and 1 is Hispanic. But then I also think of their backgrounds and their experiences for instance, where they and/or their families originate, where they have worked previously, different things about their environment early on in their personal lives in terms of different careers that they had...different industries. So I think everybody is different and...that is good, [because] the different opinions allow you again to get the best product.

ORGANIZATIONS: THEIR ROLE IN DIVERSITY AWARENESS

Sponsoring organizations have had varying experiences with inclusion in the workplace and the reasons for selecting young professionals to participate vary. Some sponsors send individuals knowing that their experience with diversity is limited. Some sponsors who send persons lacking experience with diversity want those individuals to experience a more diverse setting and learn how to work within it, hoping that that experience will influence cultural or attitudinal shifts. Many business organizations see that additional experience with diversity serves as a business advantage, and they understand the need to be responsive to changing customer clienteles. They call for the use of the talents of all and realize that that will make the workplace more productive. Many organizations not only see diversity as an appreciation of diverse cultures and points of view but also want to advance multicultural understanding.

An emerging leader notes how diversity of experience can enhance one's understanding:

One thing I learned working in this company is that someone of a liberal arts background and somebody of an engineering background—have completely different way of thinking of things, and never the two shall meet. It's almost like these guys are from different planets, and I've appreciated having a liberal arts background so the approach of an engineer is completely different. It's not worse, it's not better— just different. That one thing we did talk about...putting yourself in somebody else's shoes and trying to think in their shoes. I definitely have learned that and I appreciate that. It's just a different diversity—different way of thinking.

Another observes.

I've been in banking for the last several years so there's just so much diversity you get in banking. [Bank name] was really good in that it really put its money where its mouth was when it came to hiring a diverse group of people. The percentage of people coming from diverse backgrounds—whether it be race, sexual orientation, color—it seemed to be more diverse, as far a bank goes… This bank here is ok, but I would say they can go a long way to making it more diverse… I wish there was more diversity around me all the time, it just makes you more aware and in touch with what's going on in the world when we have some people with other focuses and other walks of life around you, and I think some of us tend to forget about that sometimes when 80 percent of the people we work with are white, even male or female—you tend to not focus so much on what might be going on in some other part of the world or even your own neighborhood.

Other comments are also instructive:

I have always worked in a bank, and banks are probably matching up poorly with our society is as far as the make-up of people… we've got slightly more than 50 percent male to female, there is not a lot of diversity other than that. I mean everybody is Caucasian and the same economic profile—everybody lives in the suburbs, and so clearly it's not the same mix of people as you have in the ELP.

I just got into the… Minority Management Development Program. I never in a million years would have applied for that program if I hadn't done the ELP… I never thought of myself as being a minority, or diverse—never really recognized that there are people who aren't as lucky as I am, and that have issues with that, and they had an interesting perspective that I want to hear about.

I would say [the ELP] afforded [me] the opportunity to work in diverse groups. I probably was capable before but definitely I don't think I would have continued in the current job that… I am in now, I don't think I would have been exposed to that opportunity to work in a diverse group.

In our region nonprofit organizations and government agencies have more diverse workforces. So some sponsors select individuals who have experience with diversity with the hope of further enhancing other skills for those people.

… this agency is—a very diverse agency, working in a very diverse community. Boston is a majority minority city and our staff members are out night after night after night working with people of Boston, so they are working with a diverse community… Nominator R.

This particular individual [nominated Fellow] is outstanding at working in that [diverse] environment, so with those demonstrated skills and other experiences [will show] even more potential... Nominator Q.

Many of the sponsoring organizations have diversity awareness programs and the leadership development experience complements those efforts. Linda Hite and Kimberly McDonald (2006) find that large organizations often have more productive programs than smaller organizations, but they also express concern that many organizations fail to move beyond basic programs to explore more intensive strategies for overcoming workplace discrimination.[14] We are pleased that so many of the organizations recognize the need for diversity awareness and take steps to see that individuals in those organizations have additional exposure and awareness programs. But we are acutely aware from conversations with individuals of color that more leadership is needed from white managers to bring about organizational changes for creating an atmosphere conducive to diversity. The young professionals tell us that when they as people of color take the lead, they are aware that they run risks and this is not something they can do on a regular basis without support. Awareness is the first step, but beyond that organizations need to move to eliminate bias and to create multicultural workplaces.

DIVERSITY AND INCLUSIVENESS: A BUSINESS ADVANTAGE

Bennett, Bennett, and Landis (2005) remind us to see diversity in the most expansive context.[15] And organizations throughout society—business and nonprofit—recognize the importance of a renewed focus on diversity and inclusiveness. William Bowen and Derek Bok (Bowen, Bok, and Burkhart 1999), former presidents of Princeton and Harvard respectively, argue that a diverse and culturally aware workforce is both a business and moral imperative. They assert the need for leaders from all aspects of the spectrum and note the inherent creativity that diverse teams exhibit. They see diversity as a business necessity "because it affects competitiveness."[16]

Most organizations today move well beyond compliance and see the business case for such work. This means leveraging talent and retaining it as well as responding to expanded customer bases. It is our goal that young professionals experience diversity in a variety of ways and learn to appreciate its many facets and that they will see diversity as an advantage in their workplaces and personal lives. Generations X and Y are more inclusive generations than previous ones and diversity is viewed by many of them as the advantage that it should be. In conversations we repeatedly hear that they see many benefits in working in a diverse group and that this setting has opened their minds about how a focus on inclusiveness can bring positive benefits to organizations.

Francisco discusses the value of inclusive structures and his belief that differences can be overcome—something he is committed to doing. Paul's experience and his recent launching of his own company speak to the goal of many organizations. Francisco, who with a colleague has turned entrepreneur, describes the challenge this way:

> *Boston is a diverse city in the sense that the population is 51 percent minority. But the source of power and influence in this city remains primarily white. According to Partnership, Inc., [a leadership program for professionals of color] in order for a company to be truly diverse, at least 30 percent of top management must be composed of professionals of color. That's the magic number to create an open and supportive workplace. Many companies talk diversity, but when it comes to their numbers, representation in leadership positions is sorely lacking. We need to elevate those companies to the 30 percent mark and further develop the powerful executive minority that is emerging in Boston.*

Francisco will focus on improving the climate for persons of color:

> *I left Bank of America in 2005 to take a senior position at Veritude, a Fidelity Investments company, as a vice president within the Client Relationship Management Group, providing strategic guidance and client relationship management to Veritude client companies. I specialized in Recruitment Process Outsourcing (RPO), managed staffing services and consulting services for a range of industries including IT, healthcare, insurance and finance.*
>
> *By the summer of 2008, I finally realized my dream: Foster & Francisco LLP, my diversity recruitment business, came to fruition. Foster & Francisco was the brainchild of my dear friend Emerson Foster and me.*
>
> *...we intend to reach our primary goal of making Boston a more welcoming city for minorities. The visibility of professionals of color in key positions is a critical component of creating a thriving community. I am proud to take part in changing the landscape of this city.*
>
> *... Over the years, I've learned a great deal about character, integrity and vision—the qualities of great leaders. I have an extended family in Honduras and the game of football to thank for teaching me the fundamentals of leadership: how to inspire others, earn their respect, and gain their trust to lead them to a win. On the field, every member of the team has a vital role. No matter where we come from or what color our skin is, each of us makes a valuable contribution.*

Others agree concerning the importance of diversity for national and international competitiveness. Andrew Park (2008) states: "the smartest organizations in the world are recognizing that their diversity can be a source of competitive strength." He notes that successful organizations implement "holistic strategies that seek to better understand their employees' backgrounds, styles, and perspectives, then leverage them for real business benefit."[17] Dolezalek (2008) notes that diversity training can enhance productivity and that it helps people of different backgrounds work together in a more productive manner.[18] Many businesses have appointed chief diversity officers to lead the way in harnessing the creative ideas of their various groups. They see that diversity has a direct tie to market share and that an inclusive climate assists that company in reaching beyond traditional markets. And successful efforts at inclusiveness mean that the officers of the company (who may be white) are also involved in these issues.[19] Debbe Kennedy describes the efforts toward enhancing diversity as a new frontier for business. Effective organizations focus on diversity, inclusion, and innovation and understand that innovation "lies at the intersection of human differences." Diversity is broadly defined and the challenge is to put diversity to work in innovation.[20]

Although most agree that diversity plays an important role for staying competitive in the national and international arena, achieving diversity at all levels in organizations is a more challenging task. In the greater Boston region the issue is clouded by the recent past. With the busing controversy of the early 1970s and other more recent incidents, the region has not always been seen as a welcoming place to live and work for people of color. Statewide surveys of racial and ethnic attitudes and experiences in Massachusetts support that concern and the Gates incident mentioned above did not help. And the issues now are not only black and white as other ethnicities come into play. Although the discussion frequently focuses on black/white issues, we also hear from Latinos and Asian Americans that they face similar problems and worry about the paucity of individuals in major leadership positions in organizations. The problem continues.

However, our hope is for a growing appreciation of the benefits of multiculturalism. We agree with the words of Ron Takaki who penned these words in an essay in 2008:

> Moreover, as a historian of multicultural America, I welcome Obama's affirmation of America as a nation peopled by the world. He personifies diversity as America's "manifest destiny." A leader of vision, Obama has reached for the ties that bind—Lincoln's "mystic chords of memory," seeking to unite us as a diverse people belonging to one nation. Crossing racial, economic, and political boundaries, Obama has already inspired millions of us, both young and old, to be audacious in our hopes for changing America and the world.[21]

On the local level efforts again are underway to bring about positive change. Business and civic leaders in the greater Boston area are aware of the negative reputation that developed in previous years and want to see it reversed.

Evidence outlined in a recent study of the composition of boards of directors shows the dominance of white males and the underrepresentation of persons of color on corporate boards and nonprofits and highlights one aspect of the issue.[22] In light of the data and concerns, the Commonwealth Compact was founded in 2007 by Steve Crosby, dean of the McCormack Graduate School of Public Policy at the University of Massachusetts Boston, Ralph Martin, former Suffolk County district attorney and now a managing partner in the Boston office of Bingham McCutchen and then-chairman of the Greater Boston Chamber of Commerce, and Steve Ainsley, then-publisher of the *Boston Globe*. Its goal is "to help make Massachusetts a location of choice for people of color and women in the belief that their contributions are vital to the region's social and economic future." Organizations throughout the region have joined the Compact and made a commitment to diversity and agreed to monitor and report their progress.[23]

The Compact recently prepared a comprehensive report that benchmarks where we are and points directions for the future. Some 111 organizations in Massachusetts submitted data for the report. One hundred percent of these indicate that they value a diverse workforce and customer base. In addition, 97 percent of CEOs say they are actively engaged in diversity efforts and 79 percent say diversity is explicitly referenced among the organization's values or goals. Although 80 percent note that workplace diversity has improved in the past five years, they believe there is still a long way to go with only 49 percent indicating satisfaction with the diversity of their leadership team. Although 98 percent believe that women now advance as fast as men, only 76 percent believe that non-whites advance as fast as whites.

Clearly more can be done. Persons of color represent 34 percent of all employees of organizations responding to the survey but hold only 22 percent in managerial positions and above. Moreover, persons of color are most heavily represented in clerical and technical positions. And among Compact organizations, 23 percent had no person of color on their leadership team, and 11 percent had none on their governing board.[24] The Commonwealth Compact initiative is the first of its kind in the country and clearly has a potential to make Massachusetts once again a location of choice for people of color to work and live. With the renewed commitment to recruitment, hiring, management, and governance practices that increase diversity, the future should reflect a workplace that better mirrors the demographics.

WHAT NEXT?

When we meet with young professionals in focus group settings or in more general conversations, the topics of diversity and inclusiveness are frequently raised. They understand the concerns of colleagues and peers who continue to experience racism, applaud the efforts of many organizations to bring diverse points of view into the conversation, and welcome this openness. They do admit that managing the various issues of race, gender, age, and cultural differences is a challenge for managers, but it is a challenge that they are prepared to meet. One said: "You can't have any hang-ups about difference." They want to be in organizations that are open to hearing diverse perspectives and they stress the need for a "unified global community." Their attitude in support of inclusion may help overcome the subtle discrimination that continues to exist in many organizations. They note that the sessions in the program provided a constant opportunity to "open your mind." One notes, "I am able to look through several different lenses now" and that makes me "more effective in dealing with a multitude of people from various backgrounds." Another positive sign is that an African American woman from a recent cohort also mentioned that she is supported in her efforts on behalf of persons of color in her organization.

As emerging leaders, Gonçalves, Bailly, Halbert, Bell, Meléndez, and Francisco and the other young professionals featured in this book, as well as those of Generation X and Y who will be their colleagues, understand that organizations that practice inclusiveness and celebrate diversity will most likely be those that are successful in the future. Young professionals of Generation X and Y can help them get there. They are ready to lead.

CHAPTER 6

THE VIEW FROM GENERATION X: ORGANIZATIONS NEED TO CHANGE

WHAT CHALLENGES DO EMERGING LEADERS SEE FOR ORGANIZATIONS IN THE future, what would they like to see changed and what obstacles do they see in their own career paths?

LEADERSHIP: MOVING FORWARD

We asked about personal progress in meeting leadership goals and the alumni survey shows encouraging results for the paths to leadership for young professionals. Most respondents (see table A6.1: "Progress toward career goal" in the appendix) report feeling that they are making some progress (46 percent) or a lot of progress (39 percent) toward their career goal in their current organization. Fewer respondents said that they were making only a little (11 percent) or no progress (5 percent). There was some difference by gender and race. For the gender comparison, the differences were in the more extreme answers, with men more likely to report a lot of progress and less likely to report no progress. For the race comparison, the differences were more in the middle responses "some" and "a little" showing higher responses for people of color than for whites.[1]

BARRIERS TOWARD GOALS

We also asked about barriers encountered. As shown in table 6.1, respondents who reported making some, a little, or no progress are also asked

Table 6.1   Major factor holding back progress

What is the major factor holding you back from making a lot of progress towards your career goal in your current organization? (% reporting Yes for each)	Gender		Race/Ethnicity		Total (n=80)
	Male (n=32)	Female (n=48)	White, Not Hispanic (n=47)	Other (n=32)	
No opportunities to move up	34	31	32	31	33
Issues of work/family balance	19	17	19	16	18
Lack of support from boss or supervisor	13	10	13	9	11
Lack of necessary skills	3	4	2	6	4
Own lack of motivation or drive	3	4	6	0	4
Discrimination	0	2	2	0	1
Reluctant to take on responsibilities of leadership role	0	0	0	0	0
Lack of encouragement	0	0	0	0	0
Other	28	31	26	38	30

what they believe is the major factor holding them back from making a lot of progress toward their career goal in their current organization. Nearly one third of young leaders (33 percent) cite lack of opportunity as the major factor holding back their progress. Another nearly one in five (18 percent) cite issues of work/family balance as the major barrier to progress. Many respondents report other factors that impede their career progress, such as lack of support from their boss (11 percent), lack of necessary skills (4 percent), and their own lack of motivation (4 percent). Only one person reported discrimination as a barrier to progress at work. But when we discuss barriers in focus group settings, the picture changes. Comments from both women and people of color note the double bind that exists as discussed in chapters 4 and 5. They are conscious of how others view them through gender and racial lenses and how these factors may impact their careers. Similarly, in focus group settings and conversations the work/family balance issue is raised to a greater extent than the survey results indicate. We hear this issue again and again from both female and male participants, but more so from females. Nearly one third of respondents (30 percent) name a barrier that was not pre-listed in the survey such as lack of time, being unsure of their career goals, and organizational politics so respondents recognize both personal and corporate barriers to their career advancement. There are only small differences when comparing by gender and race.

Hurwitz also makes an interesting observation about what may hinder progress, and she wants young professionals to assume responsibility for their career paths.[2]

The "quick fix" mentality that has evolved in my generation—the need for instant gratification—could pose a threat to some young professionals' careers. Playing a game of job hopscotch to avoid a challenging or unpleasant job could, at times, be necessary, but at other times, it could be a mistake. The leaders of the future need to beware of quick fixes available to them, be they technology or other temptations, and remember that some of their greatest learning could come from a place outside their comfort zone.

PROMOTIONS AND
INTERPERSONAL CHANGES

In addition to this self-reported assessment of career progress, we ask about promotions received while or since attending the Emerging Leaders Program. Over half of the respondents (51 percent) report being promoted while or since participating. Males and females are close in their rates of promotion (53 percent and 49 percent, respectively), but the race groups are further apart (58 percent for white and 39 percent for others). These data are encouraging except for people of color. We also ask about promotions in conversations and in focus groups, and regularly over half in every group have positive stories to report about promotions and changes in job responsibilities. And in a recent discussion we were pleased to hear that one of the black males reported a major promotion. As we discuss in chapter 5, efforts need to continue to see that more people of color are promoted to leadership positions.

We also want to know about interpersonal changes that occur after concluding leadership development efforts. The list is quite extensive as interviews with alumni show. In most cases these statements note improvement on a variety of personal behaviors and are in line with the positive changes noted previously in the LPI results.

- *Gaining more credibility with more senior managers*
- *Improved relationships with colleagues and ELP mentor*
- *Increasing visibility within the organization by getting involved with more high-level civic engagement*
- *Gaining appreciation for the work of colleagues who have been influential in supporting the Fellow over his career*
- *Acknowledgement from supervisors, colleagues and/or family of seeing more confidence and maturity in the Fellow*
- *Change in group dynamic style from taking charge to allowing the conversation to flow and trying to "lead from the back"*
- *Positive impact from utilizing team building and leadership techniques and accepting the difference in approaches and styles among colleagues*

- *Experiencing both soured and improved relationships (where the Fellow became assertive and succeeded in helping one supervisor with goals to the upset of a direct supervisor)*

And one of the alumni in this interview provided a summary of some of the positive skills that were enhanced.

I have a stack of [new tools] that I think allow me to run meetings better, not just from the chaotic manner in which teams went on but also seeing how some of the monthly meetings were put together. It really helped me to understand the importance of an agenda, and bullet-points and making sure that things are clear...that people have involvement and goals...I really appreciate the power of networking and that's something that I hadn't given any credence to prior to my involvement in the program. I guess I would say that the meeting, how to run a meeting, how to involve people would be another.

ORGANIZATIONAL CHALLENGES

Young professionals are concerned about making progress in their own leadership journeys, but also are cognizant of the challenges corporations and other organizations face. As displayed in table 6.2, young professionals anticipate a number of upcoming challenges in the next ten years.

By far the biggest problem they foresee is retaining qualified workers (93 percent), followed by dealing with global economic pressures (89 percent). The finding concerning talent retention holds for both the corporate and nonprofit sectors and echoes conclusions cited in many current studies dealing with organizational challenges. Interestingly, the challenges of finding and retaining qualified workers was also identified as the number one challenge in our region when we surveyed greater Boston business

Table 6.2   Challenges for organizations

For each of the following, please indicate if you expect it to be a major leadership challenge for business in the next 10 years. (% Yes for each)	Gender		Race/Ethnicity		Total (n=131)
	Male (n=58)	Female (n=72)	White, Not Hispanic (n=78)	Other (n=51)	
Retaining qualified workers	93	93	90	98	93
Dealing with global economic pressures	90	88	90	86	89
Keep up with technological advances	76	76	81	69	76
Environmental issues	74	73	78	67	73
Dealing with diversity and inclusiveness	68	78	68	82	73
Hiring qualified workers	72	71	76	64	72
Effective teamwork	70	69	72	66	69
Dealing with difficult people	53	61	63	50	57
Other	32	22	24	29	27

leaders in 2001. And the issue will not go away. The Chamber issued a study in 2008 *Greater Boston's Challenge: Sustaining the Talent Advantage* that discusses the efforts of employers to sustain a highly skilled and talented workforce and remain globally competitive. And in fall of 2008 the *Boston Business Journal* continued that theme noting that good employees are hard to find at any time, but even harder to locate in a difficult economic climate.[3] In discussions with young professionals, they express their concerns about talent retention in their roles as managers and realize that members of today's Generations X and Y are very mobile and do not plan to stay at one company for lifetime employment, as do many Boomers. One notes. "Generation X is a whole new crop of people—unlike our parents they jump jobs—does that make them disloyal to people, to companies?" However, they also believe that their companies can and should take positive steps to retain talent, and they have suggestions about how that can be accomplished.

Pauliina Swartz, portions of whose essay are quoted in an earlier chapter, expresses her particular concerns as she reflects on her experience of immigrating to the United States from Finland. She cites cultural differences in organizational values between the United States and Finland, and the benefits that accrue to organizations when they help young professionals emerge as leaders, which also helps them retain talented individuals.

> *...Many organizations do not take advantage of the talent in their midst and one reason is that many organizations focus too much on predetermined external factors such as race and gender versus internal capabilities and talent when choosing, developing, promoting and rewarding their employees.*
>
> *To promote emerging leaders, organizations should consider an individual's internal strengths and accomplishments (both inside and outside the office), the transferability of these skills and relevant life experience. Organizations should ask if the individuals have leadership experiences in the community that can be leveraged in the workplace. Also does the person have life experiences... and/or experience in a foreign culture that make them uniquely suited for certain opportunities within the organization. Additional factors to consider include a willingness to express divergent opinions and an ability to work with a diverse group of people. These are strengths and provide benefits for organizations that seek not just to post numbers but also to benefit from diversity.*
>
> *...A direct, confident, and articulate communication style is highly valued in American society. But I come from a culture where there is less emphasis on developing such skills and style. In my native Finland, silence is actually considered a virtue!...An organization that is open to different styles of communication is more likely to promote leaders with diverse cultural and ethnic backgrounds compared to an organization that is less tolerant. As a woman, an immigrant, and the first college graduate in my family, I have at times struggled to fit in to a corporate work environment. I sometimes wonder whether I should openly*

express my sense of humor (which some may consider unconventional) or whether I should, as I have seen many other women do, adapt my style to a less spontaneous and more composed style. In my family, formal suits were only worn to funerals. As a result, I have grappled reconciling my sense of style with the expectations of the company dress code. If I follow my instincts, do I run the risk of appearing too dressed down, leading some to believe I am not committed to the organization and advancement?

An organization that balances its talent management efforts will help emerging leaders succeed and in turn help retain them for the organization. It does this by broadening the pool of candidates considered "qualified" for key opportunities. Such an organization will experience improved employee engagement, retention, and job satisfaction by creating a more inclusive workplace. People management is a priority within the organization... Here is my list of what organizations need to do to promote and retain talent:

Provide opportunities to emerging leaders to prove themselves. An organization can systematically develop emerging leaders by providing them with challenging job assignments, access to training and development opportunities, exposure to different types and levels of people and to different parts of the organization, and non-job specific leadership roles. To provide opportunities for emerging leaders takes time and effort. Sometimes organizations may choose to keep leaders from emerging than having to deal with the added work of creating the opportunities.

Be open to multiple paths to success. The trade-offs that are required to achieve success in an organization vary and one way to turn emerging leaders away from an organization is to insist that there is only one way to succeed. Leadership that is homogeneous and fails to represent the greater population of employees, clients or community will not be successful. Organizations need to celebrate diverse stories of success, especially at the senior levels of the organization, so that there are living examples and role models for emerging leaders.

Promote a culture that celebrates true diversity. Differences, whether of gender, ethnicity, or opinion, should be seen as a source of strength as opposed to a threat or a compliance exercise. Is the organization comfortable with people who look or sound different and also who question the status quo and are willing to disagree with each other? Dedication to diversity needs to be driven from the top of the organization.

Provide access to committed mentors. Young professionals—emerging leaders—benefit from mentors. Navigating an organizational landscape and doing so skillfully is important and is especially the case in organizations that do not actively promote emerging talent.

Foster a performance culture. Emerging leaders have a great deal to offer. High performance should be rewarded.

Promote collaboration as the best way to get things done. Collaboration is a skill that emerging leaders bring to the organization and collaboration is in the best interest of all the stakeholders but often becomes the casualty of egos, turf battles, distrust, and disrespect.

Swartz provides useful advice to organizations from the vantage point of an emerging leader herself—one who has been selected by her financial institution as a promising young leader. Her concerns also indicate that she will be a leader who will engage her peers and her direct reports and give the feedback that will improve everyone's performance. Her advice is in line with that suggested by many human resource managers and is seconded by Joseph Bower (2007) as he argues that organizations must pay more attention to the emerging leaders within their organizations. He advises, "grow insiders" and give them challenging and complex assignments.[4]

Dance too outlines the importance of working with upcoming leaders. He wants managers to spend time coaching.

> *Show some patience with junior members and be willing to coach. Changes in resources in the twenty-first century will happen faster than before. Gone are the days when someone was hired and expected to work at the same firm until retirement. As new resources come into the workplace, the leader must be willing to take the time to work with junior members. But it doesn't stop there; leaders must show a willingness to coach and mentor. This will be a challenge in our I-needed-it-yesterday world. But effective leaders will know how to manage so as to get the results that are needed on a day-to-day basis. In the long run, resource retention should rise. Key resources will be more willing to stay put if they feel they are an important part of the team.*

The importance of global economic issues, which came in number two on the survey, has been confirmed in subsequent meetings. They are eager to participate in specially organized sessions dedicated to doing business in countries such as China and India, and they are very aware of the need to take a global perspective. Many of them travel internationally frequently on business and are eager to understand other cultures. They also know that international work is beneficial to their careers, and they welcome the opportunity to work with colleagues in the various cohorts who have immigrated to the United States from a variety of countries in Europe, Africa, Asia, the Caribbean, and South America. In discussions they stress the importance of taking a global perspective and point out that one may be called to manage a team the members of which you may never meet in person. So diversity is of greater importance, but it is a wider definition of diversity—one that also stresses cultural differences as well as an appreciation of differences in styles. They note that they will need to use different and expanded techniques to get the best out of workers whose cultural orientations may be quite different from their own. And they welcome this challenge.

Tolikas reminds us that all of us need to assume roles of global citizens.

"I am not an Athenian or a Greek, but a citizen of the world," said Socrates in Plutarch's Of Banishment. And there cannot be a more accurate description of my personal understanding, experiences, and path in leadership; a continuous process that is extending my world beyond the professional growth and higher positions and titles of an organization; but also a self-transforming process, one of the most dynamic "unfoldings" in my life, as I constantly challenge my inner self to positively influence thinking and action in my community and even in the wider context of society.

... "I am not an Athenian or a Greek, but a citizen of the world." This cannot be more real than today, as we are all becoming citizens of an expanding world and participants in a truly global economy. And although the impact of the Internet on globalization and sovereignty is under growing debate, the ability to quickly, simply, and constantly connect to others from a mobile device almost everywhere has enhanced our efficiency to build networks and connections. Information access and exchange can ignore and defy country borders and traditionally prevailing forces, to weaken ideas and beliefs in one geographic location while strengthening them in another. The stereotype of a single, perhaps privileged, individual making history is being challenged by the ability to quickly learn, create, connect, and influence at any age, within most social or economic contexts. And technology and globalization have resulted in every country on the planet having emerged on the world map, a collage of entities of various needs and means, claiming their own ranking and impact along political, cultural, and economic dimensions.

And similarly Gonçalves has made a strong personal commitment to global issues and continues to work with communities in Cape Verde.

...in 2003, I had the opportunity to meet the prime minister of Cape Verde. He was visiting Boston University and I was invited to attend a breakfast in his honor. He spoke about the challenges Cape Verdeans were facing with slow economic development and lack of education. As I listened to him, the wheels in my brain started turning. The following week, I called a strategic planning meeting with a dozen friends of mine: the President of Bridgewater State College, some folks from UMass Dartmouth and Bentley College, and local Cape Verdean community leaders. The two issues on my agenda were how to address the educational needs of Cape Verde, including identifying resources and funding, and how to address the economic development needs of Cape Verde, including infrastructure projects and agricultural requirements. We strategized around creating partnerships with key institutions to help us meet our goals.

A few weeks later, we proposed a workplan to the prime minister of Cape Verde and he was thrilled. To implement our plan, we applied for and were awarded a $110 million grant from the Millennium Challenge Corporation in Washington, D.C. Due to that funding and the determination of forward-thinking community leaders, I'm proud to announce that we just opened the doors to the University of

Cape Verde, the nation's first public institution of higher education. My next goal is to obtain a second phase of MCC funding to complete an economic development planning framework for Cape Verde focusing on municipal projects.

. . . In addition to my work in Cape Verde and at the BRA, I'm deeply committed to developing more effective local government practices abroad. With that goal, I serve as managing director of International Development Consortium, providing knowledge services to government agencies throughout West Africa, Latin America, and Southeast Asia. For the government of India, we provided an in-depth study that acted as a blueprint to form a privately held institute for preventative health care, public health education, and counseling to women and children. These nonprofit services are provided by voluntary primary health care physicians who supply free medicine for underprivileged rural residents. In Sri Lanka, we completed an evaluation of the country's technical and vocational training program, which resulted in the implementation of education and sartorial reforms with skills-based training and job-creation programs that correspond with private sector employment requirements. For my homeland of Angola, we developed a comprehensive five-year market reform analysis while creating public and private partnerships with national government agencies and local business leaders. This resulted in the construction of a 24-hour state-of-the-art industrial bread factory, which provides sustenance and quality jobs in the region.

The survey responses also listed as other important issues for the future: keeping up with technology (76 percent), addressing environment concerns (73 percent), dealing with diversity (73 percent), and hiring qualified workers (72 percent). These young professionals are regular and constant users of technology for a wide variety of business functions from team meetings across national boundaries to daily dealings with colleagues. They understand its importance and welcome it as a business tool. They are also are very aware of some of the possible downsides of technology, and they often talk of the dangers of putting too much personal information in blogs or onto Facebook and MySpace. They know that some entries meant for humor or as sarcasm can be misinterpreted.

One interesting challenge related to technology that they cite is that of managing Boomers, Generation X, and Generation Y in one unit. Some have called the current workplace a "multigenerational melting pot."[5] Managing Boomers appears to be the greater challenge. Of particular note is the lack of technological sophistication and adaptability of some Boomers and their unwillingness to embrace new technologies in the workplace even when such would enhance their ability to accomplish certain tasks. Because younger leaders are much more adept at using technology, ongoing workplace issues develop. Gen X and Gen Y can become impatient with their less technologically competent colleagues.[6] The frustration shows in this comment from an alum. "Technology is layered onto this—cell phones are used now more for other functions than for calls. We pay everything online. As technology changes, people change. My parents don't have it [internet, a computer]—it's ok with them but it drives me crazy. The world evolved and we have both groups of people and we need to be able to work with both."

We also hear many stories about "bosses" who don't use email regularly, Boomers who do not get their news in a timely basis from the Web, and of the reluctance of Boomers to share information. The young professionals want all the information they can get as soon as they can get it and do not have patience with those whose styles are more traditional. One also reports how he tried to work with his Dad to get him comfortable with technology since that was the direction his father's organization was moving. The parent could not adjust and ended up losing his job. The generational difference noted here is significant and highlights the direction organizations are following as using technology in all operations and helping their workers maximize its use becomes the norm. These young professionals obtain their news via technology also. We asked for a show of hands recently to ascertain who had read the morning newspaper. Only one hand went up. The rest use the Web, or radio, or TV for their news and information. They believe that technology empowers people in new ways, expands the range of networks, and creates community. Many advocate regular use of LinkedIn, Facebook, and Twitter with the caution expressed above. They note how successful President Obama was in using technology in the 2008 campaign and that there are lessons to be learned from that endeavor. With technology the workplace truly becomes global and increases the need to be sensitive to other cultures and ways of doing business, they argue.

Emerging leaders also understand that training must accompany technological changes, for themselves as well as for others. Online learning works better for the younger generation than the "boss telling you what to do."[7] In focus groups, however, they also voice the concern that too much technology decreases human contact and interaction and that this can be a downside. They admit that like Boomers they can benefit from face to face interaction. Focus group discussions are particularly valuable to them as a way to reconnect with professional colleagues and to share recent business experiences. They also continue to create their own business networks across sectors and find them particularly useful as they move ahead.

Concern for the environment also comes through in meetings and conversations with these young leaders. They want their companies to have a commitment to "being green." Many cite examples of what companies are doing and some suggest that we hold some of our leadership development sessions at a green building such as the new Genzyme building in Cambridge, Massachusetts. Individuals from both the business and nonprofit sectors emphasize environmental issues, and many express a concern about working in an organization that does not have "green" high on the agenda.

Another interesting finding has to do with diversity. Here we see a notable difference in responses by gender in our survey. Women are more likely to see diversity and inclusiveness as a future concern than men are (78 percent for women and 68 percent for men). Women also find less progress in the area of diversity than they would like to see. However, when young professionals of both genders are asked if race and gender still matter, their reaction is a resounding yes. They tell us that it (diversity) often is the "elephant" in the room and needs much more realistic discussion in organizations. (This concern is an ongoing one in line with previous observations from Tulgan.) In spite of issues with diversity, young professionals note that they want to see people valued for their individual talents and recommend that all individuals be respected.

Responses to the survey also indicate some differences between the two race groups. Non-whites are more concerned about diversity issues than whites, 82 percent versus 68 percent. Yet in their conversations both whites and non-whites discuss diversity and racial issues in an open manner. As noted in chapter 5, many whites remark that their participation in leadership development has been one of the first times that they have been in such a diverse setting and that they are now much more conscious of subtle forms of discrimination that continue to exist. As these young professionals move into positions of increased power and responsibility in their organizations, diversity challenges will continue, but they appear to be better prepared to deal with them than previous generations. They are more aware of the need to resolve some of the long-standing issues and to eliminate subtle forms of discrimination. And we need this action because we hear from individuals of color that it is hard to be the major force calling for more diversity in your organization. As noted in the previous chapter, to stand out may even hurt one's career progress in some organizations.

In our survey we found that there were additional differences between the two race groups in several other areas, including some where non-whites are more concerned than whites (retaining qualified workers, 98 percent versus 90 percent), and some where whites are more concerned than non-whites (keeping up with technological advances, 81 percent versus 69 percent; environmental issues, 78 percent versus 67 percent; hiring qualified workers, 76 percent versus 64 percent; effective teamwork, 72 percent versus 66 percent; and dealing with difficult people, 63 percent versus 50 percent). The survey findings overall are in line with comments we hear at focus groups and in other conversations. These emerging leaders display many of the characteristics outlined by Jay Conger and Bruce Tulgan when they describe differences between Generation X and Boomers.[8]

A further challenge concerns the consequences of dealing with an aging workforce in areas beyond technology. The health problems of an aging workforce are one area. In addition, some worry about job availability as they see that some Boomers do not want to leave their positions. Reports of the many vacancies to occur shortly may be exaggerated as the economic climate becomes worse. Intergenerational differences in work and leadership styles are also issues of concern. Particular stressful management challenges occur when Boomers, Generation X, and Generation Y have different goals for how to organize and run a unit. One young professional noted that some workers do not appear to want to be empowered; some Boomers seem to be putting in their time, which contributes to their unwillingness to change. How to deal with staff members who are not able to change their work style and adjust is a problem. One said (and others agreed), "Managing down is difficult." Others also did not like it when an older supervisor talked down to them. Deal (2001) notes that some of the conflict between generations comes from a difference in values and that there are differences between Generation X and older groups in the way each "perceives authority in the workplace." Some companies are making positive responses to this generational mix in the workplace and have developed strategies to assist Generations X and Y and Boomers in working together. At NSTAR (an electric and gas utility company in Massachusetts) they have created "Engaging the Generations" workshops to enhance collaboration. They find that there are shared values among the groups and that that information is helpful to all involved as they work together in a variety of circumstances. And a recent study points out that older workers show greater "resiliency in a recession-battered workplace" and because they can draw on past experiences, they can help others with these challenging times.[9] So it is not all bad news.

As noted above, young professionals lean more toward a collaborative style, which was highlighted in chapter 3 as one of the skills they value. Authoritarian and top down management styles are not for them. They welcome and want to hear many points of view. Dissent and discussion are not seen as negatives. In fact, they argue that they can disagree on issues but still work well with others that do not agree with them, and we have watched this happen as they work in teams on joint projects. (These observations follow those made by Greenberg, Rodriguez, and Bennis.)

In spite of the many challenges, emerging leaders also believe that more can and should be done to fully utilize the skills and wisdom of the Boomers. Some of the young leaders recognize that Boomers have valuable experience and are willing to learn from them. Many are looking for mentors and Boomers can often fill that role. Experience has its benefits and needs to be valued as part of an inclusive strategy. Organizations need to help individuals understand and deal with generational differences in the workplace because generational differences like differences of race and ethnicity can and should be used to an advantage.

LEADERSHIP QUALITIES AND VALUES

Earlier studies have noted that we need to know more about what young professionals want in their leaders so we asked them what leadership qualities they value. Survey respondents were asked to use a 1-to-10 scale to rate how much they value eleven leadership qualities. As shown in table 6.3, the quality that young leaders report valuing the most is honesty and integrity, which had a mean rating of 9.8. These emerging leaders are very clear that honesty and integrity need to be central to the values of organizations where they work and of the ones that they want to lead. They see honesty and integrity as not only the major value in leaders whom they respect but also in the kind of leaders they want to be. Seeing integrity as the most important quality was reinforced in conversations and during focus group discussions. They have been impacted negatively by the lack of trust they feel in our institutions, particularly financial ones. Whether concerning the Madoff scheme, Fannie Mae and Freddie Mac financial meltdowns or some of the bank failures, they want to see more integrity in leaders and ethical behavior in organizations in the future. They concur with observations of James O'Toole and Warren Bennis (2009) that an important role of leaders is to rebuild trust in their organizations.[10]

Seven of the qualities have rankings from 9.4 (setting the vision for the organization) to 8.9 (encouraging creativity and innovation and implementing strategies to move the organization ahead). Again our findings are in line with those of Kouzes and Posner who find that after surveying what people want in their leaders, being "forward-looking is second only to honesty." Honesty and providing a vision for the future are a must.[11] Also high on the list are collaboration and teamwork and managing change. Three qualities are somewhat lower on the scale—practicing inclusiveness (8.5), maximizing

Table 6.3   Ranking of leadership qualitie

Please rate how much you value each of the following qualities in a leader. Use a scale from 1 to 10 where 1 means not at all and 10 means extremely.	Mean rating (SD) (n=128–131, varies by item)
Honesty and integrity	9.8 (0.6)
Setting the vision for the organization	9.4 (0.9)
Developing the organization's people	9.3 (0.9)
Managing change	9.2 (1.0)
Teamwork and collaboration	9.1 (1.0)
Dealing effectively with conflict	9.1 (1.0)
Encouraging creativity and innovation	8.9 (1.1)
Implementing strategies to move the organization ahead	8.9 (1.1)
Practicing inclusiveness	8.5 (1.6)
Maximizing profit for the organization	8.3 (1.4)
Networking	8.2 (1.5)

profit for the organization (8.3), and networking (8.2). These overall results suggest that young leaders see all these as necessary qualities with honesty and integrity topping the list.

The general rank orderings are not very different for men and women. Honesty and integrity are highest for both groups, and the same three: inclusiveness, maximizing profits, and networking are rated lower on the scale by both groups. Women give higher ratings to networking than men—a finding that is also evident in focus group conversations. (See table A6.2: "Ranking of leadership qualities—Women versus Men" in the appendix.) Women see the need for access to the many more informal networks that exist in organizations as well as to the more established professional networks. Women also generally give higher and more uniform ratings than the men. For nine of the eleven qualities, women give higher mean ratings with lower dispersion (lower standard deviation). For one other, the mean rating is equal between men and women (maximizing profit) and women had slightly lower dispersion. For only one quality is the mean lower for women (encouraging creativity and innovation), but the difference is minor.

There are also some race differences (see table A6.3: "Ranking of leadership qualities—White, non-Hispanic versus Others" in the appendix) as well, though the general rank ordering of qualities was about the same between the two race groups. Consistently, honesty and integrity have the highest mean rating, followed by setting the vision for the organization. Inclusiveness, maximizing profits, and networking are not rated quite as high. As with gender, there is a pattern in that for ten of the eleven qualities, white respondents give lower mean ratings with more variation in answers. But for many qualities, the difference is very small (.2).

Over one fourth (27 percent) of respondents say there are other leadership qualities that they value a great deal. Some of the qualities they report include humility, compassion, courage, good decision making skills, good communication skills, and charisma.

Respondents were also asked to evaluate how closely their own leadership values match the values of their organization. (See table A6.4: "How closely leadership values match values of the organization" in the appendix.) Respondents feel that their values are a complete match (7 percent), a very close match (42 percent), or a somewhat close match (41 percent), leaving only 10 percent who reported that their values were somewhat or very far from their organizations' values. There is an interesting difference between how men and women respond to this item, with men more likely to say their values very closely match that of their organization, while women tend to say "somewhat close." This finding is not surprising as we hear from many women that some organizations remain places where subtle forms of discrimination continue to exist and that women wrestle with how best to deal with these issues on a daily basis. There are no differences between how the two race groups respond.

Another way leadership values are measured is by asking respondents what leaders they most admire and why. Respondents named over thirty leaders, with many choosing former presidents of the United States (such as John Kennedy, Ronald Reagan, or Franklin or Theodore Roosevelt) or civil rights activists (such as Martin Luther King, Malcolm X, or Rosa Parks). Additional choices include other political figures (such as Robert Kennedy or Hillary Clinton), and foreign leaders (such as Tony Blair and Winston Churchill) as well as a number of other individuals. In focus group settings that took place just before the 2008 election, we also heard many comments about Barack Obama. And in the 2009 group discussions on leadership his name is often at the top of the list. (His name was not listed in the survey, which was completed before he was nominated.) The reasons that respondents say they admire these leaders vary widely. Qualities that respondents write in range from "believability" to "spirited perseverance" to "motivational," and ones frequently mentioned were honesty, intelligence, passion, and charisma. A few recurring themes include the ability to collaborate, to inspire people with a common vision, and to overcome difficult circumstances. We also note an increase in interest in political activity and in discussing politics by young professionals during the period leading up to the 2008 election. This increase is also a factor with college students and this interest of the younger generations is confirmed in the 2008 presidential election that saw college freshmen involved in political affairs at an increased level. This bodes well for Generation X working with Generation Y in the future as they share a common concern here. And we are pleased to report that one of our male alumni as well as one of the members of the 2010 cohort both ran for City Council in 2009. So interest in politics also extends to running for office.[12]

OUTREACH, COMMUNITY INVOLVEMENT, AND PHILANTHROPY

Additional areas of inquiry are the role of the corporate leader in the community and the role of organizations in corporate social responsibility. As shown in table 6.4, when asked what they think is the most important role a corporate leader should play in the community, respondents choose: active involvement on community projects (39 percent) at the top of the list, active involvement on boards (24 percent) second and encouraging employees to be involved in community service (22 percent) next. All these suggest important ways in which young professionals hope to see corporate leaders actively involved. There are only small differences in the gender and race comparisons.

Table 6.4   The role of corporate leader in the community

What is the most important role a corporate leader should play in the community? (%s total down the columns to 100%)	Gender		Race/Ethnicity		Total (n=130)
	Male (n=58)	Female (n=71)	White, Not Hispanic (n=77)	Other (n=51)	
Active involvement on community projects	38	41	43	33	39
Active involvement on charitable boards	24	24	23	26	24
Encouraging employees to be involved in service	24	18	18	26	22
Monetary contributions	7	11	9	10	9
Other	7	6	7	6	6

In focus group conversations the importance of community and connections to likeminded professionals are noted. Similar comments appear in their essays.

Nate Pusey of Citibank describes how his strong views on the necessity for leaders to show evidence of civic commitment and community engagement has been partially developed by his parents:

> ... my parents were quite involved in the community of Canaan. My father had a seat on the town zoning board, while my mother worked in the court system, sat on the library committee and the budget committee. They sang in the local Methodist church for forty years. Although they were active in town politics, they assumed support roles for local leaders rather than taking on leadership positions themselves. They didn't actively encourage me to become a civic leader, but being raised in an environment with self-driven parents clearly had an effect on me.

He continues:

> In recent years, I've found an ideal way to give back to the community by merging my passion for music and my financial capabilities. I serve on the Board of Directors of the Boston Children's Chorus, a remarkable nonprofit arts organization. Since 2005, I've devoted a significant amount of energy to the BCC, because it's an organization I believe in: the mission of the BCC is to provide an intensive musical education for Boston children, with the goal of empowering them to achieve social change. By singing together, young people learn about teamwork, communication, and leadership. And the chorus helps to transcend social barriers by bringing together all kinds of children from Boston's diverse neighborhoods, focusing on their commonalities instead of their differences.
>
> ... I have served as the Treasurer of the Finance Committee and as an Executive Committee member, which enabled me to become involved with all aspects of the organization, from hiring recommendations to fiscal analysis.
>
> ... The chorus started with 20 children and has grown to 300 multicultural youth. Today the singers make up nine choirs and have performed over 150

concerts, including ones in Mexico and Japan. Another tour is planned for the Middle East...

...Working with the Boston Children's Chorus has been extremely meaningful for me. When you enter the performance hall for a Boston Children's Chorus concert, all colors of people sit together and experience beautiful, inspiring music as one large family. At those concerts, there are no limitations of social class or race or ethnicity. Sitting elbow to elbow with people that are different in so many ways, while listening to the same captivating music, is a pivotal community-building event. Whether we're bankers or street cleaners, elementary school teachers or welfare recipients, we're all gathered to hear one thing: the eloquent, majestic voices that will someday, hopefully, become tomorrow's leaders.

Pusey's statement, advocating the need for community involvement, is echoed by others.

One writes that

...you gain a sense of wanting to contribute more to the community. You get to meet people who, as busy as they are, spend a lot of time volunteering and getting involved in the things that are going on in Boston and the needs of the Boston community.... you do your work and you go home, and you are in your own little bubble, and there is so much other stuff out there that you don't realize you could be doing. I want to get more involved.

Alumni discussing the importance of civic engagement note. "I couldn't believe the people doing good work... it helped bring balance to me—that leadership is about giving back..." Another describes a recent personal experience. "I am planning a baby naming (it's a tradition even though the baby has a name) and I will be asking people to give to Children's Trust Fund (rather than gifts to me and the baby). I had the instinct before ELP but would not have known where to put it."

Another alum relates how important it is to demonstrate civic commitment to one's children. "With my children—creating leaders...that's when I'm the most powerful leader—where we volunteer, give...the circle of giving. It's helping me create the next generation of civic-minded leaders."

Not only do the emerging leaders stress civic engagement, but individuals who sponsor persons share this view. One of the sponsors captures the spirit of the need for civic engagement.

We want to build a base of people in this city or in this region who want to know more about their world, and want to know more about what is going on and so we think anything we can do to contribute to civic engagement—people being involved in their community, and then individual leadership skills of course will be important for the future of the city,... That's in a nutshell why we chose civic engagement as one of our priority areas...Nominator RR

The female from financial services, who wishes to remain anonymous, wants to use her leadership skills to bring about needed changes in our society.

> *To me, the new model for leadership is having the courage to work diligently for what's right and using the power of one's passion to change the world, one small step at a time. This is the type of leader that I strive to become. I believe that leadership is neither a switch that suddenly turns on and off nor a skill that one is born with. It is an art, cultivated over one's lifetime through a series of experiences lived, relationships developed, opportunities seized, and risks taken. It also, however, is within the reach of all who seek to attain it, via proactive steps to challenge themselves to develop their own leadership style and path.*

She also has put her values into operation:

> *I consider it a tremendous honor to have been recently invited to serve on two not-for-profit boards, where I can further develop my skills as a leader and also give back to the community. In addition, I offer my time as a mentor to other parents of autistic children via a number of special-needs parent groups. I have also served as a mentor to several women beginning careers in the financial services industry. . . . My long-term goal, however, is to utilize both my leadership and autism advocacy skills to improve upon the services and opportunities for autistic children both in my own community and nationally.*

It was not surprising that almost all young leaders believe that community service is necessary to be a true leader. Specifically, 57 percent feel that it is absolutely necessary and 39 percent feel that it is somewhat necessary. There are a number of ways to demonstrate community leadership, and serving on a nonprofit or charitable board is one way to demonstrate such involvement. A little over one third of respondents (37 percent) serve on a nonprofit or charitable board. Of these volunteers, most serve on one (46 percent), two (29 percent), or even three (15 percent) boards. Almost all respondents (79 percent) who serve on a charitable board feel that their service helps them professionally.

Table 6.5 summarizes the gender and race comparisons about community service and service on charitable boards. There seem to be some attitudinal differences, with men and whites more likely to say that community service is only a little or not necessary to be a leader. Non-white respondents are most likely to say that service is absolutely necessary, and they support that attitude with action, as they are twice as likely to report sitting on a charitable board (26 percent for whites versus 51 percent for others). In addition to serving on boards, many volunteer for a variety of projects, and as noted earlier in this chapter, some are trying to set examples to their children of the value of volunteering in a variety of ways.

Table 6.5   Community service and service on charitable boards

To be considered a true leader, how necessary do you feel it is to do community service work?	Gender		Race/Ethnicity		Total (n=131)
	Male (n=58)	Female (n=72)	White, Not Hispanic (n=78)	Other (n=51)	
Absolutely necessary	59	56	47	73	57
Somewhat necessary	33	44	46	28	39
A little or not at all necessary	9	0	6	0	5
Item 3: Do you serve on any nonprofit or charitable boards? (% Yes)	41	32	26	51	37

These emerging leaders note that Corporate Social Responsibility (CSR) is moving from "window dressing" to reality, and they see CSR as a more significant issue in the years ahead than it has been in the past. They also realize that corporate social responsibility is an issue where they might have a personal impact as aspiring board members. The current difficult economic climate may impede efforts at CSR, but as budgets are scrutinized, we hope that companies will keep their eyes on goals for the long term. Many young professionals want to work in organizations where this is a priority. As individuals they care deeply about the culture and values of organizations. It is their belief that the younger generation of workers is more focused on CSR and that these individuals are making conscious decisions to want to "do good" and have their organizations follow suit.

Closely related to their ideas on community outreach and corporate social responsibility is their view that strong and consistent corporate philanthropic efforts are another way that organizations can attract and retain young professionals. As discussed in chapter 3, in 2008, 49 of them worked on the topics of CSR and philanthropy for nine months and prepared reports that were shared with organizations such as the Massachusetts Business Roundtable and The Bank of New York Mellon Foundation. The team that worked directly with the Massachusetts Business Roundtable saw its research cited in the May 2009 roundtable report and also circulated nationally. One of the findings was that incorporating social responsibility initiatives into business plans is useful for recruiting and retaining workers. These young professionals are committed to working in organizations that value outreach and involvement.

When young professionals are involved in philanthropy, they build new skills and practice teamwork while also serving community needs. Our work supports that of John Quelch and Katherine Jocz (2009) in which they advocate the importance of social responsibility even in an economic downturn and the Rajendra Sisodia (2007) book *Firms of Endearment* that reiterates the importance of organizations having a "vision of service" and a "passion of their leaders for doing good while doing well." Kanter's recent book (2009) *Supercorp* also shows the connections between high levels of business performance and social good.[13] In focus group settings, we hear similar themes. Many report personal examples of community service and note that their own activities occur as a result of learning about opportunities from their peers as well as hearing from established leaders about the importance of involvement in the community. They understand that helping their communities is also a way to enhance their skills.

Conclusions

Emerging leaders have distinct ideas about the kind of organizations where they want to work and are concerned about finding and keeping talented individuals in their organizations. They cite this as a major area of concern even in the economic downturn of fall 2008. They also worry about how best to deal with generational difference in the workplace, especially when technology is involved. They look for organizations where collaboration is the norm. They cite honesty and integrity as the top qualities they want to see in a leader and they want to be that kind of leader—a leader who values integrity. And correspondingly they want organizations where they work to value integrity and to have strong ethical principles. They are also very aware of the challenges of dealing in a world where global economics and global concerns predominate. This is a challenge they are ready to meet. Moreover, they want to work in organizations that take corporate social responsibility seriously and many of them are already involved in their own communities. Many of them see community involvement as a necessary component of leadership and believe that this will grow in the future.

And what is very important now and in the future is to foster leadership whenever and however we can. Swartz provides a good summary:

> The... benefits of getting emerging leaders to emerge are also important. The success of emerging leaders can lead to better decisions. These leaders can bring in the perspective of "outsider" to the decision-making processes. This is especially valuable if there is a mismatch between the organization and the clients that the organization serves.... The mentoring of emerging leaders can benefit mentors as much as mentees. It allows senior executives to stay in direct touch with a population with whom they may not have a natural connection. In general, I believe getting emerging leaders to emerge is a powerful way for current leaders to create a legacy. As Tom Peters said, "My point is not that 'people are cool,' 'people are important.' It is that... 'people' (their talent, creativity, intellectual capital, entrepreneurial drive) is...all the hell there is."

The main barriers perceived to be holding them back are lack of opportunity and work/life balance issues. These are areas where organizations need to make changes—the kind of changes that will assist them in retaining these young leaders. So we have some interesting answers to the questions of what young leaders want to see in their leaders, what kind of leaders they want to be, and what values they want in organizations with which they are associated.

CHAPTER 7

LEADERSHIP FOR THE FUTURE: PASSING THE TORCH

NEW LEADERS

Leadership is on the national and local agenda in a way that it has not been for some time. In 2008, the presidential candidates continually spoke about leadership and their personal views on what kind of leaders they would be. All this suggests that the leadership patterns that we will see in the future will look quite different from that practiced by many individuals who held leadership positions in the past. Leadership also is on the agenda because more than ever people realize that for organizations to be successful in the future, they must discover and develop human talent. Find those high potentials, engage them and retain them is the message. Knowledge assets are the ones that will count. Managing talent is the mantra for the future and that will be one of the major roles of a leader.[1]

In the last few decades, a variety of responses to the quest for new models of leadership are occurring, and many leadership programs have been developed on college and university campuses for undergraduates as well as graduate students. Moreover, at last count some 39 business and management schools have leadership degree programs. In addition, there are excellent community leadership programs throughout the United States as well as a variety of programs run by Chambers of Commerce. Leadership development also is part of the culture of many companies. Fay Hansen (2008) discusses several successes in the corporate sector including Whirlpool, Unilever, and GE. These include formal training, mentoring and rotating assignments as well as intensive teamwork. And senior leaders devote a large percentage of their time to cultivating new leaders. Organizations and corporations are aware that they must be attentive to the future leaders in their organizations.[2]

It is our hope that all organizations, profit and nonprofit, will put a major focus on leadership development for their young professionals (as well as their more senior managers) in the days and years ahead. The stakes are high and, as we have said in prior pages, leadership for the future cannot be left to chance. We know that young leaders have their own ideas about leadership. When we query young professionals on what kind of leader they will be and how their approach may differ from current patterns, their answers are clear. New models are emerging. Here is some of what they say.

Gonçalves begins with the need for honesty and integrity, which was also number one in our survey. His words are also in line with discussions that occur when ethics issues are raised. In addition, his ongoing commitment to playing a global leadership role is a theme heard again and again from emerging leaders.[3]

> *In an ideal environment, a leader is supposed to be honest and adhere to ethical standards, but this is not always welcomed at the workplace, because being honest and ethical does not always generate positive results. In some cases, being honest and ethical can put one's job on the line. But for someone like me, who was raised on a coffee farm in Angola, it's impossible to operate without an ethical compass. In order to achieve professional and personal satisfaction at work, I've learned to develop a fluid style of leadership. This has helped me address situations involving shifting motives, because at times it can be difficult to distinguish between private interests and community objectives. I am convinced that my presence and honesty have made a tremendous impact in the manner in which the BRA [Boston Redevelopment Authority] conducts business in communities of color. Under my leadership, there is significantly more accountability, although more is clearly needed.*
>
> *. . . I'll never forget where I came from, and I can't ignore the impoverished conditions that many people endure their entire lives. I look to my mother, a Cape Verdean farm girl who finally learned to write her first name after months of laboring at her kitchen table with a pad of paper and a pencil. That same drive and determination—identifying a problem, establishing a goal to address the problem, and persevering until that goal is achieved—is at my core.*

Francisco, too, notes how as a future leader he will be a global citizen and one who practices and promotes inclusive leadership.

> *When I look to the future, I see leaders becoming increasingly diverse and globally focused with a culturally friendly lens. This includes gaining language skills beyond English and developing an appreciation for other countries and ways of life. Since business borders are rapidly diminishing around the world, our leaders need to understand the interdependencies of the global economy and take institutional responsibility for our energy consumption and its implications for future generations. Most important, leaders of the twenty-first century need to have*

compassion and become involved in not-for-profit causes that improve the overall human condition.

Like Francisco, Tolikas sees the necessity for leaders to respond to the wider world.

Perhaps our perception of the world today is larger and more complex than Socrates' perception of the world. But the need to let our thinking and actions become more global and bigger in scope is as crucial as in the ancient times, as issues such as poverty, lack of human rights and justice, war, climate change, nature and animal conservation, and disease affect us all, even though they may not appear to influence our own lives and status. There is tremendous opportunity: to act, to transform, to help. In the context of the American philosopher Sidney Hook, today one has more of an opportunity to be an "event-making man" taking action to change the world rather than be an "eventful man" just observing and living the present as it happens to unfold. But there is also tremendous challenge: the world complexity and the urgency to act have multiplied. The potential for conflict is becoming even greater as the diversity in values, capabilities, and expectations can be overwhelming. America's sustaining a leading position in different markets or even accessing new markets is being questioned and challenged. And at the individual level, accepting the challenge to become a citizen of the world means challenging yourself more than ever to stand your ground, to become even more dynamic and decisive, to be prepared to face tremendous competition while establishing and nurturing an ever-increasing number of connections.

Qualities and behaviors essential to leaders that are discussed in earlier chapters are confirmed by other writers. Renee LeFevre is a lawyer at the Boston Redevelopment Authority (BRA) and outlines how she will practice collaboration and foster open communication when she occupies a major leadership position.

What would I do, or what changes would I make if I were promoted to CEO/ Director/Head of my company? And here is my answer: I've worked in the public sector my whole career, first as an intern for Congresswoman Nancy Pelosi, then as legal counsel for the City of Boston Assessing Department and now as legal counsel for the Boston Redevelopment Authority; I think my answer is applicable to any public sector or private company. As a CEO/Director, the first thing I would do would be to make sure that all lines of communication from the bottom up are open and that all workers know that communication is a top priority. I would hold meetings with all my head deputies to hear their perspectives on the company goals and to make sure that all of us understand the universal goal(s) of the company and what we are striving to achieve. A good leader listens to all perspectives, but also must articulate back to the team the vision and goal of what is to be achieved. I would then meet with the different departments separately to listen to the other workers' perspectives and to also talk to them in person about what the team vision and goal is and talk to them about what their roles are in achieving such vision and goal. I think that it is essential for workers to hear and meet with their leader to foster a sense of participation, ownership and also to be motivated to want to work hard.

The communication I would strive for is not just about meetings, but also about encouraging different groups to work together across the board. The communication I would strive for would be about sharing different ideas. I would strive to make every worker from the receptionist to the deputy or vice president feel like they are a part of a team and that their role is essential to getting the job done. A good leader really listens and takes the time and commitment to communicate with his/her fellow employees.

LeFevre's thinking is in line with those who see leadership as learner centered. Members of an organization learn and lead together; leadership is shared.

Sonal Gandhi, also from the BRA, highlights the importance of communication, empathy and vision as she moves into roles of increasing responsibility.

A true leader is one who is able to communicate with people at all levels, who is empathetic, human and approachable, not afraid to take risks and be transparent and thus to be truly visionary. I believe these qualities are really put to test when things are not going well or when an organization is facing a critical challenge. Challenging times are when a leader (by the above definition) is most needed and can truly make a difference. A leader has many choices to make when dealing with challenging situations, and one of the key things is to decide how to make decisions and then how to communicate them to those who are under him/her.

Bailly's view of the future is in line with her colleagues as she sees the need for relationship building.

Leaders of the future must be skilled in building and maintaining relationships at all levels of the organization. They must be comfortable moving outside their tier to establish deep and wide relationships on and off the golf course. They must show genuine interest in those who are outside the inner circle and keep the interest of the next generation of young talent. They must be approachable, open to difference, and willing to lead. Life Lesson: It's all about relationships.

Building on the relationship theme, Chi Huang looks ahead to the role health care leaders must play. He calls for health care leaders who display empathy—ones who exhibit a high degree of emotional intelligence and are self-aware. Huang also sees the need for leadership development for physicians and wants to make it a required part of medical education.

Business and industry have applied many innovative approaches to the way they operate. Successful physician leaders should be able to demonstrate proficiency and mastery in three essential areas—people, strategy-operations, and crises. Studies of the top CEOs around the world demonstrate that one of the commonalities among them is their ability to self-identify and self-regulate their emotions and also to understand the social dynamics of various groups of people, and this lends itself to effectively managing people. Also, physician leaders should be adept at developing and mentoring those with potential within the institution, as well as being able to identify change agents within the institution.

. . . The true character and integrity of leaders are demonstrated during times of extreme challenges. Crises in businesses and healthcare come in all forms—ethical, moral, fiscal, and labor-related. How the physician leader handles such challenges not only sets the tone and culture of the work environment but also explicitly sets boundaries regarding what is allowed and what is not allowed in the workplace. Paradoxically, crises must be handled not only in a transparent manner but also with a sense of confidentiality in order to prevent erosion of the trust of those within and outside the institution.

. . . The medical profession requires strong leaders with clinical and managerial skills. These leaders should be able to look around the corner and realize a vision of tomorrow. Our nation is not only facing clinical healthcare crises but also fiscal and managerial crises. Sadly, $2.3 trillion spent does not provide world-class healthcare to every individual in the United States. At best, healthcare in the United States is anemic, unable to meet even the simplest metrics or performance evaluations. Tomorrow's leaders must not only be clinically competent but also be able to manage people, develop strategy, and navigate through crises. The time has come to place leadership development on the same level of importance as research and teaching in our medical schools, residencies, and academic centers.

Ron Bell reinforces the concept that leadership can be learned and describes how as a leader he vows to learn from his mistakes.

I've heard it said that certain people are born to be leaders. No. I don't believe leaders are born. People become leaders. We're human, like everyone else. We make mistakes and we're not perfect. Like anyone, we learn through experience, through observation, through education. I didn't come out of my mother's belly and say, "I'm a leader." Yes, I had leadership qualities and was able to capitalize on them because of my upbringing, but also because of my experiences. I've become a better leader because I've made mistakes and have learned from them. And I've tried to surround myself with community mentors like Hubie Jones and Charles Ogletree. I've listened to them, found inspiration in their victories, and learned from their failures.

Emerging leaders also understand that leadership brings with it many challenges and that meeting these challenges and learning from them is a true test of leadership.

Rawan writes:

As one progresses in life and has opportunities to lead, there will certainly be challenges to overcome; encountering these challenges are defining and developing moments. I have found that at times I am put in situations by design because others feel that I will be able to lead through to the objective. Having this trust and faith placed in you to lead creates a tremendous sense of responsibility.

Challenges play an important role in defining our character. How we face them, what we do, and what we learn from them are some of the toughest questions we ever answer. There is a great quotation from the movie Wall Street: "Man looks into the abyss, sees nothing staring back at him. It is at that point man finds his character, and that is what keeps him out of the abyss." I have thought back to that quotation at numerous times when facing difficult leadership challenges.

I have not met or exceeded expectations in every challenge I have had but, I do not consider the situations as "failures" because I have been able to learn from these experiences and apply that knowledge to other challenges. True failure would be an experience where no value can be gained from any of those associated with it. By taking this approach, all challenges can be seen as opportunities for growth and success and can be measured by the amount of value gained from the experience.

DeAngelis stresses that leadership involves social responsibility, "True leaders are drawn to causes that make things better for others. Something that speaks to their values and that they have passion about." Yameen follows with her view that leaders need to be agents for change. "As leaders, we are trying to bring about positive change. Making change is difficult, since our old habits exert a fairly strong influence. Actually writing in a different format and continuing to do things differently when appropriate sends a strong message."

Leaders will be heavily influenced by technology according to Halbert, and in line with DeAngelis and Yameen, he also will be a leader with a strong social conscience. He rejects the top down leader model and calls for a more collaborative style.

As technology has become more diffuse it has leveled the playing field for individuals and nations. Information, now the most valuable of commodities in effecting change, is more accessible than at any time in human history. While this change has been rapid, and has been a boon for humanity overall, it has also brought countries and cultures into contact, and sometimes conflict, at a breathtaking pace.

Gone are the days when being well-traveled had more to do with one's savvy about the world than being well-read. Advances in telecommunication have created an environment where subsistence farmers in underdeveloped rural lands are just as likely to gain their understanding of the larger world from satellite images and transcontinental conversations with relatives, as those in developed Western countries. To be sure, those in the developed world have much greater and easier access to these assets, but the near-impenetrable barriers of access that were once such an impediment to underdeveloped nations are rapidly falling away.

The new model of effective leadership demands not only that leaders be decisive and judicious, but also that they have a strong sense of social awareness. Citizens want to be proud of the strength and accomplishments of their nations, but they also want their nation to be viewed in a positive light by people of other lands.

In these fields, as well as science, religion, education, and many others, the leaders that find themselves successful in today's world are those who truly embrace the fact that the way they see the world is often less important than how the world sees them. An understanding of the views of others has an import now that it has never had before in defining effective leadership. Having this ability not only allows a leader to react to challenges and opportunities before them, but also allows them to communicate in a way that is easily understood. With so much opportunity for miscommunication and misinterpretation, the leaders who can think and speak in the mindset and voice of those they deal with have the advantage.

This is a tall order. What they tell us is that as future leaders they will be leaders who above all value honesty and are persons of integrity. They aspire to be global leaders and practice global citizenship. The world is changing and they value and appreciate cultural differences. Support for inclusion is a given. Collaboration is another must and working in teams is the natural way to go and also more productive. Leadership is shared and leaders cannot and should not go it alone. Excellence in communication, that includes listening as well as being forceful presenters, also is essential. And they advocate broad and frequent communication and stress that information must be widely circulated to all in an organization. They care about social responsibility, and outreach to the broader community must be part of the role of effective leaders. The growing role of technology and its usefulness as a communication tool is part of the package. They also want to learn from each other, learn from mistakes, and be leaders who are constantly learning.

Moreover, Generation X and Y leaders understand the importance of reflection and self-awareness. They value relationships and understand the importance of developing one's people by coaching them and helping them to be successful. They want to develop talent in others and tell us that it is important to empower staff and those below on the organizational chart. One notes that as the leader you are responsible for managing other people's time and for keeping them engaged and helping them learn. Another states it this way. "A leader is someone who brings people along and encourages them to do things that they may not know they can do." So those in Generation X are ready to give the feedback that Generation Y is seeking.[4] As they coach, they note the power of listening to people who look at things in different ways. They believe this will help them be successful and help their organizations progress.

New Organizational Priorities

As they look ahead, one of the greatest challenges that they report has to do with working within current organizational structures as they also try to change them in ways to make them more humane, collaborative, and inclusive. This comment highlights the issue. "I can influence people who report to me but with my boss...he sees collaboration differently–it's tough to persuade him to see the value of it. If you are not in a position to effect change because you are at a lower level, it's real tough...implementing change."

Yet other emerging leaders stress that it is important not to give up. They advocate leading from the middle or, as they say, to lead from where they are in the organization. They suggest bringing one's ideas to the table and being prepared to defend them while figuring out the best ways to get those ideas into play. Laurita Crawlle, from the 2009 cohort, calls it "leading from your seat." They do not believe that leadership is reserved for the CEO or the person whose title says that he/she is in charge. As mentioned in earlier pages, they see Leadership as the capital "L" as well as the small "l" and call for an appropriate mix and balance. Leadership in the future will include many more of the small "l's" with more and more individuals playing leadership roles in organizations. The talents of all persons need to be valued, utilized, and retained.

As they look to new ways to lead, they also predict that organizational structures will have a broader focus. Although they understand that businesses need to make a profit, they hope to see changes in the overall structures of organizations that see profit as one goal along with creating responsive organizations in other areas. Halbert's observation is of particular note.

In business the eternal quest for the highest return with the lowest cost is slowly giving way to models that are more holistic. No longer can the large corporation dictate and define what the consumer, and to an extent employees, will and will not have. Options in the marketplace, combined with a genuine desire to have companies do well by doing good, have created a business climate where ideas like corporate social responsibility are not simply public relations clichés, but increasingly a part of the core philosophy of successful participants in the free-market economy.

What else do they see for the future? Because they want to be leaders who take social responsibility seriously, any organization they head will have Corporate Social Responsibility high on the list. Flexibility and family friendly environments will be encouraged and such policies will be utilized by both genders. In addition, they see a change in the nature of work. Rather than going to work at a location distinct from home, now work can take place at home or in other settings. In May 2009, *Time* carried a special story,

"The Way We'll Work," and the flexibility, the increased use of technology, and the focus on "green" organizations described are in line with what these young professionals recommend. They would approve of Janet Reid's observation that, "In 2019 Gen X will finally be in charge. And they will make some big changes."[5]

Those of Gen X and Gen Y are more than ready for that to happen. And as their numbers increase, change in leadership styles and organizational priorities will become a reality.

What we also observe over eight years is a commitment to inclusiveness that is refreshing and this will have a major impact on organizations. Because males and females work together and earn the respect of each other as colleagues, gender stereotypes are minimized and a renewed commitment to equality, not only in a legal sense but because it makes for stronger organizations, emerges.[6] These males, as they move into positions of increasing responsibility, see tangible benefits of inclusive structures. Both males and females want the talents of all brought to the table and welcome diverse points of view. Both support family friendly work policies because many males have increased their own roles in their families and along with their female counterparts are also responsible for children or aging parents.

This spirit of inclusiveness for gender also extends to race and ethnicity. Again as we watch whites work for several months with African American, Latino/a, Asian American, and multiracial colleagues, we see racial attitudes change and people valued for who they are and what they contribute. Barriers break down across the board. Because of the expanded networks at work, social networks also begin to expand.[7] Generation Y, similar to Generation X, value inclusiveness and diversity and are the most ethnically diverse generation in American history—40 percent are African American, Hispanic, Asian, or mixed race. They also are not bound by traditional gender roles. Theirs is a very tolerant generation. The "spirit of 'one for all' and concern for the group is the signature belief…"[8] Clearly having a diverse group of young professionals interacting for over a year with follow up in frequent alumni events creates a spirit of inclusiveness that benefits all.

And we see the enormous benefits of the cross sector networking that we have discussed in other chapters. Recently we became aware of an interesting example. One of our fellows is a headmaster in a charter school and she has successfully added five Emerging Leader alumni to her board! These individuals bring enormous skills to the board and all are young professionals she would never have met in her normal course of activities. Stories like this are frequent and add a new and positive dimension to how organizations will function in the future. Generation X and Y have expansive and productive networks and they know how to use them.

PASS THE TORCH

We are hopeful. Members of Generation X are moving into leadership positions as Boomers retire, and they will be managing Boomers, Generations X, and Y. This will be both a challenge and an opportunity because there will be a mix of skills and viewpoints available to organizations that, if used and managed correctly, will be of great benefit. Different skills in technology will be found in many organizations and new leaders will need to assist some Boomers with enhancing these skills. Many attributes that Generation X possesses are also valued by Generation Y and this bodes well for these two groups working together. Generation Y and Generation X are both technologically savvy and are changing the ways in which we communicate. Moreover, for both groups collaboration is the norm rather than hierarchical structures. They also are entrepreneurial and innovative and civic minded and want to be engaged with their communities. And Tulgan estimates that the combined percentage of Generation X and Y in the workforce will continue to grow beyond the over 50 percent they now number so this combination will be a powerful force.[9] Hewlett and her colleagues (2009) see another benefit from this multigenerational workforce and point out that new relationships will form as those in Generation Y (Millennials) interact with Boomers. This will be a good match because these two groups have a lot in common and many of those in Generation Y are comfortable with Boomers as mentors.[10]

These young professionals are well prepared for what lies ahead. Challenging times also are ones where innovation flourishes. Diverse workforces will bring many new points of view to the table and hierarchical decisions will not be the norm. We have planted the seeds of a new leadership model in over 400 individuals and believe that they are prepared to use the tools needed to meet the challenges. We know that they will face struggles as they move into leadership roles because collaboration is not easy, and society overall has yet to fully embrace diverse and inclusive structures. These are talented and committed young professionals and when we ask them what kind of leaders they will be, their answers are clear and point the way to new leadership models. None of them recommends a top down model. They agree heartily with this statement from Kouzes and Posner (2006), "No one ever got anything extraordinary done alone."[11] And they do not want to do it alone whether that is defined as work, family obligations, or service activities. For them collaboration is the norm. They represent what Mary Uhl-Bien calls "collective leadership" and "co-leadership."[12] This refreshing model of leadership will bring change to individuals as leaders and to organizations.

It is time for many Boomers and others to welcome a new generation of leaders. Those of Generation X and Generation Y envision a world where collaboration and inclusion are practiced not only on the local level but also worldwide, and they want to be part of bringing about that change. We believe that they will be. New leaders are needed for the new century. We have found those leaders and so can you. Find them, encourage them, and be ready to "pass the torch."

APPENDIX TO CHAPTER 1

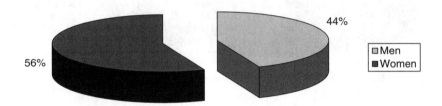

Figure 1.1   Breakdown by gender 2002–2009 data

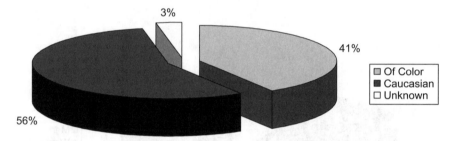

3%

41%

☐ Of Color
■ Caucasian
☐ Unknown

56%

Figure 1.2   Breakdown by ethnicity 2002–2009 data

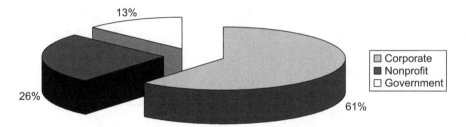

13%

26%

61%

Corporate
Nonprofit
Government

Figure 1.3   Breakdown by organization type 2002–2009 data

APPENDIX TO CHAPTER 2

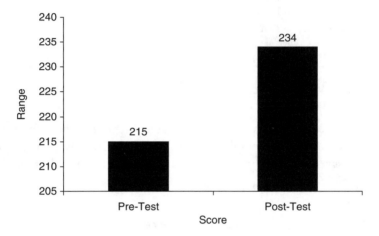

Figure 2.1   Mean LPI 1 and LPI 2

Table 2.1   Cohort summary

Cohort	LPI-1	LPI-2	N	Cohort	LPI-1	LPI-2	N
Cohort 2002	207	234	27	**Cohort 2006**	229	247	12
Male	203	229	15	Male	208	242	4
Female	212	239	12	Female	240	249	8
Cohort 2003	230	245	10	**Cohort 2007**	210	235	28
Male	225	228	3	Male	206	239	16
Female	232	252	7	Female	215	230	12
Cohort 2004	214	225	34	**Cohort 2008**	214	233	38
Male	218	233	14	Male	211	231	19
Female	212	219	20	Female	216	235	19
Cohort 2005	222	237	25	**All Cohorts**	215	234	174
Male	215	238	14	Male	211	234	85
Female	231	235	11	Female	219	234	89

Note: N=number of respondents

Table 2.2   Five leadership practices

Five Leadership Practices	Mean LPI-1	Mean LPI-2	Gain
Inspire Shared Vision			
Verbalizing Vision	17.43	19.53	2.10*
Personal Philosophy	19.53	22.94	3.41*
Model The Way			
Modeling Behavior	32.45	33.33	0.88*
Encourage the Heart			
Praise/Feedback	44.07	47.76	3.69*
Challenge The Process			
Innovation & Risk	34.59	37.92	3.33*
Reasonable Goals	21.47	22.67	1.20*
Enabling Others To Act			
Empower Others	33.02	34.02	1.00*
Constantly Learning	14.49	15.35	0.86*

Note: *at or beyond the .01 level of significance

With a possible 300 points, the scores in table 2 represent the mean for each cohort as well as for all 174 students who participated in the survey. Summary data for all seven cohorts show an LPI-2 mean score of 234 for both male and female participants.

ALUMNI SURVEY

The charts and results in chapter 2 are based on 131 completed interviews (conducted by the Center for Survey Research at the University of Massachusetts Boston) out of a possible 295 (44.4% return rate). The 2002–2007 cohorts were surveyed in summer 2007. The 2008 cohort was surveyed in the summer of 2008. Two respondents did not complete the items on race and ethnicity, so are omitted from those analyses. There are other missing data as well, which means that some analyses are based on fewer than 131 respondents. The analyses that compare across race/ethnicity use two groups: white/non-Hispanic versus all other groups. There are not enough cases in the data to make any further breakdowns. Throughout we use the shorthand White versus Others or nonwhites and refer to this as the race comparison.

The full report is found in: Bogen, K. (2008) *Analysis of Data from 2007 and 2008 UMass Boston Future Leaders Survey,* (Center for Survey Research, October 2008).

Table 2.3 Demographics

		Gender		Race/Ethnicity		Total (n=131)
		Male (n=58)	Female (n=72)	White, not Hispanic (n=78)	Other (n=51)	
Gender	Male			44	45	45
	Female			56	55	55
Race	White	64	67			66
(does not add up to	Black or African American	25	21			23
100%; could select	Asian or Pacific Islander	7	7			7
more than one race)	Amer. Indian/Alaska Native	2	1			2
	Other	5	3			4
Ethnicity	Hispanic	7	10			9
	Non-Hispanic	93	90			91
Education	Some college or 2-year degree	3	6	5	4	5
	4-year college graduate	48	39	44	41	43
	Masters degree	41	43	42	43	42
	JD	0	4	3	2	2
	PhD	0	7	4	4	4
	MD	5	1	1	6	3
	Other	2	0	1	0	1
Age	Less than 30	12	6	8	10	9
	30–34	21	27	26	22	24
	35–39	37	34	30	43	35
	40–44	25	23	27	18	24
	45 and older	4	11	9	8	9
	Mean age in years	37	38	37	37	37

Note: Numbers shown in cells are percentages, except for mean age.

Table 2.4 Organizational categories

What kind of organization do you work for? (columns add down to 100%)	Gender		Race/Ethnicity			Total (n=131)
	Male (n=58)	Female (n=72)	White, Not Hispanic (n=78)	Other (n=51)		
Corporate, for profit	48	42	58	26		45
Nonprofit health care	19	18	14	24		18
Nonprofit charitable	14	19	12	26		17
Government	14	14	12	18		14
Other	5	7	5	8		6

Table 2.5   Leadership style

Please indicate if you possess each of the following leadership styles. (% Yes for each)	Gender		Race/Ethnicity		Total (n=129–131)
	Male (n=57–58)	Female (n=71–72)	White, Not Hispanic (n=77–78)	Other (n=50–51)	
Collaborative	98	100	99	100	99
Adaptive	97	97	97	96	97
Authentic	91	99	95	96	95
Inclusive	85	93	89	92	89
Agent of change	79	81	77	84	79
Decisive	76	76	74	78	76
Strategic	85	69	72	84	76
Charismatic	74	56	60	71	64

Table 2.6 Satisfaction with your leadership style

Overall, how satisfied are you with your own current leadership style(s)? (%s total down the columns to 100%)	Gender		Race/Ethnicity		Total (n=131)
	Male (n=58)	Female (n=72)	White, Not Hispanic (n=78)	Other (n=51)	
Extremely satisfied	5	3	5	2	4
Very satisfied	43	46	39	53	44
Somewhat satisfied	47	47	53	39	47
A little satisfied	5	4	4	6	5
Not at all satisfied	0	0	0	0	0
Do you want to change anything in your leadership style? (%Yes)	71	78	81	67	75

Table 2.7 What needs to be changed?

What do you want to change in your leadership style? (% answering Yes to each)	Gender		Race/Ethnicity		Total (n=94)
	Male (n=39)	Female (n=54)	White, Not Hispanic (n=60)	Other (n=33)	
Improve decision making	21	19	20	18	19
Have more confidence	10	19	18	9	15
Improve communication	18	11	13	15	14
Be more strategic	8	15	17	3	12
Have more patience	10	7	7	12	9
Be more inclusive	10	6	8	6	7
Be more inspirational	8	6	8	3	7
Improve time management	8	6	7	6	6
Manage change more effectively	5	6	7	3	5
Be more active in the community	3	6	5	3	4
Improve conflict resolution	3	6	3	6	4
Other	23	26	23	27	24

Table 2.8 Leadership style influences

Who have been the three strongest influences in your life on your leadership style? (% Yes for each)	Gender		Race/Ethnicity		Total (n=130)
	Male (n=57)	Female (n=72)	White, Not Hispanic (n=77)	Other (n=51)	
A former boss or supervisor	51	64	60	55	58%
Observing other leaders	54	51	48	59	53%
Father	53	35	51	31	42%
Mother	32	31	30	33	31%
A current boss or supervisor	23	26	27	22	25%
Spouse or partner	14	17	20	10	16%

Table 2.9 Mentor roles

What kinds of things does your mentor do for you?	Gender		Race/Ethnicity		Total (n=55)
	Male (n=22)	Female (n=32)	White, Not Hispanic (n=33)	Other (n=21)	
Gives me advice and feedback	86	94	94	86	91%
Opens doors for future opportunities for me	68	66	70	62	66%
Points out my strengths and/or weaknesses	64	59	70	48	62%
Meets with me on a regular basis	73	53	64	57	62%
Enhances my network	59	31	36	52	42%
Other	14	25	18	24	20%

Table A6.1   Progress toward career goal

How much progress are you making towards your career goal in your current organization? (%s total down the columns to 100%)	Gender		Race/Ethnicity		Total (n=131)
	Male (n=58)	Female (n=72)	White, Not Hispanic (n=78)	Other (n=51)	
A lot	45	33	40	37	39
Some	47	46	50	39	46
A little	9	13	8	16	11
None	0	8	3	8	5
Somewhat far	7	7	8	6	7
Very far	2	4	3	4	3

Table A6.2   Ranking of leadership qualities—women versus men

Item 6: Please rate how much you value each of the following qualities in a leader. Use a scale from 1 to 10 where 1 means not at all and 10 means extremely.	Mean rating (SD) for MALES (n=57–58, varies by item)	Mean rating (SD) for FEMALES (n=70–72, varies by item)
Honesty and integrity	9.6 (0.8)	9.9 (0.5)
Setting the vision for the organization	9.3 (1.1)	9.5 (0.9)
Developing the organization's people	9.0 (1.0)	9.5 (0.7)
Managing change	8.9 (1.1)	9.4 (0.8)
Teamwork and collaboration	9.0 (1.1)	9.2 (1.0)
Dealing effectively with conflict	8.9 (1.1)	9.3 (0.9)
Encouraging creativity and innovation	9.0 (1.1)	8.9 (1.1)
Implementing strategies to move the org. ahead	8.7 (1.3)	9.1 (1.0)
Practicing inclusiveness	8.1 (1.8)	8.7 (1.5)
Maximizing profit for the organization	8.3 (1.5)	8.3 (1.3)
Networking	8.0 (1.7)	8.3 (1.4)

Table A6.3   Ranking of leadership qualities—White, non-Hispanic versus Others

Please rate how much you value each of the following qualities in a leader. Use a scale from 1 to 10 where 1 means not at all and 10 means extremely.	Mean rating (SD) for WHITE (n=77–78, varies by item)	Mean rating (SD) for OTHER RACE (n=49–51, varies by item)
Honesty and integrity	9.8 (0.7)	9.7 (0.6)
Setting the vision for the organization	9.3 (1.0)	9.5 (0.9)
Developing the organization's people	9.2 (0.9)	9.4 (0.8)
Managing change	9.1 (1.0)	9.3 (0.9)
Teamwork and collaboration	9.0 (1.1)	9.2 (0.9)
Dealing effectively with conflict	9.0 (1.1)	9.3 (0.9)
Encouraging creativity and innovation	8.6 (1.2)	9.4 (0.9)
Implementing strategies to move the org. ahead	8.8 (1.1)	9.0 (1.2)
Practicing inclusiveness	8.3 (1.8)	8.8 (1.3)
Maximizing profit for the organization	8.2 (1.4)	8.5 (1.3)
Networking	7.9 (1.6)	8.6 (1.4)

Note: n=number of respondents

Table A6.4 How closely leadership values match values of the organization

How close do you think your leadership values are to the leadership values of your organization? (%s total down the columns to 100%)	Gender		Race/Ethnicity		Total (n=128)
	Male (n=57)	Female (n=70)	White, Not Hispanic (n=77)	Other (n=49)	
Completely match	5	9	7	8	7
Very close	58	30	40	45	42
Somewhat close	28	50	43	37	41
Total	91	89	90	90	90

NOTES

INTRODUCTION

1. A. J. Bauer, "Molding Leaders," *Patriot Ledger*, July 11, 2007, 21–22. A history of the program is found in Philip L. Quaglieri, Sherry H. Penney, and Jennifer Waldner, "Development of Future Business and Civic Leaders: The Emerging Leaders Program," *Management Decision*, 45, no. 10 (2007); Sherry Penney, "Urban Universities and Urban Leadership," *Metropolitan Universities* (December 2003), and in Sherry Penney, Jennifer Leigh, and Vinai Norassakundt, "New Leaders for the New Century," *Building Leadership Bridges* (2002) International Leadership Association, 48–58.

1 WHO AND WHERE ARE EMERGING LEADERS: WHAT DO WE KNOW ABOUT THEM?

1. Bobbie Dillon, Perspectives: Presenting Thought Leaders' Points of View, 2009, www.nacubo.org. 2–3. Accessed May 25, 2009. Dillon has excellent descriptions of each group and lists characteristics for each. Her report is based on discussions at a February 2009 NACUBO (National Association of College and University Business Officers) conference: Thought Leaders Program: Changing Demographics, Changing Workplace; also see Carolyn Martin and Bruce Tulgan, *Managing the Generation Mix: From Urgency to Opportunity*, 2nd ed. (Amherst, MA, HRD Press, 2006); Jay Conger, "How "Gen X' Managers Manage," *Strategy and Business*, 10 (1998): 21–31. These authors define each group but with some slight modifications.
2. See appendix for charts on demographic make up of the group.
3. Jennifer Deal, Karen Peterson, and Heidi Gailor-Loflin, *Emerging Leaders: An Annotated Bibliography* (Greensboro, NC, Center for Creative Leadership, 2001), 1–3; Stuart Crainer and Des Dearlove, "Death of Executive Talent," *Management Review*, 88, no. 7 (1999): 8–13 in Deal (2006), 30; Introduction, *Leader to Leader*, Special Supplement (San Francisco, Jossey-Bass, 2006), 2–3, 14; European Foundation for Management Development newsletters, May 2008, February 2009; *The Enterprise of the Future* (2008) Global CEO Study, ibm.com/enterpriseofthefuture; The 2009 Top Companies for Leaders Study Officially Launches in China to Recognize Organizations with Innovative Leadership Programs, http://www.hewittassociates.com/Intl/AP/en-CN/AboutHewitt/Newsroom/

PressReleaseDetail. Accessed May 2009; JoslynHeather, "A Growing Leadership Gap: Need for Qualified Executives Persists Even As Charities Trim Staffs," *Chronicle of Philanthropy*, April 23, 2009, 29.

4. Evan Dobelle, "Bring Back the Vault," *Boston Business Journal*, http://www.bizjournals.com/boston/stories/2005/07/11/editorial2.html; Sherry Penney's interview with Alan Macdonald, Executive Director, Massachusetts Business Roundtable, July 15, 2009; Barbara Kellerman, "What Every Leader Needs to Know About Followers," *Harvard Business Review*, 85, no. 12 (2007): 84–91.

5. U.S. Census Bureau, www.census.gov/main/www/cen2000.html. Accessed June 2, 2009; Meghan E. Irons, "Workplace Diversity Grows But Not at the Top, Report Says," *The Boston Globe*, May 19, 2009, B5, B11.

6. Marshall Carter, "Growing Boston's New Leaders," *Boston Business Journal*, http://boston.bizjournals.com/boston/stories/2006/11/20/editorial2.html/.

7. Rick Friedel, "Nurturing a New Generation of Business Leaders," *Boston Business Journal*, http://boston.bizjournals.com/boston/stories/2004/03/01/editorial3.html

8. Patricia Akemi Neilson, "Asian American Models of Leadership and Leadership Development in U.S. Higher Education," Lin Zhan (ed.), *Asian American Voices: Engaging, Empowering, Enabling* (New York, National League of Nursing, 2009), 195; Richard Couto's interview with Chao C. Chen, about *Leadership and Management in China: Philosophies, Theories and Practices* (London, Cambridge University Press, 2008) in *Member Connector*, May 2009, International Leadership Association, 5–12; Edwin Hollander, *Inclusive Leadership* (New York, Routledge, 2009); 3–5, 195–198. Hollander quoting Heider (1980) for the Lao Tsu quote, 34; Patricia Neilson's interview with Chris Martin, Vice President of Sales and Administration, and Steve Dodman, Director of Business Development, from Greater Boston Manufacturing Partnership on June 24, 2009.

9. James MacGregor Burns, *Leadership* (New York, Harper & Row, 1978), Warren Bennis, *On Becoming a Leader* (Cambridge, MA, Perseus Books Group, 2003), 130–131; Warren Bennis, *Why Leaders Can't Lead* (San Francisco, Jossey-Bass, 1990); Daniel Goleman, *Emotional Intelligence* (New York, Bantam Books, 1996); James Austin, *The Collaborative Challenge* (San Francisco, Jossey-Bass, 2000); Joseph Raelin, *Creating Leaderful Organizations* (San Francisco, Berrett-Koehler, 2003); Hollander (2009), 3–5, 195–198; John Gardner, *On Leadership* (New York, Free Press, 1990); Scott Quatro, David Waldman, and Benjamin Galvin, "Developing Holistic Leaders: Four Domains for Leadership Development and Practice," *Human Resources Management Review*, 17 (2007): 427–441.

10. Jay Conger, Gretchen Spreitzer, and Edward Lawler, *Leader's Change Handbook* (San Francisco, Jossey-Bass, 1999), 223, 323, 344–365; Hollander (2009); Joan Tonn, *Mary Follett: Creating Democracy, Transforming Management* (New Haven, Yale University Press, 2003), 287–303; W. C. H. Prentice, "Understanding Leadership," *Mind of the Leader* (Cambridge, MA, Harvard Business School Publishing, 2005), 151–167.

11. Jay Conger (1998) and Hollander (2009).

12. Burns (1978), Bernard Bass, *Leadership and Performance Beyond Expectations* (New York, Free Press, 1985); Quatro (2007); Cynthia McCauley, Wilfred Drath, Charles Palus, Patricia O'Connor, and Becca Baker, "The Use of Constructive-Development Theory to Advance the Understanding of Leadership," *The Leadership Quarterly*, 17 (2006): 634–53. See also Peter Northouse, *Leadership: Theory and Practice*, 4th ed. (Thousand Oaks, CA, Sage, 2000), 189, and David Day and Stephen Zaccaro, *Leader Development for Transforming Organizations: Growing Leaders for Tomorrow* (Mawwah, NJ, Lawrence Erlbaum Associates, 2004), 383–399.

13. Bruce Tulgan, *Managing Generation X* (New York: Norton, 2000); Bruce Tulgan, *Not Everyone Gets a Trophy* (San Francisco, Jossey-Bass, 2009); Martin and Tulgan, *Managing the Generation Mix* (2006); Ron Zemke, Claire Raines, and Bob Filipczak, "Generations at Work," *American Management Association* (Atlanta, GA, AMACOM, 2000); Claire Raines, *Beyond Generation X: A Practical Guide for Managers* (Menlo Park, CA, Crisp, 1997); Deal, Peterson, and Gailor-Loflin (2001) ; Warren Bennis, Gretchen Spreitzer, and Thomas Cummings (eds.), *The Future of Leadership* (San Francisco, Jossey-Bass, 2001), 147–48, 153–154.

14. Bennis, Spreitzer, and Cummings (2001), 147–48, 153–154. *The Chronicle of Higher Education*, January 30, 2009, A18–19, notes the increase in political interest and activity among today's college students, noting that it was up from the same measure in the 2002 and 2004 elections.

15. Conger (1996); Joanne Cole, "The Art of Wooing Gen Xers," *HR Focus,* 76, no. 11 (1999): 7–8; Pam Withers, "What Makes Gen X Employees Tick?" *BC Business*, 26, no. 3 (1998): 2–6; Jim Rapp," Managing Generation X: As Employees, As customers," *Office Systems*, 16, no. 8 (1999): 14–18; Jeffrey Cufaude, "Cultivating New Leadership," *Association Management,* 52, no. 1 (2000): 73–78; Mark Murphy, "New Article: Managing Generation 'WHY'?" *Leadership IQ,* June 3 (2008); Markmurphy@leadershipiq.com. Accessed July 31, 2009); <http://click.icptrack.com/icp/relay.php?r=70262264&m sgid=410066&act=PUJ7&c=503690&admin=0&destina tion=http%3A%2F%2Fwww.leadershipiq.com%2Findex.php%2Fupcoming-events%2Fgen-y>.

16. Paul Rodriguez, Mark Green, and Malcolm Ree, "Leading Generation X: Do The Old Rules Apply?" *Journal of Leadership and Organizational Studies*, 9, no. 4 (2003): 67, 73–74.

17. Pixie Anne Mosley, "Mentoring Gen X Managers: Tomorrow's Library Leadership Is Already Here," *Library Administration & Management*, 10, no. 4 (2005): 185–192.

18. Ron Carucci, "Building Relationships That Enable Next-Generation Leaders," *Leader to Leader*, 42 (2006): 47–53.

19. Karl Moore, "Kids These Days," *Marketing*, 111, no. 29 (2004): 14.

20. Byron Reeves, Thomas Malone, and Toni O'Driscoll, "Leadership's Online Labs," *Harvard Business Review*, 86, no. 5 (2008): 58–66; Elizabeth Agnvall, "Hitchhiker's Guide to Developing Leaders: Technology Is Changing the Way Manager's Gain Skills and Knowledge," *Human Resources*, September (2008): 121–122.

21. Tulgan, *Not Everyone Gets a Trophy* (2009), Dillon, (2009).
22. Lev Grossman, "Time's Person of the Year: You, *Time*," December 13, 2006.

2　HOW DO EMERGING LEADERS SEE THEMSELVES AS LEADERS?

1. Sherry H. Penney, "What a University Has Learned from 4 Years of Financial Stress," *Chronicle of Higher Education,* May 5, 1993, B1–2; Sherry Penney and Jean Mac Cormack, "Managing on the Edge," *Journal of Higher Education Management,* Winter/Spring (1992): 23–51.
2. Paul Michelman, "What Leaders Allow Themselves to Know: Warren Bennis Unveils Some New Thinking on the Filters that Govern Decision Making," *Mastering the Challenges of 21st Century Leadership* (Cambridge, MA, Harvard Business School Publishing, 2003), 2–4; Peter Drucker, "Managing Oneself," Leadership Fundamentals, *Harvard Business Review* (Article Collection, 2005), 7–16.
3. Daniel Goleman, *Emotional Intelligence* (New York, Bantam Books, 1995), 46–49; Joseph Raelin, *Creating Leaderful Organizations* (San Francisco, Berrett-Koehler, 2003), 59–66.
4. Sherry Penney and Patricia Neilson (eds.), *Voices of the Future: Emerging Leaders* (Boston: Center for Collaborative Leadership, 2009). See the About the Participants section for brief biographies of essay authors. Excerpts from essays in this chapter are from Rawan, Huang, Hurwitz, DeAngelis, Yameen, Tolikas, Young, Halbert, Bailly, Bell, Trojan, King, Swartz, Dance, Drummond, and Gonçalves. Persons who were interviewed and others who wrote statements on surveys are not identified.
5. Goleman (1995); Daniel Goleman, "What Makes a Leader," *Mind of the Leader* (Cambridge, MA, Harvard Business School Publishing, 2005), 97–121.
6. *The Leadership Practices Inventory: Theory and Evidence Behind The Five Practices of Exemplary Leaders*, 13–18, http://media.wiley.com/assets/463/74/lc_jb_appendix.pdf/. Accessed December 2008; James Kouzes and Barry Posner, *The Leadership Challenge*, 3rd ed. (San Francisco, Jossey-Bass, 2002); James H. Kouzes and Barry Z. Posner, *A Leader's Legacy* (San Francisco, Jossey-Bass, 2006), 29, discusses setting goals and having a purpose as part of one's legacy.

The sample for this analysis includes 174 individuals across seven cohorts of participants from 2002 to 2008. Each participant completed the Leadership Practices Inventory (LPI). Relevant charts are in the appendix. Summaries of the LPI surveys were prepared by Tom Robinson, "The Emerging Leaders Program: Results from Seven Years of Learning and Practice," (unpublished paper, 2008) and John Lozada, "Report on the Results of the Leadership Practices Inventory Survey of Emerging Leaders Program Fellows in the Classes of 2002–2008," (unpublished paper, 2008). Interviews with organizations that have sent participants and alumni from those organizations were also helpful. Interviews were conducted by graduate students Ben Donner and Meredith Evans from the doctoral program in psychology. Respondents are not named for reasons of confidentiality.

7. Paired-sample t-tests of means were conducted on the mean LPI-1 and LPI-2 scores for all cohorts. In each circumstance, the mean increases in leadership aptitudes were significant at the .01 level of significance or better. The increases from LPI-1 to LPI-2 represent increases across all of the categories in the Kouzes and Posner's (2001) instrument. There has been much discussion in the literature about what accounts for increases in scores, and we realize that the leadership development experience itself may have contributed to the increases, but also that other factors may have been involved. In 2002, we also had a control group and the increases for ELP participants were greater than for the control group. See Jennifer M. Leigh, *Developing Diverse Collaborative Leaders: An Empirical Program Evaluation* (Doctoral Dissertation: University of Massachusetts Boston, 2002). For other years, we do not have control data.

8. Interviews with alumni from 2002–2004 cohorts conducted by graduate students Ben Donner and Meredith Evans; Kouzes and Posner (2006), 28.

9. "A Conversation with Leadership Expert Joseph S. Nye, Jr.," *Harvard Business Review*, 86, no. 11 (2008): 55–59.

10. Karen Bogen, "Analysis of Data from 2007 and 2008 UMass Boston Future Leaders Survey," (Center for Survey Research, University of Massachusetts Boston, 2008).

11. Joanne Cole, "The Art of Wooing Gen Xers," *HR Focus*, 76, no. 11 (1999): 7–8; Kouzes and Posner (2006), 34.

12. Kouzes and Posner (2006), 34.

13. Jeffrey Cohn, Rakesh Khurana, and Laura Reeves, "Growing Talent as if Your Business Depended on It," *Harvard Business Review*, 83, no. 10 (2005): 63–70.

3 WHAT QUALITIES MAKE EFFECTIVE LEADERS?

1. Kouzes and Posner (2006), 118.

2. "College Presidents Meet with Weld on Welfare Cuts," *Boston Globe*, December 31, 1991, B1; "Women Presidents Help Reinstate AFDC Child Care Support," *Radcliffe News*, March 30, 1993 (Presidents Linda Wilson of Radcliffe and Nan Keohane of Wellesley were part of the network). Fay Hansen, "Building Better Leaders...Faster," *Workforce Management*, 87, no. 10 (2008): 1–9. For an interesting discussion of trait theory and of a critique of it, see Marshall Sashkin, Ayman Tarabishy, and Michael Harvey, "Stogdill 60 Years Later: The Role of Character in Leadership Effectiveness," *Member Connector*, International Leadership Association, January/Februay (2009), 12; also see Richard Barker, "How Can We Train Leaders if We Do Not Know What Leadership Is?" *Human Relations*, 50, no. 4 (1997): 343–362.

3. Hollander, *Inclusive Leadership* (2009), 12, 24, 49.

4. Robert Cross, Roger Martin, and Leigh Weiss, "Mapping the Value of Employee Collaboration," July 2006. *The Mc Kinsey Quarterly*. http/www.mckinsey-qrarterly.comarticle_print.aspx?L2=18&L3=31. Accessed September 18, 2008.

5. Hollander (2009), 83–84.

6. Kotter (1996), 175.

7. Penney and Neilson (2009). Excerpts of essays in this chapter are from Yameen, Young, Drummond, Dance, Anonymous, Hurwitz, King, Huang, Pusey, Bailly, Trojan, Francisco, and Meléndez.

8. Perri Petricca and Sherry Penney, "A Core Value That Helps the Bottom Line," *Boston Globe*, May 30, 2009, A13; Mary Moore, "Study: More CEOs Say Good Works Boost Recruiting," *Boston Business Journal*, May 25–June 4, 2009, 14; *Corporate Social Responsibility and Employee Recruitment and Retention: A Primer*, Massachusetts Business Roundtable and the UMass Boston Emerging Leaders Program Team, Spring (2009); "Talent Retention: Chamber Co-hosts a Special Event with the Federal Reserve Bank of Boston" policy@bostonchamber.com. Accessed July 29, 2009; Paul Connolly and Paul Guzzi, "Setting Boston Up for the Future," *Boston Globe*, July 29, 2009, A11.

9. Anne Field, "Diagnosing and Fixing Dysfunctional Teams," *Harvard Management Update*, 14, no. 3 (2009): 1–4.

10. Diane Darling, *The Networking Survival Guide* (New York, McGraw Hill, 2003). Darling is an alumnae of the program.

11. Stephen Denning, *The Secret Language of Leadership* (San Francisco, Jossey-Bass, 2007), 22–23.

12. Melissa Raffoni, "Framing for Leadership," *Mastering the Challenges of 21st Century Leadership*, Harvard Business School Publishing, reprint No. C0212B (2003), 39–40.

13. Ronald Heifetz, *Leadership without Easy Answers* (Cambridge, MA, Harvard Business School Press, 1994), 253; Anthony Mayo and Nitin Nohria, "Zeitgeist Leadership," *Harvard Business Review*, 83, no. 10 (October 2005): 45–60.

14. Bill George, *True North* (San Francisco, Jossey-Bass, 2007); Jerry Porras, Stewart Emery, and Mark Thompson, "The Cause Has Charisma," *Leader to Leader*, no. 43 (2007): 26–31.

15. Goleman (1995); Stephanie Cote and Christopher Miners, "Emotional Intelligence, Cognitive Intelligence, and Job Performance," *Administrative Science Quarterly*, 51, no. 1 (2006): 12–18; Kevin Groves, "Developing and Measuring the Emotional Intelligence (EI) of Leaders," *Journal of Management and Development*, 27, no. 2 (2008): 225–249.

16. Deborah L. Rhode and Amanda K. Packel, "Ethics and Nonprofits," *Stanford Social Innovation Review*, Summer 2009, www.ssireview.org/site/printer/ethics and nonprofits/, 1, 3. Accessed May 27, 2009; Bowen McCoy, "The Parable of the Sadhu," *Harvard Business Review*, 75, May/June (1997): 54–64.

17. Rosabeth Moss Kanter, *Confidence: How Winning Streaks and Losing Streaks Begin and End* (New York, Crown Business, 2004).

18. Steve Sample, "When the Buck Stops, Think Contrarily," *Chronicle of Higher Education*, October 19, 2001, B 11.

4 WOMEN AND LEADERSHIP: PROGRESS AND ROADBLOCKS

1. Bogen (2008).

2. Linda Coughlin, Ellen Wingard, Keith Hollihan (eds.), *Enlightened Power* (San Francisco, Jossey-Bass, 2005), xxi, xxv, xxvi; Joyce Fletcher, *Disappearing Acts:*

Gender, Power, and Relational Practice at Work (Cambridge, MA, MIT Press, 1999), 12, 108–112, 132.

3. Barbara Kellerman and Deborah Rhode (eds.), *Women and Leadership: The State of Play and the Strategies for Change* (San Francisco, Jossey-Bass, 2007), 1–35; Deborah Rhode (ed.), *The Difference "Difference" Makes* (Palo Alto: Stanford University Press, 2003); Rich Tetzeli, "The Lessons of Adversity," *Fortune*, 159, no. 9 (2009): 63.

4. Carol Hardy-Fanta and Donna Stewartson, *A Seat at the Table? Racial, Ethnic & Gender Diversity on Corporate, Hospital, Education, Cultural & State Boards* (Research Report, Center for Women in Politics & Public Policy, McCormack Graduate School, University of Massachusetts Boston, 2007).

5. Kellerman (2007), 50 (footnote 100) lists several relevant studies and Linda Carli and Alice Eagly, "Overcoming Resistance to Women Leaders," in Kellerman (2007), 72, 127–148; Vicki Donlon, *Her Turn: Why It's Time for Women to Lead in America* (Westport, CT, Praeger, 2007), 16.

6. Alice Eagly and Linda Carli, "Women and the Labyrinth of Leadership," *Harvard Business Review*, 85, no. 9 (2007): 83–71.

7. Regina Maruca, "Say's Who," *Harvard Business Review*, 75, no. 6 (1997): 15; Rebecca Shambaugh, "Achieving Diversity at Senior Levels," *Leader to Leader*, 50 (2008): 39, 39–44; Rhode, *The Difference "Difference" Makes* (2003). 7–10.

8. Patricia Ohlott, Marian Ruderman, and Cynthia McCauley, "Gender Differences in Managers' Developmental Job Experiences," *Academy of Management Journal*, 37, no. 1 (1994): 46–67.

9. Data collected at forums for ELP (2006, 2007, 2008, and 2009).

10. Cecilia Ridgeway, "Gender, Status and Leadership," *Journal of Social Issues*, 57, no. 4 (2001): 637–655.

11. Deborah Kolb, Judith Williams, and Carol Frohlinger, *Her Place at the Table* (San Francisco, Jossey-Bass, 2004); Deborah Tannen, *You Just Don't Understand* (New York, Ballentine Books, 1991).

12. Elizabeth Parks-Stamm, Madeline Heilman, and Krystle Hearns, "Motivated to Penalize, Women's Strategic Rejection of Successful Women," *Personality and Social Psychology Bulletin*, 34, no. 2 (2008): 237.

13. Cases were prepared by Professor Colvin of Christopher Newport College in Virginia and administered to the 2006 and 2007 cohorts.

14. Ronald Heifetz, "Leadership, Authority and Women," in Kellerman, 311–327.

15. Alice Eagly, HBR (2007).

16. Penney and Neilson (2009). Essays in this chapter are from Bailly, Gonçalves, Swartz, Francisco, Anonymous, DeAngelis, Yameen, Bell, Rawan, and Young.

17. Michael Gurian with Barbara Annis, *Leadership and the Sexes* (San Francisco, Jossey-Bass, 2008), 30, 33, 39–40, 62–3.

18. Fiona Moore, "Work/life Balance: Contrasting Managers and Workers in an MNC," www.emeraldinsight.com/0142–5455.html/. Accessed on May 9, 2009; Claire Shipman and Katty Kay, *Womenomics: Write Your Own Rules for Success* (New York, HarperCollins, 2009).

19. Carolyn Clark, Rosemary Caffarella, Peggy Ingram, "Women in Leadership: Living with the Constraints of the Glass Ceiling," *Initiatives*, 59, no. 1 (1999):

65–75; Maggie Jackson, "Fessing Up to Being a Mom Can Backfire on Job Seekers," *Boston Globe*, August 2, 2009, G1.

20. Dillon, Perspective*s* (2009), 4.

21. Herminia Ibarra and Otilia Obodaru, "Women and the Vision Thing," *Harvard Business Review*, 87, no. 1 (2009): 62.

22. Eric Westervelt, "In Norway, Law Promotes Women in Boardroom," http:// www.wbur.org/news/npr/111673448. Accessed August 10, 2009. Rebecca Tuhus-Durrow, "The Female Advantage," *Boston Globe*, May 3, 2009, C1–3; Tuhus-Durrow, "The XX Factor: Why It Makes Sense for Companies to Promote Women," *Lola*, July 2009, 18–20; Linda Basch, "Mistresses of the Universe," (letter to the editor), *New York Times*, February 12, 2009. See also Catalyst studies.

23. Dillon, Perspectives (2009), 4.

5   INCLUSIVE LEADERSHIP

1. U.S. Census Bureau. Profiles of General Demographic Characteristics: 2000 Census of Population and Housing (Washington, DC: US Census Bureau); 2000 as quoted in Ellen Foster Curtis, Janice Dreachslin, and Marie Siniorsis, "Diverse and Cultural Competence Training in Health Organizations: Hallmarks of Success," *The Healthcare Manager*, 26, no. 3 (2007): 255–262.

2. Holly Dolezalek, "The Path to Inclusion," *Training*, 45, no. 4 (2008): 52–54.

3. Curtis (2007), 255–262.

4. Jennifer Leigh, Ester Shapiro, and Sherry Penney, "Developing Collaborative Leaders: An Empirical Program Evaluation," *Journal of Leadership and Organizational Studies* (accepted for publication in June 2009); Anne Donnellon and Deborah Kolb, "Constructive for Whom: The Fate of Diversity Disputes in Organizations," *Journal of Social Issues*, 30, no. 1 (1994): 139–155; Lynn Weber, "A Conceptual Framework for Understanding Race, Class and Gender and Sexuality," *Psychology of Women Quarterly*, 23 (1998): 15.

5. Peter Kiang, "Voicing Names and Naming Voices: Pedagogy and Persistence in an Asian American Studies Classroom," Vivian Zamel and Ruth Speck (eds.), *Crossing the Curriculum: Multilingual Learners in College Classrooms* (Mawwah, NJ: Lawrence Erlbaum, 2003), 209, 207–220.

6. Ibid., 211.

7. Interviews of alumni and sponsors of the program were conducted by graduate students Ben Donner and Meredith Evans from the doctoral program in psychology.

8. Alec Wilkinson, *Protest Singer: An Intimate Portrait of Pete Seeger* (New York, Knopf Doubleday, 2009), 117.

9. Oluremi Ayoko and Charmine Hartel, "Cultural Diversity and Leadership: A conceptual model of leader intervention in conflict events in culturally heterogeneous groups." *Cross Cultural Management*, 13, no. 4 (2006): 347; Peggy McIntosh, "Unpacking the invisible knapsack." http://www.case.edu/president/ aaction/UnpackingTheKnapsack.pdf/. Accessed June 9, 2009.

10. Ayoko and Hartel (2006).

11. Penney and Neilson, *Voices from the Future* (2009). Excerpts of essays in this chapter come from Gonçalves, Bailly, Halbert, Bell, Meléndez and Francisco.

12. Keith Caver and Ancella Livers, "Dear White Boss: What It Is Really Like to be a Black Manager," *Harvard Business Review*, 80, no. 11 (2002): 78, 76–81.

13. "Sotomajor's Cautious Supreme Count Audition," *The Week*, 9, no. 422 (July 24, 2009): 2; see also the *Boston Globe*, July 23–31, August 2–3, 2007, *New York Times*, July 24, 25, 2009; Georgianna Meléndez and Robert L. Turner, "The Unfinished Work of Equality," *Boston Globe*, http://www.boston.com/bostonglobe/editorial_opinion/oped/articles/2009/07/22/the_unfinished_work_of_equality/ Accessed July 23, 2009.

14. Tracy Robinson, "Insurmountable Opportunities," *Journal of Counseling and Development*, 76 (2007): 7–8; Linda Hite and Kimberly McDonald, "Diversity Training Pitfalls and Possibilities: An Exploration of Small and Mid-size US Organizations," *Human Resource Development International*, 9, no. 3 (2006): 365–377.

15. Milton Bennett, Janet Bennett, and Dan Landis (eds.), *Handbook of Intercultural Training* (San Francisco, Sage, 2005).

16. William Bowen, Derek Bok, and Glenda Burkhart, "A Report Card on Diversity: Lessons for Business from Higher Education," *Harvard Business Review*, 77, no. 1 (1999): 141, 139–149.

17. Andrew Park, "Making Diversity a Business Advantage," *Harvard Management Update*, 19, no. 4 (2008): 1–5.

18. Dolezalek (2008), 54.

19. Frans Johansson, "Master of the Multicultural," *Harvard Business Review*, 83, no. 10 (2004): 18–19.

20. Debbe Kennedy, "How to Put Our Differences to Work," *Leader to Leader* no. 52 (Spring 2009): 49–55.

21. Ron Takaki, who died recently, wrote this essay on March 4, 2008 http://www.asiansvote.com/entrie/000244.shtml/. Accessed July 31, 2009.

22. Carol Hardy-Fanta and Paul Watanabe, *Transformation and Taking Stock: A Summary of Selected Findings from the McCormack Graduate School Diversity Survey* (A Collaborative Project of the John W. McCormack Graduate School of Policy Studies, Institute for Asian American Studies, Mauricio Gaston Institute for Latino Community Development and Public Policy, and the William Monroe Trotter Institute for the Study of Black Culture, Research Report, Boston: McCormack Graduate School of Policy Studies, University of Massachusetts Boston 2006); Carol Hardy-Fanta and Donna Stewartson, *A Seat at the Table?* (2007).

23. Carol Hardy-Fanta, *Stepping Up: Managing Diversity in Challenging Times* (The First Annual Report of Commonwealth Compact Benchmark Data, Commonwealth Compact, University of Massachusetts Boston, May 2009). The Compact organizations are not a representative sample of the entire state but are a significant group. Included in the 111 are 12 of the 35 largest organizations on the *Boston Business Journal* list of the state's largest employers. Representation from two of the state's key sectors, health care and higher education, is particularly strong.

24. Ibid.

6 THE VIEW FROM GENERATION X: ORGANIZATIONS NEED TO CHANGE

1. Bogen (2008).
2. Penney and Neilson (2009). Excerpts of essays quoted in this chapter are from Gonçalves, Hurwitz, Swartz, Dance, Tolikas, Anonymous, and Pusey.
3. "Greater Boston's Challenge: Sustaining the Talent Advantage," Greater Boston Chamber of Commerce, 2008; Jennifer Leclaire, "Shortage of Top Talent Worsens Despite Soft Economy," *Boston Business Journal* (September 5–11, 2008): 31; Penney, Leigh, and Norassakundt (2002).
4. Steven Bates, "Unique Strategies Urged to Keep Emerging Leaders," *Human Resources* (March 2002): 14–15; Joseph Bower, "Solve the Succession Crisis by Growing Inside-Outside Leaders," *Harvard Business Review*, 85, no. 11 (2007): 90–96.
5. "The Challenges of a Multigenerational Workplace," *Boston Globe* (supplement) *Diversity Boston*, Spring 2009, 4–5.
6. Frances Kunreuther, Helen Kim, and Robby Rodriguez, *Working Across Generations: Defining the Future of Nonprofit Leadership* (San Francisco, Jossey-Bass, 2008); Tamara Erickson, "Gen Y in the Workforce," *Harvard Business Review*, 87, no. 2 (2009): 43–49.
7. Elizabeth Agnvall, "Hitchhiker's Guide to Developing Leaders: Technology Is Changing the Way Managers Gain Skills and Knowledge," *Human Resources* (2008): 121–126.
8. Jay Conger, "How 'Gen X' Managers Manage," http://www.strategy-business.com/press/16635507/9760?tid=230&pg=all/. Accessed on June 4, 2009; Carolyn Martin and Bruce Tulgan, *Managing the Generation Mix* (2006).
9. Jennifer Deal (2001), 7, 9; "Older Employees Add Strength in Economic Downturn," The Sloan Center on Aging and Work, age.work@bc.edu, Accessed June 29, 2009; Chris Carmody (Senior Vice President for Human Resources, NSTAR) to Sherry Penney, June 30, 2009 and July 1, 2009, emails.
10. James O'Toole and Warren Bennis, "What's Needed Next: A Culture of Candor," *Harvard Business Review*, 87, no. 6 (2009): 54–61.
11. Kouzes and Posner (2006), 99.
12. *Chronicle of Higher Education*, January 30, 2009, A18–A 19; *USA Today*, January 23, 2009; Kenneth Cooper, "The Connectors," *Globe* (magazine) July 17, 2009, 16–21.
13. ELP team PowerPoint presentation at Federal Reserve Bank of Boston, October 14, 2008; *Corporate Social Responsibility* (2009). Mary Moore, "UMass Eyes Philanthropy to Lure Young Professionals," *Boston Business Journal* (October 24–30, 2008): 19 and Mary Moore, "Study: More CEOs Say Good Works Boost Recruiting," May 29, 2009, 14; John A. Quelch and Katherine E. Jocz, "Can Corporate Social Responsibility Survive Recession?" *Leader to Leader*, 53 (Summer 2009): 37–43; Rajendra S. Sisodia, David B Wolfe, and Jagdish N. Sheth, *Firms of Endearment: How World-Class Companies Profit from Passion and Purpose* (Philadelphia, Wharton School Publishing, 2007), xvi. Rosabeth Moss Kanter, *Supercorp* (New York: Crown Business, 2009),1.

7 LEADERSHIP FOR THE FUTURE: PASSING THE TORCH

1. Peter Cheese, Robert J. Thomas, and Elizabeth Craig, *The Talent Powered Organization: Strategies for Globalization* (London and Philadelphia, Kogan Page, 2008), v, 8, 46, 50; Julie Gebauer, Don Lowman, and Joanne Gordon, *Closing the Engagement Gap: How Great Companies Unleash Employee Potential for Superior Results* (USA: Penguin Group, 2008).
2. Hansen (2008), 1–9.
3. Penney and Neilson (2009). Essays and quotes in this chapter are from Gonçalves, Francisco, Tolikas, Huang, Lefevre, Gandhi, Bailly, Bell, DeAngelis, Rawan, Yameen, and Halbert.
4. Tulgan, *Managing the Generation Mix* (2006); Tulgan, *Not Everyone Gets a Trophy* (2009). discusses the challenges for Generation X in Managing Generation Y.
5. "The Way We'll Work," *Time*, May 23, 2009, 48, 39–51.
6. Tulgan (2006; 2009).
7. Lynn Weber, "A Conceptual Framework for Understanding Race, Class, Gender, and Sexuality," *Psychology of Women Quarterly*, 23 (1998): 28.
8. Michael Hais and Morley Winograd, "Millennials Are About to Give American Politics an Extreme Makeover," February 7, 2008, www.hufffingtonpost.com/. Accessed June 23, 2009; Morley Winograd and Michael D. Hais, *Millennial Makeover: MySpace, You Tube, and the Future of American Politics* (Piscataway, NJ, Rutgers University Press, 2008).
9. Tulgan (2006; 2009).
10. Sylvia Ann Hewlett, Laura Sherbin, and Karen Sumberg, "How Gen Y and Boomers Will Reshape Your Agenda," *Harvard Business Review*, 87, nos. 7/8 (July/August 2009): 71–76; Murphy (2009). Mark Murphy, http://click.icp-track.com/icp/relay.php?r=70262264&msgid=410066&act=PUJ7&c=503690&admin=0&destination=http%3A%2F%2Fwww.leadershipiq.com%2Findex.php%2Fupcoming-events%2Fgen-y/.
11. Kouzes and Posner (2006), 11.
12. Richard Contu's interview of Mary Uhl-Bien, *Member Connector*, June/July 2009, International Leadership Association, 8, 13.

BIBLIOGRAPHY

Agnvall, Elizabeth. 2008. Hitchhiker's guide to developing leaders: Technology is changing the way manager's gain skills and knowledge. *Human Resources.* September: 121–122.

Austin, James. 2000. *The collaborative challenge.* San Francisco: Jossey-Bass.

Ayoko, Oluremi, and Charmine Hartel. 2006. Cultural diversity and leadership: A conceptual model of leader intervention in conflict events in culturally heterogeneous groups. *Cross Cultural Management* 13: 347.

Barker, Richard. 1997. How can we train leaders if we do not know what leadership is? *Human Relations* 50: 343–362.

Basch, Linda. 2009. Mistresses of the universe. *The New York Times,* February 12: Letter to the editor.

Bass, Bernard. 1985. *Leadership and performance beyond expectations.* New York: Free Press.

Bates, Steven. 2002. Unique strategies urged to keep emerging leaders. *Human Resources.* September: 14–15.

Bauer, A J., 2007. Molding leaders. *Patriot Ledger,* July 11: 21–22.

Bennett, Milton, Janet Bennett, and Dan Landis (eds.). 2005. *Handbook of intercultural training.* San Francisco: Sage.

Bennis, Warren. 1990. *Why leaders can't lead?* San Francisco: Jossey-Bass.

———. 2003. *On becoming a leader.* Cambridge, MA: Perseus Books Group.

Bennis, Warren, Gretchen Spreitzer, and Thomas Cummings (eds.). 2001. *The future of leadership.* San Francisco: Jossey- Bass.

Bogen, Karen. 2008. Analysis of data from 2007 and 2008 UMass Boston future leaders survey. Center for Survey Research, University of Massachusetts Boston.

Bowen, William, Derek Bok, and Glenda Burkhart. 1999. A report card on diversity. *Harvard Business Review* 77: 138–49.

Bower, Joseph. 2007, Solve the succession crisis by growing inside-outside leaders. *Harvard Business Review* 85: 90–96.

Burns, James Mac Gregor. 1978. *Leadership.* New York: Harper & Row.

Carli, Linda, and Alice Eagly. 2007. Overcoming resistance to women leaders. Barbara Kellerman and Deborah Rhode (eds.), *Women and Leadership.* San Francisco: Jossey-Bass: 72, 127–148.

Carmody, Chris, "Engaging the Generations." Emails to Sherry Penney. June 30 and July 1, 2009.

Carter, Marshall. 2006. Growing Boston's new leaders. *Boston Business Journal.* http://boston.bizjournals.com/boston/stories/2006/11/20/editorial2.html/.

Carucci, Ron. 2006. Building relationships that enable next-generation leaders. *Leader to Leader* 42: 47–53.

Caver, Keith, and Ancella Livers. 2002. Dear white boss: What it is really like to be a black manager. *Harvard Business Review* 80: 76–81.

Cheese, Peter, Robert J. Thomas and Elizabeth Craig. 2008. *The talent powered organization: strategies for globalization*. London and Philadelphia: Kogan Page.

Chronicle of Higher Education. January 30, 2009: A18–19.

Clark, Carolyn, Rosemary Caffarella, and Peggy Ingram. 1999. Women in leadership: Living with the constraints of the glass ceiling. *Initiatives* 59: 65–75.

Cohn, Jeffrey, Rakesh Khurana, and Laura Reeves. 2005. Growing talent as if your business depended on it. *Harvard Business Review* 83: 63–70.

Cole, Joanne. 1999. The art of wooing Gen Xers. *HR Focus* 76: 7–8.

College presidents meet with Weld on welfare cuts. 1991. *Boston Globe*, December 31: Section B1.

Conger, Jay. How "Gen X" managers manage. *Strategy and Business*. http://www.strategy-business.com/press/16635507/9760?tid=230&pg=all/.

Conger, Jay, Gretchen Spreitzer, and Edward Lawler. 1999. *Leader's change handbook*. San Francisco: Jossey-Bass.

Connolly, Paul, and Paul Guzzi. 2009. Setting Boston up for the future. *Boston Globe*, July 29: A11.

Cooper, Kenneth. 2009. The connectors. *Globe Magazine*. July 17: 16–21.

Corporate social responsibility and employee recruitment and retention: A primer. 2009. Massachusetts Business Roundtable and the UMass Boston Emerging Leaders Program Team.

Cote, Stephanie and Christopher Miners. 2006. Emotional intelligence, cognitive intelligence, and job performance. *Administrative Science Quarterly* 51: 12–18.

Coughlin, Linda, Ellen Wingard and Keith Hollihan (eds.). 2005. *Enlightened power*. San Francisco: Jossey-Bass.

Couto, Richard. 2009a. Interview of Chao C. Chen, about leadership and management in China: philosophies, theories and practices. *Member Connector*. International Leadership Association. May: 5–12.

———. 2009b. Interview of Mary Uhl-Bien. *Member Connector*. International Leadership Association. June/July: 8, 13.

Crainer, Stuart, and Des Dearlove. 1999. Death of executive talent. *Management Review* 88: 8–13.

Cross, Robert, Roger Martin, and Leigh Weiss. 2006. Mapping the value of employee collaboration. *The McKinsey Quarterly*. http/www.mckinseyqrarterly.comarticle_print.aspx?L2=18&L3=31/.

Cufaude, Jeffrey. 2000. Cultivating new leadership. *Association Management* 52: 73–78.

Darling, Diane. 2003. *The networking survival guide*. New York: McGraw Hill.

Day, David and Stephen Zaccaro. 2004. *Leader development for transforming organizations*. Mawwah, NJ: Lawrence Erlbaum Associates.

Deal, Jennifer. 2006. Introduction. *Leader to Leader*, Special Supplement. San Francisco: Jossey-Bass.

Deal, Jennifer, Karen Peterson, and Heidi Gailor-Loflin. 2001. *Emerging leaders: An annotated bibliography*. Greensboro, NC: Center for Creative Leadership.

Denning, Stephen. 2007. *The secret language of leadership*, San Francisco: Jossey-Bass.

Dillon, Bobbie. 2009. Perspectives: Presenting thought leaders' points of view. http://www.nacubo.org/.

Dobelle, Evan. 2005. Bring back the vault. *Boston Business Journal*, http://www.bizjournals.com/boston/stories/2005/07/11/editorial2.html/.

Dolezalek, Holly. 2008. The path to inclusion. *Training* 45: 52–54.

Donlon, Vicki. 2007. *Her turn: Why it's time for women to lead in America*. Westport, CT: Praeger.

Donnellon, Anne, and Deborah Kolb. 1994. Constructive for whom: The fate of diversity disputes in organizations. *Journal of Social Issues* 30: 139–155.

Drucker, Peter. 2005. Managing oneself. *Harvard Business Review*: Article Collection: 7–16.

Eagly, Alice, and Linda Carli. 2007. Women and the labyrinth of leadership. *Harvard Business Review* 85: 83–71.

Erickson, Tamara. 2009. Gen Y in the workforce. *Harvard Business Review*. 87: 43–49.

European Foundation for Management Development newsletters. May 2008, February 2009. http://www.efmd.org/.

Field, Anne. 2009. Diagnosing and fixing dysfunctional teams. *Harvard Management Update:* 14: 1–4.

Fletcher, Joyce. 1999. *Disappearing acts: Gender, power, and relational practice at work*. Cambridge, MA: MIT Press.

Foster Curtis, Ellen, Janice Dreachslin, and Marie Siniorsis. 2007. Diverse and cultural competence training in health organizations: Hallmarks of success. *The Healthcare Manager* 26: 255–262.

Freidel, Rick. 2004. Nurturing a new generation of business leaders. *Boston Business Journal* http://boston.bizjournals.com/boston/stories/2004/03/01/editorial3.html/.

Gardner, John. 1990. *On leadership*. New York: Free Press.

Gebauer, Julie, Don Lowman, and Joanne Gordon. 2008. *Closing the engagement gap: How great companies unleash employee potential for superior results*. USA: Penguin Group.

George, Bill. 2007. *True north*. San Francisco: Jossey-Bass.

Goleman, Daniel. 1996. *Emotional intelligence*. New York: Bantam Books.

———. 2005. *Mind of the Leader*, Cambridge, MA: Harvard Business School Publishing.

Greater Boston's challenge: Sustaining the talent advantage. 2008. Greater Boston Chamber of Commerce. http://www.policy@bostonchamber.com/.

Grossman, Lev. 2006. Time's person of the year: You. *Time*. 13 December.

Groves, Kevin. 2008. Developing and measuring the emotional intelligence (EI) of leaders. *Journal of Management and Development* 27: 225–249.

Gurian, Micheal, and Barbara Annis. 2008. *Leadership and the sexes*. San Francisco: Jossey-Bass.

Hais, Micheal, and Morley Winograd. *Millennials are about to give American politics an extreme makeover*. http://www.hufffingtonpost.com/.

Hansen, Fay. 2008. Building better leaders…Faster. *Workforce Management* 87: 1–9.

Hardy-Fanta, Carol. 2009. Stepping up: Managing diversity in challenging times. The First Annual Report of Commonwealth Compact Benchmark Data. Commonwealth Compact, University of Massachusetts Boston.

Hardy-Fanta, Carol, and Donna Stewartson. 2007. A seat at the table? Racial, ethnic & gender diversity on corporate, hospital, education, cultural & state boards. Research Report, Boston: Center for Women in Politics & Public Policy, McCormack Graduate School, University of Massachusetts Boston.

Hardy-Fanta, Carol, and Paul Watanabe. 2006. Transformation and taking stock: A summary of selected findings from the McCormack graduate school diversity survey. Research Report, Boston: McCormack Graduate School of Policy Studies, University of Massachusetts Boston.

Heather, Joslyn. 2009. A growing leadership gap: Need for qualified executives persists even as charities trim staffs. *Chronicle of Philanthropy*. April 23: 29.

Heifetz, Ronald. 1994. *Leadership without easy answers.* Cambridge, MA: Harvard Business School Press.

Hewlett, Sylvia Ann, Laura Sherbin, and Karen Sumberg. 2009. How Gen Y and boomers will reshape your agenda. *Harvard Business Review* 87: 71–76.

Hite, Linda, and Kimberly McDonald. 2006. Diversity training pitfalls and possibilities: An exploration of small and mid-size US organization. *Human Resource Development International* 3: 365–377.

Hollander, Edwin. 2009. *Inclusive leadership.* New York: Routledge.

Ibarra, Herminia, and Otilia Obodaru. 2009. Women and the vision thing. *Harvard Business Review* 87: 62.

Irons, Meghan E. 2009. Workplace diversity grows but not at the top, report says. *Boston Globe*, May 19: Section B5.

Jackson, Maggie. 2009. "Fessing Up to Being a Mom Can Backfire on Job Seekers," *Boston Globe,* August 2: Section G1.

Johansson, Frans. 2004. Master of the multicultural. *Harvard Business Review* 83: 19.

Kanter, Rosabeth Moss. 2004. *Confidence: How winning streaks and losing streaks begin and end.* New York: Crown Business.

———. 2009. *Supercorp.* New York: Crown Business.

Kellerman, Barbara. 2007. What every leader needs to know about followers. *Harvard Business Review* 85: 84–91.

Kellerman, Barbara, and Deborah Rhode (eds.). 2007. *Women and leadership: The state of play and the strategies for change.* San Francisco: Jossey-Bass.

Kennedy, Debbe. 2009. How to put our differences to work. *Leader to Leader* 52: 49–55.

Kiang, Peter. 2003. Voicing names and naming voices: Pedagogy and persistence in an Asian American studies classroom. Vivian Zamel and Ruth Speck (eds.), *Crossing the Curriculum: Multilingual Learners in College Classrooms.* Mawwah, NJ: Lawrence Erlbaum: 207–220.

Kolb, Deborah, Judith Williams, and Carol Frohlinger. 2004. *Her place at the table.* San Francisco: Jossey-Bass.

Kotter, John. 1996. *Leading change.* Cambridge, MA: Harvard Business School Press.

Kouzes, James and Barry Posner. 2002. *The leadership challenge*, 3rd ed. San Francisco: Jossey-Bass.

Kouzes, James, and Barry Z. Posner. 2006. *A leader's legacy.* San Francisco: Jossey-Bass.

Kunreuther, Frances, Helen Kim, and Robby Rodriguez. 2008. *Working across generations:* Defining the future of nonprofit leadership. San Francisco: Jossey-Bass.

Leadership practices inventory: Theory and evidence behind the five practices of exemplary leaders. http://media.wiley.com/assets/463/74/lc_jb_appendix.pdf/.

Leclaire, Jennifer. 2008. Shortage of top talent worsens despite soft economy. *Boston Business Journal.* September 5: 31.

Leigh, Jennifer, Ester Shapiro, and Sherry Penney. 2009. Developing collaborative leaders: An empirical program evaluation. *Journal of Leadership and Organizational Studies* (accepted for publication).

Lozada, John. 2008. Report on the results of the leadership practices inventory survey of emerging leaders program fellows in the classes of 2002–2008. (unpublished paper).

Martin, Carolyn, and Bruce Tulgan. 2006. *Managing the generation mix: From urgency to opportunity,* 2nd ed. Amherst, MA: HRD Press.

Maruca, Regina. 1997. Say's who. *Harvard Business Review* 75: 15.

Mayo, Anthony, and Nitin Nohria. 2005. Zeitgeist leadership. *Harvard Business Review* 83: 45–60.

McCauley, Cynthia, Wilfred H. Drath, Charles J. Palus, Patricia M. G. O'Connor, and Becca A. Baker. 2006. The use of constructive-development theory to advance the understanding of leadership. *The Leadership Quarterly* 17: 634–653.

McCoy, Bowen. 1997. The parable of the Sadhu. *Harvard Business Review* 75: 51–64.

McIntosh, Peggy. Unpacking the invisible knapsack. http://www.case.edu/president/aaction/UnpackingTheKnapsack.pdf/.

Meléndez, Georgianna, and Robert L. Turner. 2009. The unfinished work of equality. *Boston Globe.* http://www.boston.com/bostonglobe/editorial_opinion/oped/articles/2009/07/22/the_unfinished_work_of_equality/.

Michelman, Paul. 2003. What leaders allow themselves to know: Warren Bennis unveils some new thinking on the filters that govern decision making. *Mastering the challenges of 21st century leadership.* Cambridge, MA: Harvard Business School Publishing. 2–4.

Moore, Fiona. Work/life balance: Contrasting managers and workers in an MNC. http://www.emeraldinsight.com/0142-5455.html.

Moore, Karl. 2004. Kids these days. *Marketing* 111: 14.

Moore, Mary. 2008. UMass eyes philanthropy to lure young professionals. *Boston Business Journal.* October 24: 19.

———. 2009. Study: More CEOs say good works boost recruiting. *Boston Business Journal.* May 25: 14.

Mosley, Pixie Anne. 2005. Mentoring Gen X managers: Tomorrow's library leadership is already here. *Library Administration & Management* 10: 185–192.

Murphy, Mark. 2008. New article: Managing generation "WHY?" *Leadership IQ.* June. http://click.icptrack.com/icp/relay.php?r=70262264&msgid=410066&act=PUJ7&c=503690&admin=0&destination=http%3A%2F%2Fwww.leadershipiq.com%2Findex.php%2Fupcoming-events%2Fgen-y/.

Neilson, Patricia. 2009. Interview with Chris Martin. Greater Boston Manufacturing Partnership.

Neilson, Patricia Akemi. 2009. Asian American models of leadership and leadership development in U.S. higher education. Lin Zhan (ed.), *Asian American Voices: Engaging, Empowering, Enabling,* New York: National League of Nursing: 191–207.

Northouse, Peter. 2000. *Leadership: Theory and practice*, 4th ed. Thousand Oaks, CA: Sage.

Nye, Joseph S., Jr. 2008. Conversation with leadership expert. *Harvard Business Review* 86: 55–59.

Ohlott, Patricia, Marian Ruderman, and Cynthia McCauley. 1994. Gender differences in managers developmental job experiences. *Academy of Management Journal* 37: 46–67.

Older employees add strength in economic downturn. The Sloan Center on Aging and Work. http://www.age.work@bc.edu/.

O'Toole, James, and Warren Bennis. 2009. What's needed next: A culture of candor. *Harvard Business Review* 87: 54–61.

Park, Andrew. 2008. Making diversity a business advantage. *Harvard Management Update* 19: 1–5.

Parks-Stamm, Elizabeth, Madeline Heilman, and Krystle Hearns. 2008. Motivated to penalize, women's strategic rejection of successful women. *Personality and Social Psychology Bulletin* 34: 237.

Penney, Sherry H. 1993. What a university has learned from 4 years of financial stress. *Chronicle of Higher Education*. May 5: B1–2.

———. 2003. Urban universities and urban leadership. *Metropolitan Universities*. December.

———. 2009. Interview of Alan Macdonald, Executive Director, Massachusetts Business Roundtable.

Penney, Sherry, and Jean MacCormack. 1992. Managing on the edge. *Journal of Higher Education Management*. Winter/Spring: 23–51.

Penney, Sherry, and Patricia Neilson (eds.). 2009. *Voices of the future: Emerging leaders*. Boston: Center for Collaborative Leadership.

Penney, Sherry, Jennifer Leigh, and Vinai Norassakundt. 2002. New leaders for the new century. *Building leadership bridges*. College Park, MD: International Leadership Association, University of Maryland: 48–58.

Petricca, Perri, and Sherry Penney. 2009. A core value that helps the bottom line. *Boston Globe* May 30: Section A13.

Porras, Jerry, Stewart Emery, and Mark Thompson. 2007. The cause has charisma. *Leader to Leader* 43: 26–31.

Prentice, W. C. H. 2005. Understanding leadership. *Mind of the leader*. Cambridge, MA: Harvard Business School Publishing: 151–167.

Quaglieri, Philip L., Sherry H. Penney, and Jennifer Waldner. 2007. Development of future business and civic leaders: The emerging leaders program. *Management Decision* 45: 1685–1694.

Quatro, Scott, David Waldman, and Benjamin Galvin. 2007. Developing holistic leaders: Four domains for leadership development and practice. *Human Resources Management Review* 17: 427–441.

Quelch, John A., and Katherine E. Jocz. 2009. Can corporate social responsibility survive recession? *Leader to Leader* 53: 37–43.

Raelin, Joseph. 2003. *Creating leaderful organizations*. San Francisco: Berrett-Koehler.

Raffoni, Melissa. 2003. Framing for leadership. *Mastering the challenges of 21st century leadership*. Cambridge, MA: Harvard Business School Publishing. 39–40.

Raines, Claire. 1997. *Beyond Generation X: A practical guide for managers*. Menlo Park, CA: Crisp.

Rapp, Jim. 1999. Managing Generation X: As employees, as customers. *Office Systems* 16: 14–18.

Reeves, Byron, Thomas Malone, and Toni O'Driscoll. 2008. Leadership's online labs. *Harvard Business Review* 86: 58–66.

Rhode, Deborah (ed.). 2003. *The difference "difference" makes*. Palo Alto: Stanford University Press.

Rhode, Deborah L. and Amanda K. Packel. 2009. Ethics and nonprofits. *Stanford Social Innovation Review*. www.ssireview.org/site/printer/ethics and nonprofits/.

Ridgeway, Cecilia. 2001. Gender, status and leadership. *Journal of Social Issues* 57: 637–655.

Robinson, Tom. 2008. The Emerging Leaders Program: Results from seven years of learning and practice (unpublished paper).

Robinson, Tracy. 2007. Insurmountable opportunities. *Journal of Counseling and Development* 76: 7–8.

Rodriguez, Paul, Mark Green, and Malcolm Ree. 2003. Leading Generation X: Do the old rules apply? *Journal of Leadership and Organizational Studies* 9: 73–74.

Sample, Steve. 2001. When the buck stops, think contrarily. *Chronicle of Higher Education*. October 19: B11.

Sashkin, Marshall, Ayman Tarabishy, and Michael Harvey. 2009. Stogdill 60 years later: The role of character in leadership effectiveness. *Member Connector*, International Leadership Association, January/February: 12.

Shambaugh, Rebecca. 2008. Achieving diversity at senior levels. *Leader to Leader* 50: 39–44

Shipman, Claire and Katty Kay. 2009. *Womenomics: Write your own rules for success*. New York: HarperCollins.

Sisodia, Rajendra, S., David B Wolfe, and Jagdish N. Sheth. 2007. *Firms of endearment: How world-class companies profit from passion and purpose*. Philadelphia: Wharton School Publishing.

Takaki, Ron. http://www.asiansvote.com/entries/000244.shtml.

Tannen, Deborah. 1991. *You just don't understand*. New York: Ballentine Books.

Tetzeli, Rich. 2009. The lessons of adversity. *Fortune* 159: 63.

The Challenges of a Multigenerational Workplace. 2009. *Boston Globe* supplement, *Diversity Boston*, Spring: 4–5.

The enterprise of the future. 2008. Global CEO study, ibm.com/enterprise of the future; The 2009 top companies for leaders study officially launches in China to recognize organizations with innovative leadership programs. http://www.hewittassociates.com/Intl/AP/en-CN/AboutHewitt/Newsroom/PressReleaseDetail/.

The way we'll work. *Time* 48: 39–51.

The Week, 2009. Sotomajor's Cautious Supreme Count Audition. July 24.

Tonn, Joan, 2003. *Mary Follett: Creating democracy, transforming management*. New Haven: Yale University Press.

Tuhus-Durrow, Rebecca. 2009a. The female advantage. *Boston Globe,* May 3: Section C1–3.

———. 2009b. The XX factor: Why it makes sense for companies to promote women. *Lola*. July: 18–20.

Tulgan, Bruce. 2000. *Managing Generation X*. New York: Norton.

———. 2009. *Not everyone gets a trophy*. San Francisco: Jossey-Bass.

U.S. Census Bureau. http://www.census.gov/main/www/cen2000.html/.

Weber, Lynn. 1998. A conceptual framework for understanding race, class, gender, and sexuality. *Psychology of Women Quarterly* 23: 28.

Westervelt, Eric. "In Norway, Law Promotes Women in Boardroom." http://www.wbur.org/news/npr/111673448/.

Wilkinson, Alec. 2009. *Protest singer: An intimate portrait of Pete Seeger.* New York: Knopf Doubleday.

Winograd, Morley, and Michael D. Hais. 2008. *Millennial makeover: MySpace, YouTube, and the future of American politics.* Piscataway, NJ: Rutgers University Press.

Withers, Pam. 1998. What makes Gen X Employees Tick? *BC Business* 26: 2–6.

Women presidents help reinstate AFDC child care support. 1993. *Radcliffe News,* March 30.

Zemke, Ron, Claire Raines, and Bob Filipczak. 2000. Generations at work. *American Management Association* Atlanta, GA: AMACOM.

About the Participants

We asked participants from the Emerging Leaders Program to assist us in learning more about their thoughts on leadership by writing essays outlining their views. Those essays were compiled and published in 2009: *Voices of the Future: Emerging Leaders*. Copies of the essays are available on our Web site (leaders.umb.edu.).

SANDRA BEST BAILLY

Author of: They Said "Do and Be the Best"

Sandra Best Bailly is the Results Management Office Project Director for Blue Cross Blue Shield of Massachusetts and oversees the full complement of active "Health and Wellness" projects. Sandra holds a Graduate Certificate in Project Management from City University, Bellevue, Washington; Masters in Social Work from Simmons College Graduate School of Social Work; and a Bachelor of Arts from Tufts University with an Undergraduate Certificate from the Community Health Program.

RON BELL

Author of: Leading From the Court

Ron Bell is the Director of the Governor's Office of Community Affairs for the Commonwealth of Massachusetts. He is the founder of Dunk the Vote and has held several other positions in the community. Ron is a Fellow at Harvard University John F. Kennedy School of Government Community Fellows Program, 2008.

ANNE MARIE BOURSIQUOT KING

Author of: So Much More to Learn

Anne Marie Boursiquot King is the director of grants at the Tufts Health Plan Foundation, the philanthropic arm of the company. She holds a Bachelor of Science in Business Administration from Suffolk University and Masters in Business Administration in International Business from the McCallum Graduate School of Business at Bentley College.

DAVID DANCE

Author of: I Needed It Yesterday!

David Dance is an IT project director at Blue Cross Blue Shield of Massachusetts. He has over 25 years of IT experience in various areas including programming, computer operations, network security, database administration, and various management roles on a variety of high visibility projects. David received his Bachelor of Science in Engineering from Virginia Tech.

LISA DEANGELIS

Co-author of: Dialogue on Leadership

Lisa DeAngelis is the Principal of Leading with Values. Prior to that she worked as the Managing Director and Lead People Strategies Partner at Shawmut Design and Construction. She has nearly 20 years of experience in the field of Human Resources across a broad range of industries. Lisa is pursuing her Masters in Business Administration at Regis University.

HUGH DRUMMOND

Author of: Teaming the Way to Success

Hugh Drummond is a Vice President at O'Neill and Associates. His work is in public relations, crisis communications, marketing, and government affairs with public and private sector experience including corporate, non-profit, technology start-up, agency, Capitol Hill, and political campaigns. Hugh received his Bachelor of Arts in Politics from De Sales University.

PAUL FRANCISCO

Author of: The New Boston: Transforming the Corporate Landscape

Paul Francisco is a Managing Director and Co-founder of Foster & Francisco LLC, a Boston-based executive search firm focusing on the recruitment of diverse talent across a number of industries and not-for-profit organizations. A former player for the NFL's New England Patriots (1994–1995), Mr. Francisco is a graduate of Boston University with a Bachelor of Arts in Political Science. He is an active member of the Association of Latino Professionals in Finance and Accounting, for which he currently serves as the Boston chapter's president.

ARMINDO GONÇALVES

Author of: From Angola to America: My Leadership Journey

Mr. Gonçalves has spent his professional career undertaking development work at the International American Development Bank, the Boston Housing Authority, and the Boston Redevelopment Authority, where he currently serves as deputy director of economic development. He earned a Bachelor of Arts degree from the University of Massachusetts in Planning and Urban Economics and an advanced degree in International Development and Regional Planning from MIT.

W. E. DAVID HALBERT

Author of: Keeping It "Real"

W. E. David Halbert served as an aide to Boston City Councilor At-Large Sam Yoon, where he was responsible for constituent service, policy analysis, and recommendations, and scheduling. David joined the Councilor's staff in 2008 after serving on the Executive Office staff of Massachusetts Governor Deval Patrick. David received his Bachelor of Arts in English/Communications from Massachusetts College of Liberal Arts.

CHI-CHENG HUANG, MD

Author of: Self-Reflections from an Emerging Leader in Healthcare

Dr. Chi Huang is currently the Chairman of the Department of Hospital Medicine at the Lahey Clinic. Prior to that he was the Associate Vice Chairman of clinical operations in the Department of Pediatrics at Boston Medical Center, Boston University School of Medicine. As founder of Kaya Children International (www.kayachildren.org), he wrote *When Invisible Children Sing*, a book about the lives of street children in Bolivia. He is currently a Massachusetts state board member of Early Education and Care. Dr. Huang graduated from Texas A&M University, earned his medical degree at Harvard Medical School, and completed his residency training at the Harvard Combined Internal Medicine/Pediatric Program.

ANDREA B. HURWITZ

Author of: Leading by Learning: A Young Leader's Quest

Andrea Hurwitz is the Assistant Director for Communications at the international nonprofit organization Facing History and Ourselves. Andrea is a Graduate of the S. I. Newhouse School of Public Communications and the College of Arts and Sciences at Syracuse University with a Bachelor of Arts in Public Relations and Sociology.

GEORGIANNA MELÉNDEZ

Author of: Heritage, Heart, Strength

Georgianna Meléndez is the Co-director for Commonwealth Compact, an initiative to make Massachusetts a location of choice for people of color. Georgianna is a graduate of Bentley College, where she earned a Bachelor of Arts in English with a minor concentration in Cultural Studies. She also currently sits on Governor Patrick's Anti-Crime Council as well as on a subcommittee of the Governor's Sexual and Domestic Violence Council.

NATHAN PUSEY

Author of: Banking on Music

Nathan Pusey is presently the Marketplace Manger of Commercial Banking in New England for Citibank, N.A. Mr. Pusey served with honor in the U.S. Navy and graduated from Boston University with a Bachelor of Science in Business Administration.

MICHAEL RAWAN

Author of: Evolution of a Leadership Style

Michael D. Rawan is Demand and Delivery Manager for Payments & Deposits Technology within the Payments and Deposits areas at Sovereign Bank, which he joined in February 2006. Michael earned his undergraduate degree from Babson College and his Masters in Business Administration magna cum laude from the F. W. Olin Graduate School of Business.

PAULIINA SWARTZ

Author of: Getting Emerging Leaders to Emerge

Pauliina Swartz, a native of Finland, is a managing director in the Structured Products Group of State Street Corporation overseeing the administration function of the Group. Pauliina received her Masters in Business Administration from the MIT Sloan School of Management and her Bachelor of Arts in Economics from Brandeis University.

MARY TOLIKAS

Author of: Path in Leadership

Mary Tolikas is Director of Operations at the Wyss Institute for Biologically Inspired Engineering at Harvard University. She received her PhD and

MSc degrees in Electrical Engineering and Computer Science at MIT in 1995 and 1992, respectively, and her Masters in Business Administration at the Sloan School of Management in 1999.

AMANDA TROJAN

Author of: Foundations for Leadership

Amanda Trojan was a Marketing Programs Manager at EMC Corporation in Hopkinton, Massachusetts. She managed worldwide product launches for EMC's Storage Division, focusing on the EMC Celerra and EMC PowerPath product line. Amanda is a Graduate of the University of New Hampshire's Whittemore School of Business with a Bachelor of Science in Business Administration and a concentration in Marketing.

DEANNA L. YAMEEN

Co-author of: Dialogue on Leadership

Deanna Yameen is the Dean for Humanities and Fine Arts at Massasoit Community College. She is a PhD candidate in Social Policy at the Heller School for Social Policy and Management at Brandeis University.

CHRISTIE GETTO YOUNG

Author of: Moving Right Along

Christie Getto Young is Senior Director of Public Policy at United Way of Massachusetts Bay and Merrimack Valley. Christie is also the author of the United Way report, "Off Welfare...On to Independence," released jointly with the Massachusetts Taxpayers Foundation in 2001. Christie is a 1991 graduate of Kenyon College in Gambier, Ohio. She also holds a Masters in Social Work from Boston College and a JD from Northeastern University.

ANONYMOUS

Author of: Work/Life Leadership

The author would like to remain anonymous. She is currently a Vice President with a Fortune 500 company. She is a member of the 2007 Emerging Leaders cohort and holds a Bachelors of Arts degree with a major in Economics.

INDEX